TOWER ABOVE ALL

THE AUTHOR

James Campbell grew up in the 1930s and has lived in Wrexham, North Wales since the early 40s, working as a Civil Servant. In 1983 he took voluntary early retirement and has since been involved in a number of charitable activities. He is the author of many articles and reports for railway and transport preservation societies, including RAILWAY PRESERVATION IN NORTH AND MID-WALES, first printed in 1977 as a joint guide to the activities of five railway organisations, and the 1980 edition of THE VISITOR'S GUIDE TO BALA LAKE RAILWAY. He is also the author of STEPPIN' OUT, an illustrated booklet published in 1988 about the Greenfield Valley Young Enterprise Centre which helps young people in Clwyd to set up their own businesses. His first major book TOWER ABOVE ALL is a charming evocation of the author's sense of fun and it is hoped will be enjoyed and shared by people of all ages.

TOWER ABOVE ALL

Personal memories of Blackpool from holiday diaries

Jimmy Campbell

Published in 1991 by
The Self Publishing Association Ltd
Lloyds Bank Chambers
Upton-upon-Severn, Worcs.

A MEMBER OF

in conjunction with
Jimmy Campbell
5 Ffordd Madoc,
Wrexham, Clwyd.

British Library Cataloguing in Publication Data
Campbell, Jimmy
    Tower above all : personal memories of Blackpool from
    holiday diaries.
    1. Lancashire (England), history
    I. Title
    942.759

ISBN 1 85421 126 9

Designed and Produced by The Self Publishing Association Ltd
Printed and Bound in Great Britain by Billing & Sons Ltd, Worcester

CONTENTS

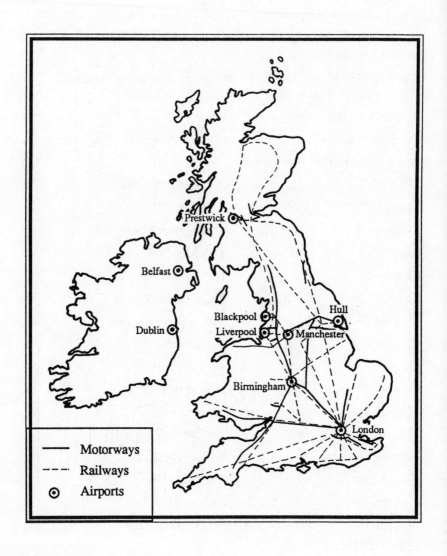

——	Motorways
- - -	Railways
⊙	Airports

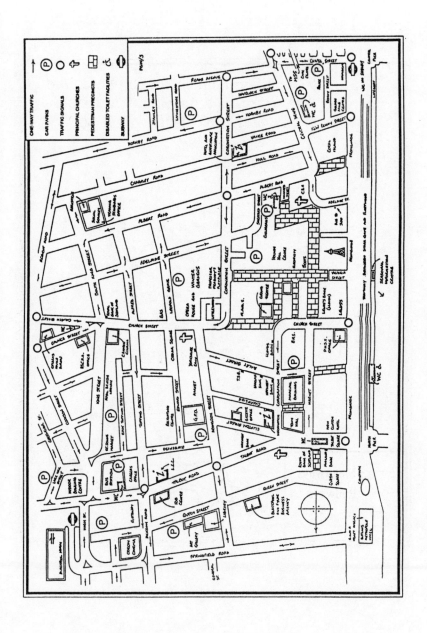

This book is dedicated to everyone who likes or provides holidays, and especially those who supply the services and hospitality to enable others to enjoy "that old Blackpool magic".

ACKNOWLEDGEMENTS

The author would like to thank everyone who has helped or contributed in any way towards this book, in particular the Self Publishing Association Limited, its founder, Mr Tony Harold and his highly qualified staff, without whose help and encouragement the whole idea would have floundered.

Special thanks also to the following:
The manager(esse)s and staff of all the hotels and guest houses where I have stayed; Mr David Banks, Manager, Clifton Hotel, Talbot Square, Blackpool; Blackpool Gazette & Herald Ltd., P.O.Box 20, New House, Preston New Road, Blackpool; Blackpool Transport, Blundell Street, Blackpool; Mr S. Brailey, General Manager, Blackpool Tower; The Reverend F. Alan Cliff, M.A., Dip Th: Mrs Rosemary Cliff; Mr Brian Crompton, Archivist, First Leisure Corporation; The late Mr Reginald Dixon, M.B.E., for kind permission to include the part about his Farewell Concert; The publishers of the farewell concert souvenir programme; Mr D.L. Ethelston, Wrexham Lager Brewery; Mr Richard Newton-Jones, Farm World, Sontley, Wrexham; Lancashire County Council, Mr J.K. Burkitt, A.L.A., District Librarian, and Reference Library staff at the District Central Library, Queen Street, Blackpool; Mr Barry Morris, M.I.P.R., FTS., Director of Tourism and Attractions, and Mr John Hall, Deputy Director; North West Museum & Art Gallery Services; Royal National Lifeboat Institution, Blackpool Branch – the late Mr J.P.M. Burslam: Mr Geoffrey Thompson, Managing Director, Blackpool Pleasure Beach Company, and Helen O'Neill, Public Relations Manager.

I would like to express appreciation to everyone who has sent good wishes for the success of this venture, and thank the people of Blackpool, whose friendliness and helpfulness have been the main reasons why every visit has been enjoyable.

Jimmy Campbell

Aerial view of Blackpool taken 1950

FOREWORD
by
Geoffrey Thompson

Many changes have taken place at Blackpool during the past forty-five years, the period written about in this book, and the introduction of many more new tourist attractions is planned for the future.

Blackpool has become the most popular tourist town in Europe. The distinguishing features, the Tower, and the Pleasure Beach, which receives more visitors than any other tourist attraction in Great Britain, have both been managed for many years by generations of local families.

Beginning in 1891 with Alderman John Bickerstaffe, the first chairman of the Blackpool Tower Company, who was succeeded as chairman by relatives during a period of over seventy years. Further details about this family and their continued support of the local lifeboats are given on later pages.

Blackpool Pleasure Beach has been owned and managed since 1896 by three generations of one local family. Founded by William George Bean, his son-in-law Leonard Thompson became Managing Director of the company in the 1930s, and a period of rapid development followed with the construction of the Grand National, the Pleasure Beach Express, Joseph Emberton's distinctive Casino building in 1939 and the creation of Blackpool Pleasure Beach's famous ice show in 1937. It is now home to hi-tech rides, as well as its famous "woodies", with the U.K.'s only bobsleigh ride, The Avalanche, and Europe's first 360 degrees "looper ride", The Revolution.

I took to the helm in 1976, and my mother, Mrs L.D. Thompson M.B.E., J.P. is now Chairman of the company, and we both enjoy continuing in the Blackpool tradition of providing first-class entertainment for all our visitors.

INTRODUCTION

Bygone Blackpool

This book is mainly a personal viewpoint of people and places at Blackpool, extracted from my holiday diaries since 1946. It records a slice of Blackpool life with no conventional beginning, middle or ending.

As there have been many changes in our ways and standards of living today compared with those of up to forty-five years ago, some explanations, recollections and comments have been added.

Why has Blackpool become so popular? Looking back to Victorian days, there were three main reasons why so many visitors were attracted:

1. Its nearness to large centres of population – Lancashire, Yorkshire, the Midlands.

2. The development of rail transport from the 1840s onwards, which enabled passengers to travel more easily and quickly. Before then the majority of working people rarely ventured more than a few miles from their homes.

3. The natural attractions of sands, sea and fresh air, especially to town dwellers. Many of them worked in harsh conditions in factories and mills and lived among depressing industrial surroundings.

Families flocked to the resort in their thousands. When the Tramway was opened it provided a most useful method of local transport in dispersing the large numbers arriving by train at the stations. Trams running frequently were able to carry railway passengers very conveniently to their local destinations.

Right in the centre of it all, for nearly one hundred years, stands the Tower. At 518 feet 9 inches high, it certainly is above all.

THE BICKERSTAFFES – A CENTURY OF LIFEBOAT SUPPORT

As any profits from the sale of this book will go to the R.N.L.I., it may be appropriate to mention a well known family who had a major influence on the resort's development, and were keen supporters of the lifeboat over a period of a hundred years.

ROBERT BICKERSTAFFE – PIONEER LIFEBOATMAN

Robert Bickerstaffe was coxswain of the first Blackpool lifeboat. He had a number of other interests as the resort was growing in popularity. He bought property to build a boatyard and the Wellington Hotel, near the Central Pier. He took over the Central Pier, which at first had been financially unsuccessful, and introduced entertainment and attractions for visitors.

The lifeboat *Robert William* was launched on 20 July 1864. During the period it was in service, from 1864 to 1885, it was launched twenty-one times and saved eighty-one lives.

On 26 February 1880 in heavy seas and a severe north westerly gale, the *Robert William* saved four men from the distressed Fleetwood Schooner *Bessie Jones*. On the way back, the sea anchor was lost and the lifeboat almost capsized, but Coxswain Bickerstaffe managed to land it safely at St Anne's. For this outstanding rescue he was awarded the Silver Medal for gallantry by the R.N.L.I.

(Blackpool Branch R.N.L.I.)
Robert Bickerstaffe, first Lifeboat Coxswain, 1864-1869 & 1876-1887.

Robert Bickerstaffe helped to form the first Blackpool Lifeboat Band in 1884. It raised large sums of money for charity.

In 1885 a new lifeboat, the *Samuel Fletcher of Manchester* was named by the Mayor of Liverpool in a ceremony which was combined with the opening of the new Blackpool Electric Tramway.

In 1886 there was a disaster involving three other lifeboats which were launched to assist the distressed German barque *Mexico* in a gale and very rough seas off Southport. The Lytham lifeboat saved twelve people from the *Mexico*, but both the Southport and the St Anne's lifeboats capsized, and the crew, except for two men, lost their lives.

The Blackpool and Lytham lifeboats put out to look for the missing St Anne's boat. In the rough seas Coxswain Bickerstaffe was washed overboard from the *Samuel Fletcher*, but managed to hold on to his rudder yokelines and was dragged back on board.

When Coxswain Bickerstaffe retired in 1887 he was awarded a second Silver Medal by the R.N.L.I. for his long and distinguished service in the lifeboats.

ALDERMAN JOHN BICKERSTAFFE, EX-MAYOR OF BLACKPOOL AND FIRST CHAIRMAN OF BLACKPOOL TOWER COMPANY.

John Bickerstaffe was one of Robert Bickerstaffe's sons. He was involved in local politics and enterprises, and was Mayor of Blackpool when the foundation stone for the Tower was laid in 1891.

He became chairman of the Blackpool Tower Company, and was confident that the Tower would become successful. He put up some of the money for it himself, and encouraged others to take shares and invest capital in the company to raise the initial building cost of £42,000. After the Tower was opened in 1894 he built up the Company, and his faith that it would become profitable was eventually justified.

To show their appreciation the shareholders of the company

(Blackpool Evening Gaz.)

Sir John Bickerstaffe

15

presented him with a handsome silver model of the Tower, which can be seen today in the Tower's "MEMORY LANE" room. He was knighted in 1926.

The sailor's cap he wore on most occasions indicated the family's connections with the sea.

CARRYING ON THE FAMILY TRADITION

After Sir John Bickerstaffe died in 1930, his younger brother, Alderman Tom Bickerstaffe, became chairman of the Tower Company. He died four years later and his body was cremated. His ashes were scattered from the lifeboat between the Central and North Piers.

Sir John's son, Robert Bickerstaffe, was the next chairman, and carried on the family tradition during the Second World War until he retired in 1945.

Tom Bickerstaffe's son Douglas was the last member of the family to become chairman of the company. Shortly after he retired in 1963 the Tower Company and its property was sold. The family connection of support for the lifeboats had ended after a continuous period of almost one hundred years.

At the present time, it is understood that there are no remaining relatives of the Bickerstaffe family living in the Blackpool area.

THE LIFEBOATS OF TODAY

Since 1965 the R.N.L.I's "D" class high speed inflatable rescue boats, have been used on service at Blackpool. Powered by a 40 h.p. outboard engine, these 15 ft. 6 in. long inshore lifeboats are capable of speeds over 20 knots, and are primarily intended for rescues involving small craft, bathers and other services where speed is essential.

At the Blackpool station there are two inshore "D" class lifeboats, which continue to give invaluable service to those in difficulty off the coast.

The R.N.L.I. are planning the introduction of new fast carriage lifeboats for their fleet in a £50 million boat building programme up to 1993. The estimated cost of one of the new lifeboats is about half a million pounds.

BACKGROUND TO POST WAR PERIOD

My first Blackpool holiday commenced on 21 October 1946, when conditions were very different from today. It was a year after the 1939-45 War had ended. Many men and women had served in H.M. Forces, and some had been demobilised. During the War over three quarters of a million airmen had been given their initial R.A.F. training at the Winter Gardens.

In 1946, price controls, food and fuel rationing and other wartime regulations were still in force. When people went away they had to hand their ration books in where they were staying or they could not obtain their share of rationed foods.

Many goods were scarce or unobtainable. People accepted these restrictions as a result of the War; we had become used to managing with whatever was available.

The five-day week had not yet been introduced in industry, and hours of work were longer than they are today. The need for a vacation was no less important than it is today, and large numbers of visitors flocked to Blackpool for relaxation and a break from austerity. I considered myself lucky to receive a total of three to four weeks holiday from work per year. A fortnight was around the average for many workers of similar age.

I am not quite sure why I chose Blackpool as the destination of my first post-war holiday. Any alternative would have had to be in Great Britain, because at the time not many people were able to travel abroad for a holiday.

Most passenger trains were still drawn by steam locomotives. From Preston, rail travellers had the choice of two different routes to Blackpool. One line ended at Blackpool North station. I travelled via the alternative route to Blackpool Central station, with stops at Lytham, St Anne's, Squire's Gate and Blackpool South.

A Labour Government headed by Prime Minister Clement Attlee was in power. The Conservative opposition party, led by wartime Prime Minister Winston Churchill, had recently held their Annual

Conference at Blackpool. Local Town Council elections were due to be held in a fortnight. Among thirty-seven candidates for the fifteen seats were a number of ex-servicemen. Altogether there were fourteen Conservatives, twelve Labour, seven Liberal, two Independent and two Communists.

At the Winter Gardens, a Local Government Exhibition organised by the Town Council and National Association of Local Government Officers, (NALGO) was held for one week. It showed how the 11 shillings in the pound rate was spent.

The exhibition was opened by the Mayor on Saturday 19th October. He welcomed guests at a civic lunch in the Baronial Hall of the Winter Gardens. In a speech of thanks, Mr C.A. Roberts, ex-National president of NALGO replied: "Things happening around us are changing day by day, but the hospitality and kindness of Blackpool goes on forever". I have every reason to agree with him.

CHAPTER 1

21st – 25th October 1946 – The First Holiday

When I arrived at the guest house on my first holiday in Blackpool, the landlady said to me, "I'll do OUR best to make you feel comfortable". She succeeded in doing so better than I had expected, in spite of limitations caused by restrictions and shortages of so many goods.

A notice was posted in bedrooms advising visitors to bring their ration books, sign the Visitors' book before leaving, and to be punctual for meals. Another notice on the wall read: "No fish and chips to be brought in".

Before my holiday I had been rather depressed after a period of ill health. After spending a few days at Blackpool I was considerably cheered up by a refreshing break from the normal routine of work, and felt that my health had improved. Most of all I was impressed by the friendliness and hospitality of the people I had met.

Monday 21st October

LOCAL GOVERNMENT EXHIBITION

After arrival at Blackpool and lunch, my first call is at the Winter Gardens and Olympia. Admission charge to the Local Government exhibition being held there is sixpence [2½p].

Exhibits of Blackpool in miniature are on show: the gas works, electricity generating station, art gallery and little waterworks.

There are also plans of local reconstruction and housing schemes; fresh flowers transplanted from parks and pleasure grounds; a dazzling illuminations display of coloured electric light bulbs from as small as a pea to as big as a football; hospital furnishings, an iron lung and children's cots; a waxworks figure of the first Health Visitor to illustrate advances in Health Services.

Schoolgirls dance to the accompaniment of loud speaker music.

Later a brass band gives a concert on a stage.

I like especially a scale model of the tramway system, with overhead wires, shelters, and a miniature tram which can be controlled from the side of the track. A tram driver shows children how to regulate the speed of the model. Afterwards he gives each one a printed card.

Written tributes from different parts of the country to the politeness and courtesy of Blackpool Transport's conductors and conductresses are on display.

Attended by local Police are hints on how to make your home burglar proof and a model of the house where a murderer was arrested.

THE MAGIC TAP MYSTERY

An ordinary household tap is suspended in mid air from four pieces of string. An endless supply of water appears to be flowing from the tap into a basin beneath. A number of mystified spectators are gathered around the attendant in charge, trying to figure out how the "Magic Tap" works.

"There's no pipes or anything attached", says the attendant.

"Well how does it do it?" asks a member of the audience.

"I'll give you a clue. What goes up must come down. Now do you get it?"

"No."

"Is that real water?" asks another.

"Of course it's real water. I'll put my pencil through it to prove it. There you are. It's come out wet. So it must be water".

"I still don't see how it's done", says a young woman who has been one of the most inquisitive.

"Well I'll lift you up and show you. Now do you see?"

"Not yet – oh yes!" she discovers the answer, "I see at last!"

"You can come down now. But don't you go telling all the other people, will you?"

Almost opposite the "Magic Tap" is a small cinema. I go inside and see some Ministry of Information films about road accidents, road planning, and juvenile delinquency in Scotland.

Upstairs in Olympia are pictures about housing and reconstruction, fragments of rocks and geological strata, and small models of Central Station before and after the proposed replanning.

Tuesday 22nd October

Examples of how to attract customers and sell goods to them can often be seen at Blackpool when there are many people about. The salesperson will talk while demonstrating what is being offered for sale. When anyone stands up in a public place and speaks loudly and persuasively, he or she will invariably attract a crowd. If something is for sale, however worthless it may appear, as long as enough spectators attend the demonstration, there is always somebody who can be talked into buying it.

LITTLEWOODS SALESMAN IN ACTION

One of the first shops in the town centre I go to is Littlewoods. At one of the counters a salesman is demonstrating how to use a particular brand of polish.

"All you have to do", shouts the salesman, "is just apply it with a dry cloth and rub like this. It doesn't get your hands dirty, ladies, and it saves months of your soap ration. You can use it for cleaning any shoes, boots or furniture, and it's not affected by water. It'll polish up your grate better than ordinary metal polish. Only a shilling [5p] a tin. There's two colours: green and black. Thank you lady. One of each, sir? Thank you. If you're not satisfied I'll refund the money."

A man who has previously bought a tin hands it to the salesman and asks for his money back. After the customer has his shilling refunded the demonstrator opens the tin and remarks, "That's the first dissatisfied customer I've had in a fortnight. I don't believe he's even tried it."

He applies some polish from the returned tin onto a piece of dirty leather and it immediately becomes clean and bright. "There you are," he says. "There's nothing wrong with that."

BARBED WIRE AT PLEASURE BEACH

In the afternoon my first visit to the Pleasure Beach finds it almost deserted, with only a few visitors wandering around. I assume that this is because the holiday season has ended. My guess may have been wrong, as the War had caused a temporary halt on new developments at the Pleasure Beach, and may have been the main reason for the lack of activity at this time.

The popular Roller Coaster, Big Dipper, Grand National, Pleasure Beach railway and numerous other exciting rides and attractions in this Amusement Park are usually a hive of activity during the summer. The only movement I notice today is that of a contraption like a two sailed windmill being tested. It appears that passengers are carried on each of the sails when it is in motion.

Workmen reconstructing some of the machines and rides ignore the holiday-makers strolling around.

Battered parts of derelict Dodgem cars are lying in the open exposed to the weather. I come to an area which seems as though it is not intended for public use, as heaps of barbed wire are lying on the ground. More barbed wire bars the exit from a sunken garden, so I have to retrace my steps and return through the entrance.

I hurl an apple core into an unoccupied boating lake which has a few empty rowing boats on it.

TOUGH STEAK AT A RESTAURANT

Before an evening performance at the Tower Circus, I go into a restaurant near the Tower, and sit down at an upstairs dining table where two men are talking.

That's the toughest bit of steak I've ever tasted", says one with a loud voice. "I've been coming here for the last fortnight and it's the worst meal I've had. Don't you think so, George?"

"That's the last time I'll have steak and chips here," agrees George, taking out a packet of cigarettes and offering one to his friend.

The waitress arrives and asks me: "What do you want?"

"I'll have Welsh Rarebit, tea and cakes."

"There's only one cake left", she says, and brings it to me.

"Better eat it quick before somebody pinches it", advises Loud Voice. "Do you know what I should like now, George?"

"What?" asks George.

"A nice plate of Gorgonzola and biscuits."

"Well why don't you ask the waitress for them? You won't get them, but there's no harm done by asking."

"I'll call her over and see what she says. You never know what might happen".

The next time the waitress passes our table, Loud Voice asks, "Could we have two plates of Gorgonzola and biscuits?"

The waitress laughs and replies, "You know very well that we haven't got such a thing!" but she does not sound offended.

"Well could we have our bill please?" asks Loud Voice.

"Yes", she replies, "That'll be seven shillings [35p] altogether."

"All right", and Loud Voice hands her a ten shilling [50p] note. "Take eight out of this".

George pushes ninepence [3¾p] under his plate for a tip and leaves with his friend.

DAYS OF RATIONING

Although other goods were rationed as well during this period – including clothing and footwear, I considered that food rationing was the most unwelcome restriction of all. Some people grumbled about it, while others made jokes, like describing a six course lunch as two chips and four peas.

Restaurants could only serve whatever foods were available, and their supplies were limited. George and his friend were partly joking and partly wishful thinking when they asked for Gorgonzola, knowing very well that imported foreign cheeses would be unobtainable.

I believe that the cheese ration was as low as one ounce per week at one time during the War, but later increased to four ounces. Other typical weekly allowances were two ounces of butter, two ounces of cooking fats, four or five ounces of margarine, four ounces of bacon and ham, a quarter of a pound of tea, half a pound of sugar, two and a half pints of liquid milk, and meat to the value of one shilling and twopence [6p]. About a pound (in weight) of sweets and chocolates per four weeks was allowed.

In wartime imported foods had to be brought from overseas in merchant ships, which were subjected to attacks from enemy aircraft and submarines. Many seamen were killed and injured, and shipping lost and damaged. It was some years after the war ended before conditions improved and restrictions caused by food and other shortages were lifted. The last foods to be de-rationed were butter, margarine, cheese and cooking fats in May 1954, and meat in June 1954.

Wednesday October 23rd

TRAM TO FLEETWOOD

On a misty morning, I decide to travel by tram to Fleetwood to find out what the town is like. The nine mile journey costs sevenpence [3p].

After a look around the quayside, market, railway station and town, I return to the tram terminus near the dock.

I board one of the older types of tram which does not have an automatic door. A cheerful middle aged driver is sitting in the front seat, smoking his pipe and talking to four young passengers.

"So you didn't get to the Isle of Man after all?" he says.

"No," answers one of the two lads, "The boat has stopped running there for the winter."

"You know," says the driver, "Some folks ask me if that's the Isle of Man over there," he points to the other side of the river.

"Is that the Ribble over there?".

"No, it's the Wyre. The Ribble's further down".

"Do you know much about the history of this place?" asks one of the girls.

25

"Yes, I daresay I could tell you a good deal about it if we didn't have to keep up a four minute service".

The driver continues talking until the conductor signals that it is time to commence the return journey to Blackpool North Station.

Thursday 24th October

"A BULLET IN THE BALLET"

On the final evening I see "A Bullet in the Ballet" at the Opera House. It is described as a comedy thriller with ballet in three acts, and is a dramatisation of a Brahms-Simon novel. It includes music by Stravinsky from Petrouchka. The ballet stars are Leonide Massine and Irina Baronova, and the main actors Barry Morse, Charles Goldner and Ivy St. Hellier.

Many famous artists in show business entertained both troops and civilians during the War. There were still enough live entertainment and theatre shows in Blackpool to attend a different one on every evening of the week. Some advertised at the time I was there included:

TOWER: Spectacular children's ballet, "Dancing Shoes", produced by Annette;

TOWER CIRCUS: The Cairolis – welcome return of famous clowns. Miss Peggy's Liberty Horses, The Tovarich Troupe. Water Ballet, "Aquamarine";

GRAND THEATRE: Ethel Revnell in "FINE FEATHERS";

OPERA HOUSE: George Formby in "STARRY WAY";

ICEDROME, PLEASURE BEACH: "ICE PARADE OF 1946".

Friday 25th October

TUNES ON PIANO

Shortly before I leave the guest house to return home, the manageress asks me, "Did you like playing on our piano yesterday?"

"Yes, I enjoy playing the piano".

"We enjoyed listening to you too. It made a change."

It does not matter how dusty or out of tune a piano may be, as long as there is some music available I can try to play something. The music I found in a piano stool included "Icicle Joe the Eskimo", "Destiny Waltz" and "Dizzy Fingers". Today, the opportunity of playing music on holiday has disappeared. With so many other leisure diversions available such as television, most hotels no longer have a piano in their lounge.

CHAPTER 2

12th – 19th JUNE 1948

Saturday 12th June

CRICKET

In the afternoon I watch a match at the cricket ground, Stanley Park, Blackpool versus Electric and Transport. Blackpool score 147 for 8 wickets in two hours and ten minutes. Admission charge is sixpence [2½p].

FINANCIAL LESSON

On the way to the Pleasure Beach I buy a choc ice and am charged ninepence [3¾p]. Sixpence is a normal average price for a similar ice cream.

WATCH OUT FOR PROFITEERS

Nylon stockings were among the goods which were scarce during this post war period of austerity, and could occasionally be found on sale on the Golden Mile. The sellers who took advantage of these shortages and made profits by selling commodities including sweets, confectionery, rock and chewing gum illegally off "points", were known as "SPIVS" or "WIDE BOYS" (from padded shoulders which were in fashion). Sometimes the culprits were caught in the act of selling by the Police and taken away to be dealt with for offences against the Ministry of Food rationing laws. However, others who were quick enough managed to get away by disappearing among the crowds of visitors.

There was no shortage of customers, as many people on holiday were glad to pay for anything on offer which was difficult to obtain, even if it was higher than the normal price.

After my experience with the choc ice, I learned in future to ask about the price of goods before buying them.

Sunday 13th June

SHRINKING SANDS

From the Central Pier I watch crowds on the beach become confined to an ever narrowing margin of dry land as the incoming tide gradually brings the sea nearer to the promenade.

Almost every available space on the sands is occupied by people enjoying themselves, as the weather is fine. Adults sunbathe or sit in deck chairs. Children amuse themselves with beach balls, and play cricket and other sports and games. Swimmers and paddlers of all ages splash about in the sea. Dogs join in the fun, chasing seagulls or running in and out of the water.

SPELLBOUND BY THE SANDS

Sand is absolutely fascinating. There is no end to the things you can do with it. You can walk on it in your bare feet and feel it soft and relaxing. You can run about on it, play games and sports like cricket, football, beachball, and it does not matter if you fall over, it is soft to land on. Or if you prefer to be less active you can lie on it, or sit in deck chairs and sunbathe.

Children can play in it, dig holes and channels for water to run in and out. Or build sandcastles and pies with spades, make designs, decorations and write messages or love letters. Afterwards all their artistic handiwork soon becomes destroyed, either by the tide coming in over it, or by other children jumping on it.

The combination of sand and salt water gives more scope for experiment. What better materials could be mixed together in a bucket to make a sloppy soggy mess?

The spell of the seaside is different every day and almost every time you look at it. The ever changing colours and patterns of the sea, sands and sky according to variations in the weather and wind. The movement of the waves, sometimes rough, sometimes smooth is fascinating to watch. No wonder it is such a great attraction to both young and old, some of whom would otherwise never see the sea but for their holiday.

THINGS AT SEA ARE NOT ALWAYS WHAT THEY APPEAR TO BE

An elderly Scotsman on the Promenade points out to sea and asks me, "What's that out there?"

"That's a bank of sand where the tide has gone out", I reply.

"Oh, and aren't there some people swimming in the sea straight out there?" He points in another direction.

"I can't see any straight ahead, but there are some people swimming further down the coast."

Monday 14th June

SOUTH PROMENADE BOATING POOL

Beyond the Pleasure Beach on the South Promenade is an open air Pool where children can sail their model boats. I see yachts, scale models of motor launches and tug boats and other sailing vessels both large and small. Children playing in the water, throwing balls to one another and splashing about, occasionally interfere with some of the boats, much to the displeasure of the owners.

Sometimes one of the children in the water falls down and gets his clothes soaking wet. The youngest usually burst into tears, and run to their parents.

One father said to his daughter, "If you fall in again, Violet, you go straight home to bed". But he did not carry out his threat when she tumbled over again.

Tuesday 15th June

ERIC'S ESCAPADE

I am sitting in a public shelter on the Promenade reading a book and enjoying the sunshine. Suddenly a boy aged about nine or ten and with a running nose approaches me.

"Could I have a penny, please?" he asks. "I want to go to the lavatory."

I hesitate at first, being mean by nature, but reluctantly decide to give him a penny. He runs off in the direction of the public lavatory, where I can hear some of his mates playing, and I think it will be the end of the episode. However, some minutes later he comes running back in distress.

"Somebody's got themselves locked in the lavatory down there," he cries, expecting me to do something about it. "He can't get out."

"Well, I suppose I'd better come and see," I reply, and follow the lad down the stairs. "Who's got locked in?"

"It's Eric," he answers, as if I'd know who Eric is. "He's locked himself in there," and points to a door behind which muffled noises can be heard. Outside the door, two young lads are standing helplessly.

I try to open the door, but without success. Then I examine the distance between the gap above the door and the ceiling, but decide that it is too high to attempt to climb.

"Put a penny in," advises the ringleader of the group.

I put a penny into the slot, draw the knob to one side and heave with all my weight against the door.

It opens easily, and out walks Eric, wagging his tail.

CHILDREN'S BALLET AT THE TOWER

The children's ballet at the Tower Ballroom is a well-known and popular feature each season. This year the title is STORYLAND. It is produced by Annette and commences at 6:00 p.m.; it lasts about an hour.

Behind the transparent curtain hung across the front of the stage a band can be seen. The lights go down, and suddenly the whole spectacle is one of youthful action and colour.

The first group of youngest girls come singing and dancing down the steps leading from the stage to the ballroom. More enthusiastic young girls follow, and soon half of the dance floor becomes filled with a troupe of agile dancers.

From the back of the top balcony two large spotlights follow the dancers. In the middle of the dance floor and around the top of the balconies a number of swiftly alternating electric lights add more colour. They change from blue to yellow, then to red, and back again to blue.

After a while the dancers return up the steps to music and make their exists at the side of the stage.

Their performance of various dances continues between turns by solo artistes. Individuals sing into some of the numerous microphones producing echoes throughout the hall, do impersonations of well-known characters on radio shows and play the drums, piano, xylophone and other musical instruments.

For the finale of this non-stop performance the whole company of about eighty girls are on the dance floor. A swing seat suspended from the roof is lowered. One of the smallest girls sits inside. She is hoisted high above the ballroom floor and waves to the audience below. The other dancers take up their positions and receive well deserved applause from the audience. The girl in the swing is lowered to the ground amid further applause. At the end of the performance she makes her exit with the rest of the young dancers.

Wednesday 16th June

SPORT AT STANLEY PARK

A bus ride to Stanley Park to watch more sport. First bowls on the bowling greens.

Then school athletics on the Oval sports field. Track races, hurdles, field events, high jump and tug-of-war. Four houses of a local school compete against one another for the most points – Chester, Durham, Lancaster and York – encouraged by cheers and shouts from their supporters.

DEATH OF STAR

Before the evening variety show I read a news headline: "Famous Star dies in Blackpool".

James Etherington was the singer in the Charlie Chester show at the Opera House. He collapsed after yesterday evening's performance and died at 5.00 a.m. this morning.

George and Alfred Black's production, "SKY HIGH", still goes on, with Frederick Ferrari taking over at short notice as the leading male singer.

"SKY HIGH" AT THE OPERA HOUSE

"Sky high" is a well-suited title to where I sit in the second row from the back in the Upper Circle. It certainly is "Sky High" above the stage!

As well as Charlie Chester, other stars in the show are Arthur Haynes, Ken Morris, Len Martin and Edwina Carrol. Frederick Ferrari deputises very well, and sings duets with Sylvia Welling.

WINTER GARDENS BALLROOM

After the stage performance I watch dancing in the nearby Winter Gardens, which may be considered to be the best ballroom for dancing in Blackpool.

Thursday 17th June

PALACE THEATRE AND BALLROOM

I see Lauri Lupino Lane and company in the stage musical, "ME AND MY GIRL". I sit in the second row from the back again, but this time in the Lower Gallery, not quite as high as at the Opera House.

After the show I watch dancing in the Palace ballroom. There are slightly fewer dancers than I saw at the Tower and Winter Gardens, but this is also a popular place for entertainment.

Friday 18th June

BINOCULARS SALESMAN ON THE GOLDEN MILE

Some of the patter from stallholders is as amusing as you can hear from comedians in theatre shows. One salesman on the Golden Mile is demonstrating a pair of binoculars.

"This is a very good pair", he says. "Useful for watching horse racing, dogs – I beg your pardon – greyhounds, or even looking for work. Though if you look for work you hold them the other way round." They are marked two pounds fifteen shillings [£2.75]. He sells them for ten shillings [50p].

CENTRAL STATION – SUPPLEMENTARY TICKET FOR SATURDAY TRAVEL

There are so many excursions on a Saturday from Blackpool that passengers have to book a supplementary rail ticket in advance from British Railways for the train on which they wish to travel. I go to Central Station to book my ticket for the 2.30 p.m. train from North Station tomorrow.

DECLINE IN RAIL SERVICE OF TODAY

Railways in Great Britain were nationalised on 1st January 1948. The deterioration in rail services since then was most noticeable on a journey I made over forty years later from Blackpool North station at a peak period during summer.

A diesel "Sprinter" train with only two coaches was grossly overcrowded. Day trippers and commuters crammed into every available space. Mothers with young children stood all the way to Preston on a hot afternoon. The half hour trip, to the sound of babies crying continuously, was one of the most uncomfortable rail journeys I have made.

It is not surprising that there has been an increased number of complaints in recent years by rail users about the decline in the reliability of services, including cancellations, delays and increases in fares. I certainly agree with the critics in view of my experience of Network NorthWest at Blackpool North station.

There is an alternative route to Preston from Blackpool South Station, along which trains stop at the Pleasure Beach station which was opened a few years ago. I have not travelled on this line so do not know what services are like, but understand that trains run less frequently than on the main line to Blackpool North.

TOWER AQUARIUM

In the afternoon I go inside the Tower again, taking shelter from the rain outside. The Aquarium is on a lower floor; it's dark inside. I look at many different species of fish and other sea creatures swimming in tanks.

In another room there is a mechanical organ inside a glass case. It plays hunting selections and other music, with drums, cymbal and triangle accompaniment.

BEACHCOMBERS ON THE NORTH SHORE

In the evening I go for a walk along the North Promenade towards the Miners Home. The shore is almost deserted except for two lads fishing in the rough sea. One casts his line, and almost immediately reels it in full of seaweed.

Later, sheltering from a shower behind some rocks, I see three men carrying bundles of drift-wood gathered from the beach. One says, "We've never had good weather since beginning of June. Ever since they restored the 'Basic'. There's no back pay for us upper class people", he jokes.

PETROL RATIONING

It was a common practice to blame the cause of a continuous spell of bad weather on any apparently unrelated reason, from the first atomic bomb dropped from a U.S. aircraft onto a Japanese city in the War, to whichever Government happened to be in power.

The beachcomber was referring to the basic petrol ration. Motorists were rationed to about 90 miles per month at this period. Petrol rationing ended on 26th May 1950. Immediately afterwards the price of petrol was increased to three shillings (15p) per gallon.

Saturday 19th June 1948

CENTRAL PROMENADE – ACTIVITY ON THE SANDS

In the morning, I take another look at the seashore. There is much activity as the tide is going out. Workmen with spades are digging channels in the sand for the water to drain away.

A beach guard in scarlet uniform unlocks the chains which bar the way to the beach at high tide. Dogs and children are the first to run down the steps to the sands, and explore what has been left on the shore.

As soon as the tide has receded far enough, Jeeps and other motor vehicles, towing ice cream stalls and caravans full of goods to sell, drive down from the promenade and fill the empty spaces on the sands. Barrows of oysters, cockles and other shellfish, horse drawn carts with balloons, toys and souvenirs, donkeys and a Punch and Judy Show take up suitable positions.

The Punch and Judy man beats his drum until the noise has attracted enough children around his stand for an audience. Then he passes the drum to his woman assistant, and disappears with his dog Toby inside his tent to prepare for the traditional show.

CHAPTER 3

18th – 22nd SEPTEMBER 1950

ROUGH WEATHER & DAMAGE TO ILLUMINATIONS

Sometimes, but not always, stormy weather occurs in the autumn, the period of the famous Illuminations. A local newspaper reported that £5,000 damage to the Lights had been caused by recent severe gales. However, no matter how bad the weather may be now you can always find someone who can remember when it was even worse.

Monday 18th September

BREEZY BLACKPOOL

Sheltering from the storm, I overhear two pensioners talking.

"We've had some rough weather this week, but I'm glad it's not as bad as it was on Saturday", said one man. "There were fourteen people taken to hospital. I saw one girl blown off her feet near Talbot Square. It was wicked."

"Aye", agreed the other. "The wind always blows strong along there", and he re-fastened the buttons of his second overcoat.

"I was wearing three coats myself that day", said the first. "You've got to keep warm somehow when you're old."

On the Golden Mile there are signs that some of the shops and stalls have suffered damage from the gales. Two men are trying to put up a new sunblind after the previous one has been blown away.

The wind blows sand well inland from the South Shore, like a sandstorm in the desert. Any movable objects are blown about. I catch one man's trilby hat. A large thick rug is propelled from an open horse drawn landau into the middle of the road near the Pleasure Beach.

PROFITABLE EYESHADES

Lots of visitors and stallkeepers are wearing plastic eyeshades to protect their eyes from the sand blown about by the gales. They are on sale at some of the stalls for sixpence [2½p] each. Whoever is supplying them must be making a good profit.

VISITORS MORE CAREFUL WITH THEIR MONEY

This year visitors seem to be more choosy in how they spend their money compared with previous seasons, and are not buying so many things. Even when they seek shelter from the wind and rain inside the amusement places on the Golden Mile, they are more careful about how much they spend on the machines.

All the main holiday entertainment and theatre shows are booked up for about two or three days in advance, except for the dearest seats which cost from seven shillings and sixpence [37½p] to ten shillings [50p].

THE ILLUMINATIONS "THE GREATEST FREE SHOW ON EARTH"

Blackpool's Tourism and Attractions Department describes the Illuminations as "The greatest free show on earth".

The first use of coloured electric lighting and slogans in Blackpool were on five Corporation tramcars introduced in 1897 to celebrate Queen Victoria's Diamond Jubilee.

The first Illuminations were introduced on 2nd May 1912 when Princess Louise opened a static display on the new Princess Parade. The display was re-erected on 8th September and lasted until the middle of October 1912. An extended display of 60,000 lamps from the South Pier to Gynn Square proved very successful in autumn 1913, but the First World War in 1914 prevented plans for further extension.

In 1925 the Illuminations were restored with a display between the Manchester Hotel and Cocker Square. They were repeated in 1928 with an extended display from South Shore to Gynn Square, and continued increasing in size each year, except for a break from 1939 to 1948 owing to the Second World War. When fuel restrictions were relaxed in 1949 they were revived, and are now the resort's greatest attraction. They are usually switched on by a well known celebrity. Champion racehorse Red Rum is among the famous who have performed the switch-on ceremony.

Tuesday 19th September

THE ILLUMINATIONS – A BRILLIANT IDEA, BUT YOU CAN'T PLEASE EVERYBODY

I think that whoever first thought of the Illuminations had a brilliant idea. Seeing them for the first time I am very impressed. I define them as "Rainbowland in glorious technicolor." A conductor as his tram stops at Central Pier announces: "Fairyland".

All the way along the promenade for about five miles from the South Shore to Bispham is a dazzling assortment of coloured lamps, scenic designs and tableaux. Trams and buses are full of sightseers on trips. The cost of a local motor coach tour is about five shillings [25p], and a similar price is charged to see the lights in an open horse drawn landau.

It is one way traffic along the promenade from south to north, well controlled by the Police, with incoming and outgoing routes clearly signposted.

In spite of recent storms there are few dark spaces where lights have failed to come on. The Corporation breakdown van is busy driving along the promenade before and after dark, and their workmen attend to any repairs they discover.

As well as promenade displays there are three brightly illuminated trams which attract attention as they are driven along the tramway. They represent a gondola, a sailing yacht, and a brilliantly lit double decker with the words "BLACKPOOL WELCOMES PROGRESS" written in large coloured lights.

It is impossible to please everyone, and there are sure to be some who criticise the Illuminations. A few complain that some of the lights are concealed behind shelters and cannot be seen from a tram. Another finds fault with one particular design in Gynn Square because he is unable to make out what it is supposed to represent.

EARLY SHUT DOWN AT THE PLEASURE BEACH

The lights at the Pleasure Beach are turned off at 10 pm each evening. I am sheltering from the rain there about that time, while stallkeepers and amusements workers are gradually putting up their shutters and closing after the day's work. The lights go out one by one, leaving blackness in place of brilliance.

Wednesday 20th September

COMPLAINTS FROM FAMILY ON A TRAM

A holiday party from Hastings, Sussex, on a tram are complaining about being charged sevenpence for a postcard. At this time the average cost of coloured postcards on sale in shops is about sixpence [2½p].

The travellers say that it is only three halfpence fare to see the Illuminations on their sea front, whereas the minimum tram fare along the Blackpool promenade is twopence.

The conductor replies: "Well you haven't got a seven mile prom like Blackpool, and not so many lights on it either. How long is your front?"

"Three miles", answers the eldest man in the group.

"Well you get the cheaper fare here," says the conductor.

The tram turns off the promenade at the Manchester Hotel and the family alight.

"Anyway it's their own fault if they pay so much for postcards", the conductor says to the other passengers. "They shouldn't buy them. I don't know why people on holiday buy so many postcards. They're only encouraging the shops to charge high prices. But those that do are not from Blackpool anyway."

NORTH PIER – "ON WITH THE SHOW"

In the afternoon I face a gale walking to the end of the North Pier. Mackintosh and headscarves are typical protective wear during the present rough weather, and even a fur coat is seen on occasions.

"On with the Show", now in its twenty sixth year, is produced by Lawrence Wright. The stars include Albert Modley and Betty Jumel. The entertainment and comedy are enjoyed by the audience.

Thursday 21st September

WINTER GARDENS – "TAKE IT FROM HERE"

At the Winter Gardens, where stars of the radio show "Take It From Here" are appearing, Dick Bentley is unable to take part owing to illness, and his place is taken by Billy Russell.

With Jimmy Edwards and Joy Nichols heading the cast, the stage performance gains plenty of laughs and applause from the audience.

Another popular act in the show is "Nino the Wonder Dog", who balances on beach balls of different sizes without help from anyone.

DANCING TO JOE LOSS & HIS BAND

After the theatre performance I go into the ballroom nearby, where Joe Loss and his band are playing dance music. Many of the audience seem to have come to watch and listen to this well known and popular band, as there are fewer couples on the dance floor than spectators seated around it.

ANOTHER VIEW OF THE ILLUMINATIONS

When there is a break in the music I go outside for a final look at the Illuminations, which continue to shine brightly until late in the evening. Lifts take people to the top of the Tower, where they can obtain a fine view. One searchlight shines from the top of the Tower, and another at a lower level scans the sea.

There are so many illuminated displays that it is not possible to see all of them during only three or four evenings. The rough weather prevents much walking about, and most of my views of the Illuminations are from a tram. They are most attractive, and it is well worth while coming to see them.

Friday 22nd September

TOWER ZOO

In the morning I make another visit to the Tower and have a look around the Zoo. The two chimpanzees, Adam and Eveline, are amusing themselves playing with a ball. A white haired keeper enters the cage and speaks to them, and they appear pleased to see him.

Ranee the tigress gave birth to three cubs in June. Two of them are playing together like kittens. The third, who does not look very well, sits in a corner of the cage and refuses to join in.

A few visitors think that it is a shame to keep wild animals in captivity. "Isn't it cruel to keep animals caged up like this?" The Zoo is rather stuffy and smells of sawdust and animals.

R.H.O. HILLS, AND RETURN BY TRAIN

I enter the restaurant on the top floor of R.H.O. Hills' store for lunch. Good food, excellent service. The bill is rather expensive, but the meal is considered good value for money.

One of the last things I do before going for the train home is buy a new cap for five shillings [25p].

I return on the 3:15 p.m. train from Central Station. The journey back is very quiet after the activity and excitement at Blackpool.

NOT SO FIERCE DOG

Among the many happy memories of my holiday, was a bulldog which sat in the doorway of a fish and chip shop near Stanley Mortensen's sports shop. It looked fierce, but was really quite friendly and allowed a bold man to stroke it.

CHAPTER 4

2nd – 12th JULY 1951

Monday 2nd July

ARRIVAL BY TRAIN AND TAXI

After travelling by train to Blackpool North Station and arriving at mid-day, I take a taxi to the guest house where I am staying for the next ten days. It is in a convenient central position in the town, between an ice cream place and the railway.

REVELRY ON THE PROMENADE

The first sign of high spirits and merrymaking is seen on the promenade, where a crowd of onlookers are gathered. They are watching a woman wearing a Union Jack on her skirt and bells on her garters encouraging other members of her party to join in dancing the Hokey-Cokey.

METHODS OF TRANSPORT TO THE PLEASURE BEACH

In the evening I travel by tram to the Pleasure Beach to see the Ice Show. There are so many people waiting for trams that taxis draw up at the queues and offer to take passengers for a shilling [5p] each. Many visitors choose to travel in open horse drawn landaus.

Tuesday 3rd July

ROCK OFF POINTS

Blackpool rock, one of the traditional seaside specialities, is as popular as ever today with children of all ages, in spite of rationing. They enjoy buying some at the rock stalls, and eating it or taking it home.

A spiv says to me: "Any rock off points? Not me. Too expensive. Too many fines. Too much gaol. Would you like some chewing gum off points?"

Why is rock so popular? A youth I overhear talking to his mates outside a fish and chip shop says: "You can't get Blackpool rock in Leeds."

The present ration of sweets and chocolates, including rock, is sixteen ounces a month. I spend my personal points coupons at a confectioner's on four four ounce sticks of rock – two different colours, red and yellow, and lettered all the way through.

In a rainstorm on the Golden Mile, I see a man in a hurry carrying a monster container of rock. It bursts open and half the contents are scattered on the wet ground. He does not notice until his companion points it out and warns him not to lose the other half.

BLACKPOOL ROCK IS MADE IN BLACKPOOL

Nowadays rock is plentiful and can be bought in all shapes, sizes, colours and flavours. Visitors can see how it is made as well as take some home as a souvenir. Two of the local rock manufacturing companies hold demonstrations on their premises showing how their products are prepared, and spectators are invited free.

It is understood that another confectionery company from nearby St. Annes on Sea holds the world record for the heaviest stick of rock manufactured, so the specialists in this skilled craft are well represented in the Fylde area.

Wednesday 4th July

RUGBY LEAGUE COMPETITION AT STANLEY PARK

In the afternoon I go to Stanley Park to see a Rugby League match between Huddersfield and Dewsbury. It is the first time I have seen Rugby League, which is played mainly in the north of England, but not normally during the summer. Others in the crowd have obviously not watched this thirteen-a-side professional sport before either, as some men are trying to explain the rules to their wives and children before the game starts.

It is a fast and hard-fought game, and most of the spectators seem to enjoy it. Huddersfield win by 27 points to 21, although they have a player off the field injured for about half of the second half.

CENTRAL PIER SHOW

In the evening I go onto the Central Pier to see Al Read in "Right Monkey".

Thursday 5th July

ELECTRIC NEWSREEL

You do not need to buy a newspaper to read the news in Blackpool. On the top of the Palatine Hotel there is an electric newsreel which spells out news items continuously throughout the day.

Three men on the promenade are looking upwards as it flashes out: "Weather forecast for tomorrow – little change".

"That's right enough", one of them laughs, "You have little change left in your pocket when you go home from Blackpool".

CRICKET AT STANLEY PARK

I make another afternoon visit to Stanley Park, this time to watch cricket. There are not a large number of spectators. Blackpool, strengthened by Australian Test players, Dooland and Tribe, are playing Lancashire Club and Ground in a two day match.

It is all over just after 4.00 p.m. on the second day. Blackpool declare at 312 for 7 wickets, Tribe scoring 161. Then the two Australians, helped by some good fielding, bowl the Lancashire side out for 100 in their second innings, and Blackpool win by an innings.

SOUTH PIER SHOW

In the evening at the South Pier, another well known northern comedian, Dave Morris, stars in "Club Night". He can also be heard on radio in a show with the same name.

Friday 6th July

STALLKEEPER ACCUSED OF SWINDLE

A showman who has a stall where a ball is rolled into numbered sections, is accused by a woman customer of running a swindle.

He replies: "A swindle? Indeed it's not. You see this number here?" He points to a card at the side of his stall. "That shows this game has been approved by the Blackpool Council. They examine these games thoroughly, and if they don't show a certain percentage of wins you don't see them back. We've got a keen Chief Constable here, you know. He won't take no nonsense from anybody. He had the Conservative Club up last week, and in a Conservative town too."

UNCLE'S ONE-UPMANSHIP & KEEN COMPETITION

There is keen competition between the two leading Bingo stallkeepers on the promenade, who are both known as "Uncle", and by chatting and joking generally manage to attract a number of onlookers. Both claim to have the finest selection of prizes. Bingo has been universally popular for many years, and one reason why so many visitors are attracted to the stalls is the desire to win a prize of goods which are still scarce.

One stallkeeper says to his audience: "If you go into the other amusement places they'll only swindle you, so why not come in here and be swindled by me? I've got the best choice of prizes in Blackpool. No penny brooch or packet of flea powder! You can have anything you see on this stall from a pair of nylons to fifty cigarettes – sixty if you smoke Woodbines."

The other "Uncle" went one up on his rival by getting his name mentioned in a national newspaper about two weeks ago. The Mayor of Blackpool went to his stall and tried to win a teapot he fancied. After spending about a pound without winning anything he bought the teapot for sixteen shillings [80p]. The newspaper printed a story about it, which gained much publicity for "Uncle".

Saturday 7th July

PALACE THEATRE EXTRA ACT

One of the funniest unrehearsed incidents I have seen at a stage show occurs at the Palace Theatre this evening. Top of the bill is ventriloquist Peter Brough, popular for his act with Archie Andrews.

In the same show are Ravic and partner, a roller skating act, who perform on a small circular drum.

After the end of the first house there are a few minutes to spare before the second performance is due to begin. Volunteer members of the audience are invited onto the stage to be whirled around by Ravic for a laugh. They hang on to his neck in turn, and the roller skater whirls them around the drum a few times at speed. Most of them become dizzy afterwards, and stagger back to their seats unsteadily.

The last male volunteer is being spun around the drum when suddenly his trousers come off and fly across the footlights. He runs for cover trouserless, and disappears into the scenery at the back of the stage to hide his embarrassment. Peter Brough calls for the curtain to be lowered. There is much laughter from everyone except the unlucky victim.

OLD TIME DANCING

After the show I go into the Palace ballroom to watch old time dancing. The music is provided by an orchestra and dances are being enjoyed by people of all ages. I see many dances that I have not seen before – the Waltz Cotillion, the Lancers and Festival of Britain waltz.

Sunday 8th July

The Pleasure Beach is not open on Sundays, but some of the amusements on the Central Promenade are.

HOW TO TAKE ADVANTAGE OF AN UNEXPECTED SHOWER

It is a warm day, but a sudden heavy shower in the morning catches by surprise many visitors, who are wearing only light summer clothing. One salesman has a plastic head cover and comb set on his stall, and sells about twenty of them for a shilling [5p] each in a very short time.

Taxi drivers also take advantage of the sudden change of weather to pick up passengers and drive them to hotels or other shelter.

These are examples of how profits can be made from unexpected happenings by resourceful individuals who seize their opportunities.

STANLEY PARK FOR OPEN AIR LEISURE ACTIVITIES

Stanley Park was designed by architect E. Prentice Mawson, and landscaped at a cost of £250,000, covering 250 acres of former waste land. It was opened on 4th October 1926 by Lord Derby, head of the Stanley family. Up to three million visitors yearly use six bowling greens (both flat and crown), thirty-two tennis courts, two eighteen-hole putting courses, a Crazy Golf course, three grass cricket squares, two concrete pitches, ten soccer pitches, four table tennis tables and numerous boats on the lake.

Stanley Park is very popular with local people as well as visitors, and is the town's largest and best known public park. Many sporting events are held there, and during Blackpool's Sports Week these include tennis, golf, bowls and Rugby League.

On a fine day it is very pleasant to wander around the beautiful rose gardens and see the various colours of the flowers reflected in the brilliant sunshine. The ornamental fountain and pond in the centre of the Italian gardens is a favourite subject for photographers.

OPEN AIR SERVICE

Members of Sunday Schools from different Churches in Blackpool, Salvation Army, Boys Brigade and Scouts march to Stanley Park for an open air service. It takes place in the Oval, where the Rugby League match and athletics meeting were held during the past week.

Monday 9th July

STALLKEEPER'S FORECAST FOR BIG FIGHT

There is much interest in tomorrow's world middleweight boxing championship between Randolph Turpin and Sugar Ray Robinson. On his Golden Mile stall, "Uncle" is in good voice, and entertains customers with his forecast. "Turpin will win. You don't want to believe all you hear about Sugar Ray Robinson. Turpin's not afraid of him. I'll have the wireless on tomorrow night, and you can all listen to the fight. If Turpin wins I'll open a bottle of whisky and give everybody a drink. If Robinson wins you can have my kind regards."

Tuesday 10th July

PALACE THEATRE AND OLD TIME DANCING AGAIN

After enjoying myself at further visits to the Tower and Stanley Park in the daytime, I get more entertainment in the evening at the Palace Theatre. There is a different variety show this week. The main stars are Peter Cavanagh, Robert Moreton and Marjorie Manners.

In the Palace ballroom, much energy continues to be used by the Old Time dancers. One of the attendants says: "You can work up a good thirst with these Old Time Dances. You can't work up a thirst at all with the modern ones". The bar is doing a good trade.

THE BIG FIGHT – RANDOLPH TURPIN v SUGAR RAY ROBINSON

I leave the Palace to find out news of the world middleweight fight. The radio commentary is due to start at 9.30 p.m.

Near the Central Station at 9.45 p.m. a crowd is gazing up at the electric newsreel on the top of the Palatine Hotel. So far no announcement has been made about the fight.

I hear a man who has just come out of a public house say, "Turpin's been warned again", so hurry back to the private hotel where I am staying.

In the lounge there is a group around the radio set listening to the fight. I arrive towards the end of the second round. Turpin seems to be doing better than expected against the powerful champion, who has already held the world welterweight title and is a hot favourite to win.

Robinson's eye is cut in the seventh round. The 23 year old Leamington Spa boxer matches his more experienced American opponent in a tremendously thrilling contest.

The fight goes the full fifteen rounds, then everyone waits expectantly for the result. When Turpin is announced the winner on points pandemonium breaks loose.

Joke about the fight: "Turpin was fined for breaking Ministry of Food regulations. He was discovered flogging 156 pounds of 'Sugar'." Sugar was not de-rationed until September 1953.

Wednesday 11th July

SQUIRES GATE AIRPORT AND HOLIDAY CAMP

Aircraft from Squires Gate Airport take visitors on pleasure flights over Blackpool for seven shillings and sixpence [37½p].

There is also a Holiday Camp at Squires Gate. Occasionally residents from the camp are seen pedalling along the roads on specially made four wheeled cycles built for two persons.

"UNCLE'S" TRIBUTE TO LANDLADIES

"Uncle" says to his customers: "When you're leaving your lodgings and come to pay your landlady, don't give her an extra ten bob. Make it a pound. They work hard for their living, you know."

CHAPTER 5

7th – 19th JUNE 1952

SHOWMANSHIP ON THE GOLDEN MILE

The "Golden Mile," that legendary length of the promenade between the Central Pier and the Tower, where fortunes are told – and made – is one of the best known localities of Blackpool. At the time, amusement arcades, bingo parlours, sideshows, striptease shows, cafes, rock and souvenir stalls are run independently. There is much competition between stallholders.

Noise is used to attract customers, amplified by microphones and loud speakers, with much shouting of what is being offered. Loud voiced showmen keep up a steady stream of patter.

One trick of the trade is to plant an accomplice among the audience to recommend a show. After his introduction, the showman goes on to something like this: "Now I know that a lot of you here may be sceptical and don't believe what I am telling you. Is there anyone who has seen this show before? You sir? And you, madam? Can you tell the audience that everything I have said is true and that this is the most amazing show in Blackpool?"

I always hope that someone will answer: "Yes, as true as my name's Donald Duck".

Saturday 7th June

SEASIDE SUNSET

From the Central Pier I observe a beautiful sunset. An orange sun is going down above a reddish brown calm sea. The tide is coming in, and waves are gently rippling towards the golden sands. Ice cream papers, orange peel, cigarette ends and other litter on the shore are being caught up by the incoming tide. Squawking seagulls squabble over anything they can find to eat.

Sunday 8th June

SUNDAY SHOW ON CENTRAL PIER

In the evening I go into the Central Pier theatre where Uncle Peter Webster is presenting a show. There are laws limiting what can be performed on Sundays, but there is no shortage of fun and laughter in this stage performance.

Uncle Peter invites a number of children from the audience to act on the stage, and some of the results are very amusing. He auditions one group for parts in an old fashioned melodrama, and the audience is invited to vote for the winners.

Some of the children make mistakes in speaking their lines. One boy taking the hero's role is supposed to say to the villain: "Unhand that woman, you dirty dog!" What he actually says is: "Unhand that dirty woman!"

Another youngster taking the part of the villain has to say to the heroine: "Marry me or I'll foreclose your mortgage". He says: "Marry me or I'll CLOSE your mortgages!"

Monday 9th June

BOATMAN'S SALES TALK

It is a warm and bright morning with a moderate breeze, and there are many people on the promenade. Boat trips on the sea are popular, as the tide is coming in and there is not much spare space on the sands. An elderly boatman tries to attract customers by shouting:

"Come along now if you're coming for a trip around the bay. Four miles for two shillings [10p]. You'll never get a smoother sea. It's not rough enough to knock the skin off a rice pudding. We never bring any passengers back sea-sick. We just dump them overboard!"

Tuesday 10th June

TRAILER RESCUED FROM INCOMING TIDE

By the South Pier people gradually move away from the beach as the tide comes in. One ice cream trailer remains until the water has surrounded it. A beach patrolman talks to the girl attendant still inside the trailer. By now the tide has almost reached the promenade, and everyone else has left the sands.

The owner of the trailer arrives on the promenade in his car, and manages to rescue the girl from the sea, but finds that the water has become too deep for him to tow the vehicle away. The final recovery is made when the Land Rover which takes people out to the motor boats arrives. With the help of two beach patrolmen it drives into the sea and tows the trailer to dry land on the other side of the Pier.

GRAND THEATRE, "BRIGADOON"

In the evening I go to the Grand Theatre to see the popular musical play, "Brigadoon". The audience, including myself, enjoy the delightful music.

Wednesday 11th June

BEACH PHOTOGRAPHER'S STORY

"I took a holiday picture of a man and his wife on the promenade, but it didn't come out too well. He had his eyes closed. When I showed the print to him I didn't expect that he would want it. But he said he'd have half a dozen copies. When I asked him why, he said, 'My wife's always telling me I go about with my eyes shut. I'll take these to show her, to prove it'!"

CHERRY TREE GARDENS

In the afternoon I take a bus ride to Cherry Tree Gardens, near Marton. Seeing the name on a bus, I am curious to learn where it goes to and what is there.

The gardens are pleasant, warm and sheltered from the cool breeze blowing from the sea. I sit on a seat by the bowling green and watch a girl painting a picture of trees and flowers. When she has finished she packs her paint brushes and artist's gear into a box and walks away.

A boy and his father are playing a game of bowls. The mother of the same family and a little girl aged about five are on a seat nearby. The greenkeeper and a youth are also watching.

Very few people come into the gardens during the afternoon. When anyone does enter, the greenkeeper goes after them to collect the admission charge of one penny.

DISAPPEARANCE OF GARDENS

Anyone looking for Cherry Tree Gardens today would be unable to find them, as I discovered on a later visit that they are no longer in existence and the area where they used to be has changed a good deal.

Exploring off Cherry Tree Road I found a modern estate with well kept red brick built houses. There were no public gardens, but green and pleasant grassy spaces between the houses and road. A notice: "Please keep off lawns. Do not exercise dogs".

On the corner of Cherry Tree Road was a modern single storey building, inside which in a dining room I saw upturned chairs stacked on top of tables. Elderly men and women were sitting in another room, and I discovered that the building was an old people's residential home. The name, "CHERRY TREE HOUSE", was above the main entrance.

Thursday 12th June

NOAH'S ARK AND THE INFLUENCE OF TELEVISION

Noah's Ark in the Pleasure Beach sprouted a couple of television aerials on top of its roof. As the number of households with television sets gradually increased after the end of the War, what was shown on television influenced and affected our way of life more widely throughout the country.

THE TOWER AND WHAT PEOPLE SAY ABOUT IT

The Tower is the most conspicuous and unique speciality which makes Blackpool different from anywhere else. You cannot avoid seeing it wherever you go. It is a landmark for miles around.

Replicas and miniatures of the Tower are on sale at every souvenir shop. There are badges, brooches, glassware, headscarves, pennants, Meccano outfits, pottery, ties, trinkets, picture postcards and in every other conceivable form and shape.

A well known comedian has said: "I go into the Tower because it is the only way I can get away from seeing it!"

Visitors seeing it for the first time stand and gape open-mouthed at it, and say: "Oh look! The Tower!"

When the Tower lift stops near the top, I stare upwards at it, and attract a group of visitors. They gaze and gasp, "Oh look! The lift is stuck". But it is not long before it starts to move again.

The Tower is a convenient topic of conversation between strangers who meet beneath it.

HIGHER-UPMANSHIP

One middle aged lady to another: "Have you ever been to top of th' Tower?"

"No, but I've been to the top of the Eiffel Tower in Paris. That's higher. I went with a party."

BUT IT'S NOT A LEANING TOWER

Boy aged about eleven, looking up at the Tower: "Just imagine that falling down!"

Friday 13th June

MARIONETTE SHOW

In addition to the Punch and Judy show, there are also Marionette shows on the sands. I watch the performance of "Little Red Riding Hood" held in the back of a mobile van. There are more adults than children looking at the show, which lasts about a quarter of an hour.

Saturday 14th June

OLYMPIC SWIMMING TRIALS AT DERBY BATHS

The Olympic swimming trials at the Derby Baths are being televised, and spectators are allowed in free to watch them. There is a queue outside the baths for tickets, and I have to wait some time before being allowed inside.

A group of young men in the queue are joking while they wait. A latecomer joins them.

"Hurry up," says one of the others, "We've just refused five tickets."

"Oh I forgot to bring my swimming costume and towel", jests the newcomer.

They see two men carrying a large case being allowed through the "Officials" entrance.

"Well that's one way of getting in easily", says one of the queuers, "Has anyone got a First Aid box or case or something?"

There are 2,000 seats around the main swimming pool and all are occupied. Television cameramen, technicians, press photographers and officials hold the best positions for viewing.

We watch swimming, diving and a water polo match in which Great Britain defeat The Rest 9-1. Some enthusiastic Scottish supporters cheer noisily when swimmers from Motherwell are in the water.

Sunday 15th June

SPORTS HOLIDAY – CRICKET

Blackpool's Sports Holiday is being held from June 14th until June 28th. Sporting events include cricket matches, tennis, an athletics meeting of the Lancashire and Cheshire Boys Clubs, Olympic swimming trials at the Derby Baths, and yacht races at sea, weather permitting.

In the afternoon I go to Stanley Park to watch part of the cricket match between Blackpool and Ilkley. Blackpool score 161 for 6 wickets and then declare.

STRANGERS ON THE NORTH SHORE

I overhear part of a conversation between two middle aged ladies who meet in a shelter near Gynn Square.

"Are you on holiday here?"

"Yes. I come from Leek in North Staffordshire. Twelve miles from Buxton. Twelve miles from the Potteries. I came by the coach. You can get a coach direct from Manchester. Where do you come from?"

"I come from Scotland – near Edinburgh. I'm staying for a fortnight."

"Are you by yourself?"

"Oh yes. I prefer to be by myself. Are you with anyone?"

"Yes, there are three of us. I've not been in very good health lately. I've had bronchitis every winter. I'm only just recovering from it. Have you got good lodgings?"

"Oh yes, splendid. The food is delicious". She goes into details of what has been served for dinner and tea, which makes my mouth water.

"How much are you paying while you're here?"

"Oh I'm staying for a fortnight. I arrived here yesterday."

"I mean how much are they charging you per night?"

"Oh it's twelve and sixpence [62½p]. How much do you pay for yours?"

"I'm catering for myself. Just having bed and breakfast. I've brought tea, butter and sugar with me. I can get some meat on an emergency card."

Monday 16th June

NEW TRAM

I am standing outside the entrance to the North Pier when a new tram, No. 304, glides along and stops on the middle track. It has already been on a trial run along the promenade. A crowd gathers on both sides of the track and stares at it.

The driver turns the trolley on the overhead wires in preparation for the next journey southwards. He also alters the indicator on the front from RESERVED to SOUTH PROMENADE VIA PLEASURE BEACH, so it appears that passengers are to be allowed on the next trip.

A Rolls Royce carrying the Mayor and Mayoress drives up and stops on the tram track. The passengers alight and are shown around the tram. The Mayor inspects the controls and spacious driving cab with interest and opens the front window. He prepares to drive the tram on its first passenger journey.

Those who are first in the queue are allowed inside the tram, and it soon fills up with passengers. Two Tramway Inspectors order some of the crowd outside away from the track. Press photographers position their cameras in readiness to take photographs of the historic occasion when the tram moves off.

The vehicle starts slowly, driven by the Mayor wearing his top hat and chain of office, and guided by the Tramway Manager. It gains speed smoothly along the Promenade towards the Pleasure Beach, and disappears out of sight among other trams and holiday crowds.

FIRST CORONATION CAR

The first new post war trams were the twenty-five Coronation cars, originally numbered from 304 to 328 – 1952 was the year Queen Elizabeth was crowned. They were very handsome looking trams, 50 feet long and about 8 feet wide; cream and green central entrance single-deckers, built by Charles Roberts of Wakefield and seating 56 passengers. I believe that only one of the Coronation trams remains at Blackpool today, re-numbered 660.

SPORTS HOLIDAY – TENNIS

Another visit to Stanley Park in the afternoon, this time to see part of the tennis tournament. According to the Sports Holiday leaflet obtained from the Information Bureau, the tennis is supposed to start at 2.00 p.m. When I arrive just before 3.00 p.m. play has not yet started.

A few minutes later some of the players come on to the courts and start playing. The weather is rather unsettled at first, which may be the reason for the late start.

Tuesday 17th June

SOUTH SHORE OPEN AIR BATHS – MANNEQUIN PARADE

Also part of the Sports Holiday fortnight programme is a mannequin parade and aquatic display held at the South Shore open air baths in the afternoon.

(Blackpool Branch R.N.L.I.)

South Shore Open Air Baths

The mannequin parade advertises what kind of ladies' clothing is on sale at R.H.O. Hills' store. Fourteen attractive models walk around the pool showing different fashions and costumes. I think mischievously that it would be fun if the cool breeze should blow one of their hats into the water. It would be transformed from a straw boater into a straw FLOATER.

AQUATIC DISPLAY

The aquatic display is given by three young members of Blackpool Amateur Swimming Club. In spite of the cold wind they produce a good exhibition of diving.

The spectators have to sit in the open air without any shelter from the weather.

After the diving display the Baths are open to the public, but only a few of the hardiest young swimmers are bold enough to venture into the cold water. One of the attendants calls four young lads over to the fountains and tells them that the water is warmer there, but they do not remain in it for very long.

CONTRAST TODAY

Conditions are very different there today. The SANDCASTLE, which has been built on the site of the former Open Air Baths, has a constant temperature of 84°F (27°C).

BOY WHO LIKES SWIMMING

I ask a young lad named Michael, who is fond of swimming, if he goes to the open air baths.

"No fear!" he replies, "I go to the Lido. I caught double pneumonia after swimming in the open air pool."

PUBLIC BATHS

There used to be four Corporation swimming baths in Blackpool, but the Lido is the only one which remains open today. The others were the South Shore Open Air Pool, and indoor baths at Cocker Street and the Derby Baths, Warley Road.

SOUTH PIER, RAINBOW PIERROTS

In the evening I see the Rainbow Pierrots on the South Pier for one shilling [5p]. It is not the best show in Blackpool by any means, but you cannot expect a star studded Command Performance at that price.

Wednesday 18th June

CONDUCTRESS KNITTING ON TRAM TO FLEETWOOD

It is an agreeable trip by tram along the promenade to Fleetwood, and many people go for the ride alone. It is not busy this morning, and the conductress even finds time to do some knitting between stops.

Thursday 19th June

A SHOE SHINE

As I am taking a heavy case to Central Station in the morning I stop for a rest opposite a shoe shine stand. A man wearing an American type shirt comes along with his wife and small son, who is carrying a model yacht.

The boy stops. "Oh look, there's a shoe shine. Have a shoe shine, Daddy," he urges.

"Oh I don't really need one", says his father, but he stops to have his brown shoes polished.

SHOE SHINE STANDS & SIGNS

There were still shoe shine stands in Blackpool. Some carried notices like: "Look both ways before you cross the road." One I passed around mid-day displayed a "Not Operating" sign while the shoe shiner was eating his lunch.

CHAPTER 6

20th – 27th JUNE 1959

Saturday 20th June

MORE HOLIDAY VISITORS ARRIVING

Returning for another holiday, I notice a number of familiar things on the way. Crowded trains to the Lancashire coast, full of confetti, empty orange juice cartons and newspapers. Children running along corridors, rubbing their hands against dirty coachwork, and peering with curiosity into compartments filled with families perspiring in the warm sunshine.

Visitors staggering with heavy luggage are met at the station by eager taxi drivers looking for customers.

Casual dress is normal, and no one bothers about what type of clothes you wear on holiday. Headgear varies from the popular "Western" or cowboy hat to broad brimmed sombreros which shade the sun from the wearer's eyes.

JUNE DAIRY FESTIVAL – RIGBY ROAD

I arrive rather late at the agricultural show held at Rigby Road. A weight lifting display is being given by a team of four hefty young local men. A small group of spectators sit on chairs in the open air, while an announcer gives out the weights and types of lift being demonstrated. He invites anyone in the audience to try and pick up the weights. No one volunteers so he has an attempt himself, but fails to raise any of them.

There are tents and marquees which contained livestock, agricultural and dairy equipment earlier in the day. A number of milk churns are lying about. I hear one stallkeeper say that he has sold all his milk, so it sounds as though the Dairy Festival has been well attended.

Messages are written on coloured balloons, which are inflated and sent up. A fair breeze carries them high into the air above the gas holder near the railway.

Sunday 21st June

CENTRAL PIER – BOY MEETS GIRL AT UNCLE PETER'S SHOW

Children accompanied by their parents are admitted free to Uncle Peter's evening show on the Central Pier. During the interval I overhear a conversation between a girl aged about eight and a boy slightly younger.

BOY: "Where do you come from?"

GIRL: "Cleethorpes."

BOY: "Where's that?"

GIRL: "Near Grimsby."

BOY: "Where's that?".

GIRL: "Don't you know? That's where the fish come from."

BOY: "What sort of a place is where you live?"

GIRL: "It's like seaside. Like Blackpool only smaller. A small holiday place."

BOY: "Where else is it near?"

GIRL: "Near Skegness."

Their conversation ends when the girl's parents return to their seats.

Monday 22nd June

TALBOT BOWLING GREEN

In the morning, rather unexpectedly I discover a bowling green next to the Talbot Hotel, in a busy area near North Station. Crown green bowling competitions are held here with prizes for the winners. The green is enclosed on all four sides, with a Bar at one end. "No betting" notices are displayed. I sit on one of the seats for a rest, while other spectators watch two bowls players, or read their newspapers.

BOWLING FACILITIES IN BLACKPOOL

There are plenty of opportunities for both crown green and flat green bowling. At present Blackpool has twenty-six municipal greens. Two of the best known crown greens are the Waterloo Hotel, the only purpose built outdoor bowling stadium in the country, which stages several top events including an autumn handicap, and the Raikes Hall, which stages the Talbot Handicap.

The £1 million Blackpool Borough Indoor Bowling Centre in Larkhill Street, near North Station, opened in 1987. It has eight rinks on carpet and offers playing facilities of international standard. In the complex there is also a modern restaurant and bar.

QUEENS THEATRE – "JOKERS ALL"

In the evening show, "Jokers All" at the Queens Theatre, the main stars are Dickie Henderson, Jimmy Clitheroe and Ronnie Hilton.

Tuesday 23rd June

NORTH SHORE BOATING POOL

The North Shore Boating Pool in a sheltered spot on the Lower Promenade, is especially popular with children. It is twopence to descend in the lift from the Upper Promenade opposite Uncle Tom's Cabin, but many people prefer to walk down the cliff footpaths.

Children can ride in motor boats, canoes, the Noah's Ark, aeroplanes and Jigsaw Train. Adults as well as children are enjoying motor boat trips. Deck chairs around the pool cost sixpence [2½p] each to hire. Parents with cameras take photographs of their children.

There are more children wanting boat rides, as it becomes warmer during the morning. Boatmen are kept busy. As soon as the permitted time for one boat ride has finished there are other customers in the queue waiting to take the next trip. Men with boathooks manoeuvre the boats into position and hold them steady while children get in and out.

CRAB CATCHING AT THE NORTH SHORE BOATING POOL

Crab catching is a favourite pastime for children at the pool, which is only eighteen inches deep. They use a simple method; first find the bait – a mussel – and break its shell in half. Then tie a piece of string to the shell and drop it into the water. If you're lucky, before very long a crab may be attracted to the mussel and pulled out of the water.

If the crab catcher is skilful enough to catch the crabs before they scuttle back into the pool, he or she usually puts them into a bucket of water. Sometimes the crabs are counted first and then thrown back into the pool. A particularly large crab causes a great deal of excitement as children crowd around to have a closer look at it.

Some confusion is caused when one small boy's bucket full of crabs is knocked over. The crabs crawl sideways in all directions, frightening the youngest children and arousing the attention of grown-ups sitting in deck chairs nearby.

If you think catching crabs is a childish activity, it is not very different from angling, which is reckoned to be one of the most popular adult sports.

Wednesday 24th June

CIRCUS ELEPHANT

As I am passing the side entrance to the Tower Circus just before the afternoon performance is due to begin, one of the elephants is standing outside surrounded by an audience who are feeding it with bread and fruit.

At first there does not seem to be any attendant in charge of it, although there are two or three Circus hands talking by the entrance door. A few minutes later an Indian trainer wearing a turban and dressed in green appears and calls it. The elephant returns to the Circus to be dressed for the opening parade.

A few minutes later the animal reappears wearing a green saddle, and looks around the spectators for more food. The trainer calls it back again, and it finally disappears inside the entrance, as it is almost time for the parade of the Circus performers.

Thursday 25th June

WINTER GARDENS THEATRE, "POT LUCK"

After tea I see Charlie Chester in "Pot Luck" at the Winter Gardens. It is mainly a quiz show with give away prizes to members of the audience who are invited to take part, but there are also a few variety artists.

EMPRESS BALLROOM, OLD TIME DANCING

After the show I go into the Empress Ballroom, where there is Old Time Dancing to the music of, alternately, a band and Horace Finch at the Wurlitzer. Old Time Dances are held in this ballroom every Tuesday and Thursday throughout the year. It is the largest ballroom in Blackpool, and although many couples are dancing there is plenty of room on the floor. From the four corners of the hall spotlights of differing colours move around and illuminate the dancers, giving a colourful and pleasing effect.

A youngish, heftily built man with a bandaged finger says to me: "This band sounds better in here than it did in the Tower. They used to play in the Tower, you know. The Palace dance floor has only been opened during the past fortnight. It was closed during the winter."

"They used to hold Old Time Dances there when I was in Blackpool last," I reply.

"Then there's the Spanish Ballroom, which was usually kept for hired parties. I was here when the ballroom floor was laid. Do you know how it was done" He describes the process in detail, naming the different types of layers and floor coverings of various thicknesses.

"Are you staying up to hear the fight tonight?" he asks.

"What fight? I didn't know there was one on."

"Between Floyd Paterson and that Swedish heavyweight," he

answers. "It's on between 3.15 and 3.45 a.m. our time, from America. I've got a portable transistor radio, a small one, in my bedroom. If I'm awake I'll listen to it. Nobody else can hear it except me. It's very quiet."

The dancing continues while he talks. A waltz cotillion is followed by the Gay Gordons. Horace Finch takes over from the band, and the Wurlitzer rises from underneath the stage while he is playing it.

"Wonderful instruments those Wurlitzers. The German type came first and then the American. They can make any sound or effect from the piano to the bagpipes. Horace plays the console at the bottom, and the pipes are right at the top of the hall behind those two panels in the roof, one on each side. The Tower Wurlitzer is exactly the same. There's one in the Odeon too, but it's not played on now."

"Blackpool's Odeon is the largest in the country, isn't it?" I ask.

"It's the largest of the original Odeon theatres, but there's one bigger in Sunderland that was taken over from another circuit."

After finishing his session Horace Finch descends beneath the stage with the Wurlitzer until they are both out of sight. Members of the band return to their places and immediately recommence playing, as the dancing continues non stop.

"Well I'd like to stay longer but I'd better go, " I say. "Does the dancing go on until eleven o'clock?"

"No, it finishes at half past ten."

CHANGES AT ODEON TODAY

In common with many other cinemas, the Odeon has since been converted to three screens to allow a choice of three different programmes. I think that the Wurlitzer is no longer there.

Friday 26th June

WEDDING PRESENT

Small middle-aged woman with Tyneside accent: "You may as well give the young ones of today a tin opener for a wedding present as they canna bake a cake".

There seem to be a good number of "Geordies" on holiday this week. Each evening after the public houses close I hear a noisy group of them returning to their lodgings singing "Blaydon Races" at the top of their voices.

Saturday 27th June

HOW CHILDREN EARN EXTRA POCKET MONEY

A busy summer Saturday. Travellers arrive and depart by all methods of transport – bus, coach, train, car and taxi. They provide opportunities for local school children to earn extra pocket money. Wheeling handcarts, soapboxes on wheels, perambulators, or anything else which would carry heavy suitcases, they mix with crowds at the bus and railway stations, looking for customers laden with luggage.

"Carry your bag please, sir?" they cry, hoping for a generous tip. They do not ask for a particular sum of money, but accept what they are given.

Sometimes they carry cases from the station a short distance only to a waiting taxi. Some of the stronger ones scorn the use of labour saving devices like handcarts and use their own muscle power to carry heavy belongings. It can be a profitable experience for the most enterprising who are prepared to work for long hours throughout the weekend.

VARIATION IN METHOD OF TRANSPORT HOME

This time my own method of travelling home is in two stages. First by taxi from the hotel because of heavy luggage. Then home by coach from Rigby Road Coach Station, having booked a seat on Wednesday.

COWBOYS AND INDIANS TEST

During a spell of warm weather there is a simple way of finding out how long visitors have been staying, by looking at them and applying the "Cowboys and Indians" test. The "red skins" are the ones who have been longest and taken advantage of the sun, and the "pale faces" are the ones who have only just arrived.

FISH AND CHIPS – MYSTERY HISTORY, BUT NO SECRET WHERE YOU CAN FIND THEM

The most famous food associated with Blackpool must be fried fish and chips. Many people eat them, especially during the evenings and after the shows are over. They make an uncomplicated, satisfying and usually reasonably priced meal for all ages.

Children request their parents: "Give me a bob to buy some chips". Parents, friends and all the family join in the fabulous fried feast. Groups wander around the streets eating out of oily bags and newspapers in the traditional way, as many believe that it tastes better while they are strolling about.

The familiar scent of fried food is borne on the breeze outside fish and chip shops, and advertises what is on sale. It is impossible to describe an odour in writing, but the smell of fish and chips is unmistakable and unforgettable, and lingers on long after they have been eaten.

As Shakespeare might have said, "If music be the food of love, I'll have sixpenny-worth of fish and chips".

There are many famous and well known couples in history and fiction whose names are linked together, such as Romeo and Juliet, Anthony and Cleopatra, Laurel and Hardy, and numerous others. Perhaps soldier and sailor may be the nearest similarity in this subject, as the potato grows on the land and fish are caught in the sea.

No one knows when the fried fish and potato chip were first sold together as a takeaway meal. Or who was the earliest to introduce the method of production and cooking which has become accepted as common today. Why should anyone wish to cover them with batter, drop them into a vat of boiling oil, and serve them out on greasy papers? Their origin is shrouded in mystery.

I wonder if the same shift workers of the mills and factories who flocked to Blackpool when the railway was opened were among the earliest customers for the fish and chip trade? The introduction of rail transport also enabled fish to be carried more easily from harbours to filleting houses and fish fryers.

Some of the earliest records of the fish and chip frying trade date back to about the 1860s. The equipment used then was very primitive compared with today – coal fired frying ranges of ordinary house bricks with a top surface of thick mortar.

Today's ranges are custom built, made from sheet metal to the fryer's own specifications. Methods and premises have improved and become more hygienic. Automatic potato peelers are quicker than the old method of hand peeling potatoes with the Lancashire potato knife. Modern restaurants have seats, dining rooms and serve a wide range of hot and cold food and drinks as well as fried fish and chips. The trade has an improved image, with staff wearing white aprons.

It is not the fault of the fish fryers that in the evenings many of the streets near the promenade are paved with dirty greasy fish and chip papers. On windy nights they may be blown some distance or onto the seashore, where scavenging seagulls search for any pickings.

However I had better not commit any further indecency on this subject. I have already written suf-FISH-ent! Sorry. That just slipped out. Perhaps it is because they are so greasy. Like the salt and vinegar that goes on them they are two of the spices of life.

CHAPTER 7

26th – 30th SEPTEMBER 1966

INCREASE IN ROAD TRAFFIC

Motor traffic was increasing at this time, and the most common form of transport to Blackpool had switched from rail to road. More people owned and drove cars, and improvements to highways made it easier to reach the coast. The first motorway opened in Britain in December 1958 was the eight mile Preston by-pass, on one of the main routes to Blackpool.

More road vehicles meant that more car and coach parks were needed, and some were introduced, including one on the site of the former Central Station closed in 1964.

Parking places were in great demand, and fees at public car parks were generally expensive. If there were no parking spaces available at the hotel where road travellers were staying, problems were likely to occur.

Monday 26th September

PARKING PROBLEMS

I travel to Blackpool by road and have no difficulty in finding the way, but the first problem is discovering somewhere to park. My hotel is in a one way street with parking allowed up to 60 minutes on one side, but all vehicle spaces are occupied. The only alternative is to look for a public car park. I find one in Corporation Street, and drive up to the top. The parking fee is seven shillings and sixpence [37½p].

GRAND THEATRE

After garaging the car and finishing tea, there is time for a look around before dark. At the Grand Theatre I arrive just before the first house is due to start at 6-15 p.m. So book a seat and see Arthur

Askey and Douglas Cardew Robinson in the comedy, "Second Honeymoon". Plenty of laughs in this holiday show.

ILLUMINATED TRAMS

After the show it is dark, and with crowds of other visitors I go onto the promenade to look at the Illuminations, then board a tram to Starr Gate at the end of the South Promenade.

Archway at end of South Promenade, 23rd June 1959

One of the most popular ways to view the lights is by tram. Specially decorated trams are among those which take passengers around during the evenings. The designs are ingenious, and eye-catching, and in addition to attracting much attention as their brilliantly lit shapes move along the promenade through the darkness, the trams advertise their sponsors as well as the Illuminations.

The Illuminations trams include the Hovertram sponsored by Shell Oil Company, a ninety-nine-seat double-decker in the shape of a hovercraft, the A.B.C. Television sponsored Western Train in the shape of an American type locomotive hauling an open platform coach, another in the shape of a space rocket, and a fourth based on a Standard tram.

Tuesday 27th September

AN AFTERNOON IN STANLEY PARK

In the afternoon I walk through the gardens at Stanley Park to the Oval, a fenced off part of the park where there is an athletics track with a covered grand stand on one side.

I go past the Clock Tower in the direction of a loud speaker which is relaying music. At intervals a voice announces: "Just in time to hear the all laughter show at the Stanley Park Bowl. Enough to make a cat laugh! Starting in five minutes time. Admission – two shillings [10p] for adults, children half price, and children under seven free. There's a comfortable deck chair waiting for you at the sheltered Stanley Park Bowl. Hurry along and take your seats, please."

The Bowl is a walled off enclosure near the lake. Some empty deck chairs can be seen inside. An indistinct noise is coming from a loud speaker.

Seen on posters outside the Bowl: "The Edwin Hicks all laughter show. Prizes given for the best photographs taken. Spot the mistakes in the adverts." There are photographs of some of the performing artists and advertisements for well known products.

OPERA HOUSE – KEN DODD

One of the guests at the hotel where I am staying tells me: "Don't miss Ken Dodd's show. It's the best in Blackpool."

In the evening the Opera House is full and all seats have been sold in advance. It is a very popular variety show, with successful Liverpool comedian Ken Dodd topping the bill. His non-stop performance of comedy and song seems to win universal approval of the audience. The supporting acts including the Bluebell Girls are spectacular and very good. Altogether it is a splendid evening's entertainment.

EMPRESS BALLROOM – DANCING CHAMPIONSHIPS

After the first house at the Opera House finishes, the audience leaving mix with crowds queueing up for the second performance about 8.30 p.m., and until the first group can reach the exit there is very little room to move.

Some people wander around other parts of the Winter Gardens. Others try to get into the Dancing Championships, which are being held in the Empress Ballroom all week. Attendants bar the way, and tell them that there is no admission without a ticket.

Bars and lounges are full. Evening dress and ballroom dancing costumes are worn by those taking part in the various contests, which include Old Time dancing, modern amateur and professional ballroom and formation dancing.

Wednesday 28th September

THEFT FROM HOTEL

At breakfast all guests in the hotel where I am staying are warned by the Manager that we would be questioned by the Police owing to a theft of money from one of the bedrooms yesterday afternoon. We were told that while tea was being served between 5 p.m. and 6 p.m., evidently an intruder entered the building and stole about £70, contained in two purses which had been left by one of the guests in her first floor bedroom.

Normally none of the bedroom doors are locked, and the front entrance door of the hotel is invariably left open during the daytime. It would have been easy for a housebreaker to gain entry and walk out unrecognised, because even if the guests had seen anyone, they would probably have thought that it was either another holiday visitor or one of the hotel workers. The hotel staff were too busy serving teas to notice any stranger.

The family who had their money stolen are naturally very upset, and all the other guests are shocked to hear about it.

Shortly after breakfast two plain clothes Police officers arrive. They go into the kitchen first to question the hotel manager and staff. Then they make enquiries from the guests, most of whom remain at their tables.

No one remembers seeing anybody entering, and there are no clues which may lead to identifying whoever took the money. It is thought that the time of the theft would have been shortly after 5.00 p.m. as one family were in a hurry to go to an evening show. They finished their tea shortly before 5.30 p.m., and then went upstairs to their bedrooms to change before leaving the hotel.

The detective in charge of the investigations tells us that three similar thefts from hotels have been reported during the week, each having taken place between 5 p.m. and 6 p.m. They were probably carried out by the same person or persons, who took advantage of the fact that people staying in a hotel may forget to safeguard their valuables.

The detective advises us never to leave money or valuables in a hotel bedroom or anywhere else which may be unattended even for a short period, and either lock them up, take anything of value with us, or hand them over to the hotel manager to be put away in a secure place until required.

After the Police officers have completed their investigations all the guests return to their bedrooms to check whether any of their belongings are missing, and to take out or lock up anything valuable.

My bedroom is on the second floor, but apparently the thief has not ventured above the first floor as nothing else is reported stolen. Another guest on the same floor as myself says that she has carelessly left some money in her bedroom but luckily it is still there.

WAS THE THIEF CAUGHT?

Although upset after this experience and Police investigation, the hotel guests became more friendly and willing to chat with one another.

I did not find out afterwards whether the offender was caught by the Police, but there was a later report of three more thefts at another hotel.

Thursday 29th September

EMETT'S WONDERFUL FLYING MACHINE

The hotel manager has to attend a funeral today, so asks his guests if they mind getting their own lunches, and everyone agrees. I obtain my lunch in the restaurant on the third floor of R.H.O. Hills' store. It is quite a decent meal although service is rather slow, perhaps because a coach party from south west England has kept the waitresses busy.

In the restaurant there is a working model of one of Emett's weird flying machines. It has a queer revolving umbrella-like framework, inside which a model aviator moves backwards and forwards in his seat operating the controls. Around him there is every imaginable invention, from a cocktail mixer to an egg frying in a saucepan over an open fire.

A TRAM COMES OFF THE TRACK

Near a promenade shelter opposite the Pleasure Beach I see a group of about a dozen Corporation Transport workmen around a tram which has apparently gone off the rails on a bend.

Three of the men are heaving a cable which has one end tied to an electricity pole and the other end to the lower part of the tram. After a lot of manoeuvring they gradually manage to pull the vehicle back onto the rails.

A tram driver enters the front cab, and very slowly and carefully moves the tram forward until it is completely straight. Then he drives it slowly onto the main northward line, and returns to the Tramway Depot without any passengers.

"BILLY'S WEEKLY LIAR"

Offered for sale on the promenade is a locally produced humorous news sheet, "Billy's Weekly Liar". It is sold by a broad-built man who shouts his wares in a distinctively loud voice, and is advertised by placards like "Dead skeleton found strangled on promenade". It is the sort of paper you may read for amusement, or to cheer you up after you have returned from your holiday.

NOW JUST A MEMORY OF THE PAST

I had seen "Billy's Weekly Liar" on sale during previous visits but had never bought a copy. I believe that it is no longer obtainable.

LURE OF THE LIGHTS

The drawing power of the Illuminations continues to attract people like a magnet. It is estimated that during a recent weekend there were a quarter of a million visitors. A small minority celebrated their stay with too much spirit and were fined, mainly for drunkenness and disorderly behaviour. One newspaper report recorded twenty-four offenders appearing in Court with a total of sixty charges, including one attempted murder and five serious wounding cases.

Spectacular twinkling, flashing, multi-coloured festoon strips and animated designs all the way along the promenade, have an irresistible effect. Crowds flock to join tours by cars, coaches, buses, trams, taxis and open horse drawn landaus; some travel on foot.

Many young people wander about in groups. Teenage youths try to get into hotels for a drink, and occasionally some are refused because they appear to be under eighteen. No doubt seeing so many drinkers inside hotel bars sitting around tables is a temptation to attempt to join them.

The Tower stands out above everything else, with a red light on the top. Sometimes a searchlight beam shoots out a narrow pencil of white light.

Friday 30th September

END OF ANOTHER HOLIDAY

It is soon time to leave the hotel and drive homewards at the end of another holiday, during which I have been lucky to enjoy fine weather. The time has passed quickly, and many happy memories remain.

AFTERTHOUGHTS – 1966 HOLIDAY

Among my souvenirs of the seaside are some of the different sounds which have been heard.

In roads where nearly every residence houses visitors during the season, the sounds of many gongs announcing meals can be heard. They remind me of the opening sequence of a J. Arthur Rank film.

I can never forget the jingle of bells around the necks of donkeys on their way to or from the beach. There are strict Council Byelaws for treatment and hours of work of donkeys for hire on the sands – "Regulations with reference to Asses on the Foreshore" – which the local R.S.P.C.A. Inspector is authorised and appointed to enforce.

Noises at the Pleasure Beach: the whirring of machinery on the rides; the rattle of amusement machines; laughter of teenagers; crying of young children and babies; jingle of money as parents pay for their children's rides; attendants shouting their wares and trying to encourage customers to buy or have a go at their sideshows; and the inescapable calling of Bingo numbers into a microphone, while players sit gazing intently at their cards.

CHAPTER 8

27th – 31st MARCH 1970

SPECIAL EASTER VISIT

I had a particular reason for coming to Blackpool for the Easter weekend instead of during the summer or Illuminations period. I had obtained in advance tickets for Reginald Dixon's farewell concert at the Tower Ballroom on Easter Sunday evening.

GOOD FRIDAY 27th March

CHANGES ON THE GOLDEN MILE

On the Central Promenade the most noticeable change since my last visit is the growth of some of the amusement palaces. They now seem to be fewer in number but larger and more expensive. Business is becoming more competitive with increases in the cost of living and introduction of Selective Employment Tax.* The general trend is for the more successful establishments to grow larger at the expense of others who fail to adapt themselves to changes and eventually cease business.

Bingo still appears to be as popular as ever and the most widespread form of amusement on the Golden Mile.

One corner displays large hoardings headed "YOU MUST SEE IT", and loud speakers blare out continuously to try and lure people inside.

There are three main exhibits, for which the admission charge is one shilling [5p] each. One is headed "IT" – allegedly found in outer space by astronauts. The second, "WAS THIS THE ABOMINABLE SNOWMAN?". The third, "THE SEVERED HANDS OF PRINCESS PATMA" – unattached to any body but supposed to be alive.

---

* S.E.T. was the forerunner of the present Value Added Tax (V.A.T.)

An example of keeping up with the times is noticed in the window of Louis Tussaud's Waxworks. There is a closed circuit television set, on the screen of which passers by can observe themselves with wax models in the background.

Saturday 28th March

The local transport workers are on strike and there are no trams and buses today. As it is raining in the morning I drive to Fleetwood, and back through Poulton-le-Fylde and Hardhorn for lunch at the hotel 1.00 p.m.

The rain stops in the late afternoon, and I go out to the Winter Gardens, and at the Opera House obtain tickets for the second performance of the evening, which is due to commence at 8.15 p.m. To pass the time before the show I go into Olympia and watch children riding on the electric cars, trams, "Flying Saucers", big wheel, Dodgems, motor cycle roundabouts and other amusements.

Queues are waiting outside the Opera House when it is time for the second house to commence. After the audience from the first house has come out we go inside, and are directed to our seats by uniformed attendants.

The theatre is full, and the show is first class entertainment. The shorter first half is taken up mainly by musical acts, including the Three Squires, a soprano singer, and a lively pianist, Mrs Mills. Ken Dodd is top of the bill, and during the hour long second half keeps the audience laughing and entertained with non stop jokes, songs and encores.

EASTER SUNDAY 29th March

NO QUEUES FOR THE CHURCH PEWS

The town is quite busy with Easter visitors. Dress varies from casual wear of holidaymakers to the more formal clothes of those who are going to Church.

The Salvation Army band lines up in the roadway outside their headquarters, "The Citadel". They march off playing Easter hymns, and parade through the town with their banners flying, while Church bells are ringing.

I go inside the Parish Church for the Easter morning service, which is conducted by the Vicar. The congregation is fairly large, but there are plenty of seats for everybody, and unlike many other places in Blackpool no queues outside waiting to go in. The local churchgoers are friendly, and particularly helpful towards the elderly, disabled, blind and physically handicapped who attend the service.

From Central Pier looking north, Easter Sunday 29th March 1970

REGINALD DIXON'S FAREWELL CONCERT AT THE TOWER BALLROOM

From all over the world tributes are paid to the famous and popular organist, Reginald Dixon, at his farewell concert. Telegrams are read out from as far away as Hollywood, California, from Bing Crosby, Miami, Florida, from Reginald Foort, and from the Sheffield Wednesday Football Club (he was born in Sheffield in 1904), wishing him a happy retirement.

Two presentations are made to him during the concert. One is from Mrs Gary Vanderwerp of Australia, who has come over from the consulate at Amsterdam. She presents a bouquet as a token of appreciation to him for being so faithful a patron of the Theatre Organ Society of Australia.

The other is made by Robin Richmond. I first learned about this farewell concert earlier on the B.B.C. radio programme he introduces, "The Organist Entertains". I am most grateful to him for the privilege of being able to attend. If I had not written in advance for a ticket to the address at the B.B.C., which he mentioned on his programme, it is unlikely that I would have been able to obtain one this evening. There is a packed audience of more than 3,000 present. Before the start long queues wait outside the Tower hoping to buy tickets.

When Robin Richmond's name is announced he rushes from the back of the ballroom onto the stage. Before he is able to make his presentation speech he has to sit down to regain his breath, which causes a good deal of amusement. On behalf of the B.B.C. he presents a replica of the Tower Ballroom Wurlitzer in silver to Reginald Dixon.

The Wurlitzer plays an important role in the evening's musical entertainment. In the concert souvenir programme (price five shillings), as well as information about the evening's musical items, Reginald Dixon's career and photographs, full details are given of the Wurlitzer's specifications. It has fourteen ranks and over a hundred stops, which can produce such a wide variety of sounds.

Organ music has always fascinated me. A full sized theatre organ can be an orchestra on its own, as it does not need accompaniment from any other instrument. The Tower Wurlitzer very conveniently provides music for dancing during evenings, and is also useful for giving the resident orchestra a break between their performances.

After Reginald Dixon's retirement, his immediate successor as resident organist will be Ernest Broadbent, who is the first artist on the concert programme. He plays non stop on the Wurlitzer for about twenty minutes. His talent is evident during that short period. The audience gives him a good reception, but their loudest clapping and cheering is reserved for the star of the evening, whose turn it is to play next.

After an introduction, Reginald Dixon appears on the Wurlitzer to a thunderous burst of applause, which continues throughout the rest of the evening whenever there is a break in the music he is playing. First he plays a medley of the melodies for which he has had the most requests, and which have captured the public imagination during the past forty years.

Tunes from popular musicals, old and modern, follow in such rapid succession that he does not have time to announce the titles of them all. He only pauses for a rest when it is time for the interval about an hour after the 7.30 p.m. start of the concert. The audience enjoy every minute of it.

During the period he has been Tower organist there can be few popular tunes which he has not played for dancing to. There cannot be any other entertainer in show business who has contributed more towards the pleasure and happiness of those at Blackpool by his music. Millions have been to applaud him, to listen and dance to his music in the Tower Ballroom. During the years he has been there I cannot remember hearing anyone who had a word to say against him.

AFTER THE INTERVAL – A SPECTACULAR STORM ON THE WURLITZER

Reginald Dixon has fans of all ages from all over the world. The large number at the concert and the reception they give him indicates his popularity.

The lady sitting on the next seat but one to me is blind. As she is on her own she asks someone else to buy a programme for her, and they immediately oblige with typical Blackpool courtesy and helpfulness.

Throughout the evening flash bulbs go off like lightning at frequent intervals as press photographers take photographs of the stage, audience, and especially Reginald Dixon playing the Wurlitzer or speaking into a microphone.

Probably the most exciting and spectacular number played during the evening is "The Storm", a musical description on the Wurlitzer of a sea voyage.

It starts with some familiar sea shanties played at a normal tempo, and then suddenly bursts into a tempestuous noise, as the mighty magical music resounds devastatingly through the ballroom like the continuous rumbling and rolling of thunder. Effective lightning flashes and changes of colour lighting by the hard working spotlight operators add visual descriptiveness to the Wurlitzer's storm sounds.

The thunder and lightning continues for a few moments, then the music becomes more tranquil as Reginald Dixon makes it sound like a natural ending to the tempest. He finishes the set piece with a wonderfully peaceful rendering of the Twenty-third Psalm, "The Lord is my Shepherd", a great and fitting conclusion which I cannot describe adequately in mere words.

During the second half of the concert Reginald Dixon is backed by the B.B.C. Northern Dance Orchestra conducted by Bernard Herrman. They play a few popular numbers, and also accompany Vince Hill, who introduces the concert as well as sings in it. He reminds the audience that part of it is being recorded by the B.B.C. to be broadcast on Radio Two tomorrow at 10 a.m.

CONCLUSION OF A MEMORABLE EVENING

Then the final session on the Wurlitzer by Reginald Dixon follows, this time with the names of the tunes announced, and finishing with enthusiastic applause from the audience every time.

The last medley of tunes he plays are mostly old time choruses for the audience to join in and sing. The words are displayed prominently on an illuminated notice board, and are changed for each different tune. The last one, of course, is his world famous signature tune, "I do like to be beside the seaside". At the end the applause is so great that he has to give an encore, "Now is the hour when we must say goodbye".

Then he gives a short speech of farewell, in which he thanks everyone for their good wishes and help. His final tune, which the orchestra and everyone joins in is "Auld Lang Syne". It is a memorable scene, with the whole audience on the ballroom floor and in the Gallery and Circle above joining hands and singing the traditional Scottish song. Then Reginald Dixon disappears beneath the floor of the stage for the last time, still playing the Wurlitzer.

It is a grand finale to the evening, with the audience on their feet, cheering, applauding and waving goodbye.

The final music to round off the entertainment is left to the Northern Dance Orchestra, who play "Beside the seaside", "The Traveller's Song", and finish with "God Save the Queen".

After the concert Reginald Dixon's dressing room is besieged by fans seeking his autograph.

I remember Mrs Vanderwerp's final words to him after her presentation: "Please, please don't leave us."

This has certainly been a wonderful and memorable evening by a grand and popular artist. Thanks for the memories and melodies. They are still with us and will live on.

MEMORIES OF THE TOWER BALLROOM

After one of the most emotional and eventful evenings that I have ever spent in Blackpool there is little that I can add, except that the Tower Ballroom was the most fitting place for it to be held – a magnificent setting ablaze with light.

It is estimated that the full power required to light the Ballroom is 200,000 watts. Following a disastrous fire on 14th December 1956, the Ballroom was restored at an estimated cost of £500,000. The Ballroom floor is 120 feet long by 102 feet wide. The decorations are similar to the original in peach and gold. The ceiling murals occupy an area of over 2,000 square feet.

Above the stage is the inscription, "BID ME DISCOURSE I WILL ENCHANT THINE EAR", which is from "VENUS AND ADONIS", a sonnet by William Shakespeare.

Among my many happy memories are those of the floor being packed with holiday couples dancing to music from the Wurlitzer or band.

DISAPPOINTED VISITORS

The number of people who came specially to hear and see Reginald Dixon playing the Wurlitzer is also memorable. One instance during my first visit: a mother with two children arrived late after the organist had finished his performance and asked me: "Has Reginald Dixon been playing the organ yet?"

"Yes," I answered, "He's just finished."

"Oh that's a pity. We came up here specially to hear him but didn't know what time he was on. We've been around looking at the Zoo and the Aquarium you know, and didn't come up here till just now, so we've missed him," she said disappointedly.

MEMORIAL PLAQUE

Visitors to the Tower Ballroom today can see a plaque on the wall near the stage which is inscribed, "In memory of Reginald Dixon M.B.E. Known to millions the world over as 'Mr. Blackpool'. From 1930 to 1970 his mastery of the Tower Ballroom Wurlitzer created a musical legend which will live for ever".

EASTER MONDAY 30th March

AT BLOOMFIELD ROAD TRANSPORT WORKERS EXPLAIN REASONS FOR STRIKE

Although it has been a generally cold Easter with a maximum temperature of about 6 degrees Centigrade (43 Fahrenheit), there is a warm welcome at the hotel where I am staying; it is comfortable, and good food is provided. After breakfast I remain in the lounge to read a newspaper and play the piano while it is raining.

In the afternoon I join the crowds making their way to the football ground at Bloomfield Road for the local team's Second

Division match against Sheffield United.

As I am crossing the car park towards the entrance a man thrusts a leaflet into my hand. It is from the transport workers' union, and gives their reasons for inconveniencing the public by striking during the Easter holiday. They are demanding an increase in their wages to keep pace with the cost of living, and a reduction in working hours to a reasonable total so that they can live a normal family life instead of having to work excessive overtime.

There are over 24,000 spectators at the football ground, one of the largest crowds of the season. They are generally well behaved, and after the match the home supporters are in good humour because Blackpool win by a single goal scored in the second half. Some of the younger fans sing as they march along the streets: "We're going to win the League". Their team are now second in the Second Division.

COMEDY FILMS AT KING EDWARD CINEMA

The evening programme at the King Edward Cinema commences at 7.00 p.m. Admission to the stalls costs four shillings [20p]. The two films shown are both comedies: the British "Carry On" team in "CARRY ON AGAIN DOCTOR", and "DID YOU HEAR THE ONE ABOUT THE TRAVELLING SALESLADY?" an American period film about inventions which went wrong.

CINEMA NO LONGER EXISTS

The King Edward was one of Blackpool's old and small Cinemas, which had an illuminated kiosk near the screen where cigarettes, confectionery and light refreshments could be bought. The increasing use and popularity of television may have led to a decline in attendances and its closure.

Tuesday 31st March

RETURN HOME – TRANSPORT STRIKE ENDED

It is time to leave Blackpool soon after breakfast and start for home by road. I drive past the bus depot where transport workers are returning to duty after their strike is over. Buses and trams are running again. It is a normal working day after the Easter holiday weekend.

CHAPTER 9

28th JUNE – 4th JULY 1981

THE NINETEEN EIGHTIES AND MORE VISITS

I could not go to Blackpool for a long time for personal reasons. It was certainly not because I had lost interest or enthusiasm for the place – that old Blackpool magic was still as active as ever.

Sunday 28th June

CHANGES AT THE TOWER

The hotel where I am staying for a week is on the South Promenade. I arrive by road at about 6.00 p.m.

After a walk through the crowded Pleasure Beach, which seems to have grown larger with more new amusements, I board a tram along the promenade to the Tower. Some roads nearby are reserved for buses and taxis only.

The admission charge to the Tower has increased to £1. I enquire what is on today, then pay to go in. No dancing is permitted on Sundays, but there is a cabaret and large bar in the Ocean Room, and live music played by the resident organist on the Wurlitzer in the Ballroom.

The bar at the end of the ballroom is open. Drinkers can take their glasses to tables at the side, sit down and listen to the music.

Another new feature is that attendants with cameras are moving around the tables and taking instant flash photographs of visitors, which can be bought as souvenirs. Record albums of the resident organist can also be purchased at the bar.

A lady vocalist sings into a microphone. Later a second organist plays a Hammond electronic organ. However, the most popular musical performance of the evening is given by Phil Kelsall on the Wurlitzer. Still only in his twenties, this young organist is a talented and versatile performer with a style of his own, and appears to have maintained the high standard of musical entertainment set by his predecessors at the Tower. One of the requests is for a descriptive and spectacular arrangement of the "Dambusters March", accompanied by aircraft sound effects which reverberate through the Ballroom.

There is plenty of room in the Ballroom downstairs, and the two balconies above are occupied by only a few spectators.

In other parts of the Tower there are new features since my last visit. The TROPICAL GARDEN has palms and pools with fountains, and flamingoes and other tropical birds in the foliage overhead. It is a pleasant room where visitors may relax, with a corner where ice cream and light refreshments can be obtained.

In the next room is the MONKEY JUNGLE, where animals of the ape family are kept in glass cages.

Next is the CHILDREN'S FUN FARM, with small domestic animals, such as Shetland ponies, piglets, rabbits and chickens in pens.

Upstairs are more electronic amusement machines in the APOLLO PLAYGROUND near the TOWER ASCENT LIFTS.

Another new diversion is a hall of distorting mirrors. I see three Asian youths laughing at their oddly shaped images as they move from one reflection to another.

Monday 29th June

KEY CARELESSNESS NO.1

On returning to my hotel bedroom after breakfast I discover a bunch of keys in the door. Thinking that I have forgotten to remove my own bedroom key I absent-mindedly turn one of the keys in the lock. Then realising that there must be someone in the bedroom, instead of entering I go out for a short walk.

I search outside to find out if there are any newspaper shops nearby, but discover only private hotels.

After returning to the bedroom about fifteen minutes later and unlocking the door with the key which is still in the lock, I discover that the young chambermaid who has come to tidy up the room is still there – I have unintentionally locked her in! I apologise as she hurriedly comes out to continue her work elsewhere in the hotel.

PEDESTRIAN SHOPPING CENTRES

With the opening of many new department stores and shops, Blackpool claims to have the largest shopping area in Lancashire. Pedestrian only zones have been established near the Tower, with flowers decorating the precincts and seats where shoppers can relax.

The new covered £10 million Hounds Hill Shopping Centre is one of the main developments. It contains "Blackpool's most exciting fashion store", and many of the country's well known retailers. Glittering new shops advertise a wide range of goods for sale, and attract many visitors walking past to stop and gaze into the windows.

A wide selection of food and drink is available. I choose the British Home Stores restaurant for a salad lunch.

A multi-storey car park with lifts for shoppers stands next to the shopping centre. Overhead is a footbridge which leads to the promenade.

Tuesday 30th June

BLACKPOOL ZOO

Blackpool Corporation's Zoo Park, which is reached from East Park Drive adjoining Stanley Park, is claimed to be the most modern in Europe. Much skill and care has been taken in planning the thirty-two acre site so that as many animals as possible can be fitted into their natural surroundings, and the best possible facilities are provided for visitors.

Trees border the main routes and footpaths through the grounds. Many of the animal enclosures are bordered with moats. The Zoo has a specially equipped kitchen where diets are prepared for the animals as near to their natural food as possible. Visitors are asked

91

not to feed the animals, as some food may not be suitable for them.

A miniature railway runs from near the Zoo entrance through woodlands to the far side of the park by the Toucan House, close enough for passengers to see some of the animals in their enclosures. Passengers can ride in the train to the station at the other end, and walk through the gardens to view the animals on their way back if they wish.

The scale model diesel locomotive which draws the open coaches on the railway, no. 279, "RIO GRANDE", is of American design. The stations have Wild West names: "Injun Creek" and "Dodge City Halt".

THE WONDERFUL WORLD OF ANIMALS

I walk around the enclosures and find plenty of subjects for photographs: elephants, giraffes, peacocks, and Jackass and Humboldt's penguins. Two laughing young girls from a party of school children talk to me by the Penguins' Pool while these birds are being fed, and ask me to take their photographs. Then they run off among the crowds to another part of the Zoo.

The Sea Lion Pool attracts a large crowd who are entertained and amused at feeding time. The young attendant walks around the pool with a bucket of fish, which he feeds in turn to the four Californian sea lions in the water.

The animals perform tricks, balancing balls on their noses, pushing a can thrown into the pool, and jumping out of the water over a wooden plank held by the attendant. One sea lion jumps high out of the pool to take a fish from the attendant's hand while he balances on a ledge.

When all the fish has been eaten the attendant says to one of the sea lions, "Give me a kiss", and it comes out of the water, stands up and puts its flippers around his waist as if to embrace him.

A bell is fixed outside one of the windows at the side of the pool. When one of the sea lions rings the bell it is rewarded with a fish.

I finish my visit to the Zoo with tea in the Buffet refreshment room. It has been a most enjoyable afternoon among the animals.

Wednesday 1st July

BLACKPOOL AIRPORT

In the morning I drive to Squires Gate Lane to visit Blackpool Airport. It is a windy morning and only a few light aircraft are airborne. Pleasure flights are advertised for £6. I observe a parachute centre, private flying clubs, and airport buildings for administrative purposes, with a restaurant and information room open to the public.

Part of the landing area and runways are fenced off, but spectators can watch activities through the wire fences. I see one Air U.K. twin-engined monoplane being fuelled and about twenty passengers going aboard, accompanied by uniformed staff and flight crew. When everything is ready for take off the aircraft's engines start and red lights above the tailplane and fuselage are switched on. The aircraft taxis along the runway out of sight, and later re-appears in the air heading westwards.

Thursday 2nd July

HEAT 6, MISS BLACKPOOL CONTEST, NORTH PIER

One of the heats of the "Miss Blackpool" contest is due to take place in the Sun Lounge at the far end of the North Pier at 3.15 p.m. It is a sunny and warm afternoon, and the sheltered enclosure is crowded. Spectators are seated in deck chairs. Some are in beach wear and have obtained drinks from the bar, which is about to close.

When the time comes for the contest to begin the stage microphone is not working, so the announcer asks the audience to be patient while another one is sent for. In the meantime the resident organist, Raymond Wallbank, plays some music.

A few spectators become impatient with the delay and shout, "Get on with it!" but after a few tunes have been played they soon calm down.

When the first competitors come onto the stage the announcer's voice cannot be heard clearly from the back of the enclosure. Later about half way though the contest, when the emergency equipment is brought into use and another microphone comes on, her voice becomes more audible.

There are twenty-one contestants in this heat, which is sponsored by Blackpool Corporation and a new 200-bedroom hotel near the Derby Baths.

The winners are chosen by a panel of three judges from the Pleasure Beach cabaret show, "Viva Hollywood" at the Horseshoe Show Bar. Their choices meet with general approval, and are applauded by the audience.

Press photographs are taken of the three cash prize winners and the whole group of competitors wearing their swim suits. It is announced that today is the first occasion this summer when the sun has shone while the contest is being held.

Friday 3rd July

"SEATING FOR ZOO?"

While looking around for somewhere to have lunch, I notice a sign in a cafe window which appears to read: "SEATING FOR ZOO". It has nothing to do with animal welfare. When I approach close enough, I find that it actually reads: "SEATING FOR 200"!

WHAT HAS HAPPENED TO THE NORTH SHORE BOATING POOL?

After lunch I drive to the North Shore and Queens Promenade near Uncle Tom's Cabin. Looking down from the cliffs at the North Shore Boating Pool below I am surprised to find that apart from a van selling ice cream, recreation facilities are non-existent. Two children's roundabouts are derelict, and there are blank spaces where other amusements have been.

The now unused boating and paddling pools are full of dirty water, with wood, rubbish and other debris floating on the top. On the far side is a small corner of muddy sand. The lift which used to carry passengers to and from the Upper Promenade near Uncle Tom's Cabin is no longer there.

One of the cliff paths is closed for repairs, and notices are posted: "Cliff paths and rockeries are dangerous. Keep to the paths."

A few sunbathers and children are in the area sheltered from the stiff breeze by a wall, but anyone who wants to sit down on seats or deck chairs has to bring their own from elsewhere.

A passing Scotsman provides a clue to how the place has become abandoned. He tells me that it is a pity that there is nothing here now, and maybe the rents which were charged for pitches were too high?

Saturday 4th July

KEY CARELESSNESS NO.2. EVERYTHING COMES IN PLASTIC WRAPPINGS

After breakfast I leave the hotel at Blackpool, and drive homewards via St. Anne's-on-sea and Lytham on a pleasant sunny morning. It is not until about mid-day at Preston that I feel in my jacket pocket and discover the hotel bedroom key which I have forgotten to hand in.

At a stationary shop near the market I buy a small notebook and envelopes in preparation for returning the key.

While eating lunch at a cake shop buffet I write a note of apology to the hotel for forgetting to return the key, and put it into one of the envelopes. The key is too large for the envelope to stick securely, so I look around for a shop where sellotape is sold, and buy a roll.

The next step is to borrow a pair of scissors at another stationer's shop to cut the sellotape, then fix two strips to seal the envelope containing the key. Finally I post the envelope in a letterbox at the bus station. Mission completed.

CHAPTER 10

25th – 28th MAY 1983

TOWER – CHANGES OF OWNERSHIP

No longer a family business since the retirement of Douglas Bickerstaffe, the ownership of the Tower has changed hands a number of times. Every time it has been sold the value has increased. In 1968 EMI bought it for £4.7 million and sold it for £16 million to Trusthouse Forte in 1980, with the Winter Gardens and Golden Mile.

Earlier in 1983 First Leisure Corporation bought the Tower, Winter Gardens complex and the three piers for £37½ million. Lord Delfont is Chairman and Chief Executive of this London-based company. His company also owns many other leisure businesses in other parts of Great Britain, including piers, theatres, dance halls, a Yacht Marina, squash clubs, ten-pin bowling centres and an amusement park.

(Blackpool Branch R.N.L.I.)

Central Beach, Tower and part of the Golden Mile

Wednesday 25th May

GAMBLING

Blackpool is sometimes described as the Las Vegas of England. I have never been to that American resort, but would not expect a bucket and spade to be on the list of essential articles to take there.

There has always been plenty of scope for gambling in Blackpool. One of the first sounds I hear when entering one of the main amusement arcades is the voice of a Bingo stallholder calling out numbers. With the growth in size of amusement palaces, Bingo is now catered for on a larger scale than ever. The Coral Island Leisure Complex includes a 1,500 seat Bingo Hall.

Every possible machine designed to persuade visitors to spend their money is on view. The amusement industry has become modernized with the introduction of betting shops, the latest computer controlled games and video recordings such as the U.S.A. Derby, on which customers are invited to place their bets.

An immense amount of money must be spent on these machines each season. According to an enquiry which I made at a shop, the cost of a single small fruit machine can be about £300 to £400.

Thursday 26th May

OLYMPIA

Looking through one of the glass doors of Olympia – part of the Winter Gardens which used to contain amusement machines and rides – I discover preparations for a major new attraction. A lot of activity is going on. Workmen are busy moving about and carrying out various jobs with tools and equipment – carpentry, woodwork, a welding machine, a ladder, hammers and nails. Newly painted scenery has a background in red and other bright colours. It looks an exciting new playground, but it is still a mystery.

According to notices outside, this is "Professor Peabody's Play Place", which is due to open in two days' time. There are to be twenty action-packed activities for children. Admission will be £1.50 for children, with adults accompanying them admitted free. Adults without children will not be admitted.

A NEW SANDCASTLE

By a coincidence today is the date for the first round of the "Miss Blackpool" contest, which used to be held at the South Shore Bathing Pool many years ago, but now takes place on the North Pier.

Today the site where the South Shore Baths used to be is not open to the public as demolition work is still going on. Behind a wire fence I can see a mound of earth and some bulldozing machines in the distance.

A new £11½ million leisure and recreational complex in the shape of a sandcastle is planned to be built on this site by Techno Sunley Leisure, Leeds, in association with Blackpool Borough Council. It will be opened in two or three years' time.

NORTH PIER – OK HERE

In the evening I take a photograph on the promenade at the entrance to the North Pier of the advertisement for the show "Bernard Delfont's Showtime – Russ Abbot, Les Dennis, Paul Ridgway, Aliki, Roger de Courcy – Nightly 6:10 pm & 8:40 pm."

Instead of "Book Here" above the box office, the sign reads "OK HERE". I comment: "The 'BO' is silent, as in 'Little .. – Peep'."

RESCUE FROM SEA

Many holiday-makers overlook how dangerous the sea can be. One example of a seaside rescue was reported in the West Lancashire Gazette on Thursday 26th May. It had less tragic consequences than a similar occurrence at the same spot in January, when three young police officers were drowned in a unsuccessful bid to rescue a man who had been swept into the sea off the North Shore.

A sixteen-year-old girl who was walking on the slade at Gynn Square was swept into the rough sea. Two boy friends and her brother dived in attempting to rescue her. A twenty-year-old Blackpool onlooker also went into the sea and managed to rescue the girl. Her brother swam to safety, but the other two lads were in danger of being swept away by the tide until a policeman wearing a harness waded in and managed to rescue them.

The two lads were taken to hospital suffering from shock and exposure, and one of them was kept overnight. A further tragedy was prevented by the bravery of the policeman and the other local man, who risked their own lives to save the others.

Friday 27th May

A LOOK AT ONE OF BLACKPOOL'S LUXURY HOTELS

In the morning I take a closer look at some of the hotels on and near the North Promenade. The largest of them all is the recently opened Pembroke, a four-star hotel near the Derby Baths, with 200 bedrooms, each with private bathroom and full amenities. The price for a multi-roomed suite is likely to be high, but there is an extremely wide choice of cheaper and alternative accommodation available.

PROFESSOR PEABODY'S PLAY PLACE – PROGRESS PREPARING PREMISES

In the afternoon I return to Olympia, where progress has been made towards tomorrow's opening of the new activity centre for children.

Two girls are dusting and polishing a brightly painted red and gold machine and slide. Overhead are ropes and pulleys with rubber rings attached. Behind wire netting is a table full of brightly coloured balls. A painter is putting the finishing touches to figures of children playing.

There is a row of motor tyres. Mysterious chutes, slides and drums are all brightly painted. People and cars – and a shaggy dog in the back seat of one vehicle – are coming and going inside the building. Everyone is busy at work on different jobs.

On the walls outside Olympia are newly painted signs, with arrows pointing to the main entrance, and drawings of the cheerful, beaming cartoon character Professor Peabody, after whom the new activity playground has been named. One of the signs reads: FUN FAIR. CHILDREN OF ALL AGES – THIS IS FOR YOU! IT'S THE CHILDREN'S HOLIDAY TOO.

Apparently the Professor aims at encouraging children to climb, crawl, explore and generally enjoy themselves tackling different activities under supervision in a safe environment.

THE RUSS ABBOT ALL LAUGHTER SHOW RULES O.K.

During the daytime I buy a ticket for the centre stalls at the opening performance of the North Pier show, which starts at 7:45 pm.

When I return to the North Pier after evening dinner at the hotel all seats have been booked, and it is a full house for the highly successful first performance of the season.

The weather is cloudy and cold, and the sea rough. Rain starts to fall and crowds hurry along the windswept pier towards the shelter of the theatre.

We are able to enjoy a first-class show with lots of comedy, singing and dancing. Russ Abbot, the star, is very popular, following his recent television series, "Russ Abbot's Madhouse", and receives a favourable reception from the audience.

Saturday 28th May

BUSY BANK HOLIDAY WEEKEND

As I prepare to drive home, many visitors are arriving for the Spring Bank Holiday weekend, in addition to the large number of people that travelled yesterday. It is the beginning of the main holiday season. Although many hotels are open all the year round, more bookings are expected from now onwards. The hotel where I stay is fully booked for next week, with about thirty guests, whereas this week the total number of people seen during meal times has not been more than half a dozen.

CHANGES IN PATTERNS OF HOLIDAYS

Blackpools aims at providing value for money accommodation for its visitors at prices that they can afford. You can find whatever type of place you are seeking if you look around for it.

There have been changes in the pattern of holidays in recent years, with an increasing emphasis on day trips and short breaks throughout the extended season.

A notable trend is the increase in self-catering accommodation, now believed to form nearly one quarter of the town's total number of hotels, guest houses and holiday flats, with a number of boarding houses changing over to holiday flatlets. A wide self-catering range is offered, from the single bed-sitting room flatlet for two, with cooking facilities and a shared bathroom and toilet, to a luxury apartment.

IMPROVEMENTS IN STANDARDS OF ACCOMMODATION

Visitors demand high standards today. Many hotels and guest houses have been modernized and improved to meet the needs of guests and the minimum standard of accommodation scheme operated by the Borough Council in co-operation with local hotel and holiday trade associations. In addition, regulations such as fire precautions must be observed.

Other amenities have been introduced, such as bedrooms with private bathroom or shower, central heating, radio, colour television, video films, telephone, power points for electric shaver, and tea and coffee making facilities. Evening entertainment, dancing to music from an organist or band, cabaret, disco with bar available may also be included without extra cost to guests.

With the increasing accent on keeping fit, some hotels have their own swimming pool, solarium, sauna, steam room, gymnasium and games room. So you can obtain practically everything in your hotel, from music to a sauna, or both at the same time.

CHAPTER 11

4th – 9th JUNE 1985

ANOTHER TRAGEDY AT SEA

The sea can change from smooth to rough very quickly, and warnings of how dangerous it can be should never be ignored.

Another tragedy was reported on the front page of the West Lancashire Evening Gazette on the day of my arrival at Blackpool. A twelve-year-old South Shore boy was feared to have drowned, after a flimsy black and yellow inflatable dinghy in which he had last been seen had been discovered empty seven miles off Central Pier by lifeboats searching throughout the night.

The alarm was raised by the police, who had found out from the missing boy's six year old brother. Fleetwood lifeboat, the two Blackpool inshore lifeboats, and coastguard units from Lytham and Fleetwood took part in the search for the missing boy. The coastguard and police superintendent heading the investigation issued a severe warning about the use of this type of dinghy, which can be bought locally for £2.99. It is really intended for use in a small pool only, and is totally unsuitable for the sea.

Tuesday 4th June

BARE NECESSITIES OF LIFE

I look around the beach at the southern end of the promenade near the Starr Gate tram terminus after arrival by car in the afternoon. The sun is shining and it is quite warm in places sheltered from the cool north easterly breeze. A number of people are sunbathing on the sands. Seeing so many wearing bathing costumes only, my first thoughts are: "You only need the bare necessities of life when it is fine in Blackpool".

UNEXPECTED CHANGE OF ACCOMMODATION – EXCELLENT HOSPITALITY

When I arrive at the hotel where I have booked a room for five days, the receptionist apologises that the Manager is away on holiday. Owing to a mix up in accommodating a party my room has been overbooked, and the hotel is full this evening. She offers the choice of looking for somewhere else myself and having my deposit refunded, or staying one evening for bed and breakfast with someone she knows who has a guest house nearby. I can return here tomorrow morning after breakfast, when one room will become vacant.

I decide to accept the second alternative. I have been coming to Blackpool long enough not to be surprised at anything unexpected happening, as the unpredictable often turns out to be more interesting.

The receptionist makes a telephone call to "Jenny", to arrange for me to stay at the guest house. The receptionist then helps to carry my luggage and show me the way to where I will be staying, which is within walking distance.

There is a sound of knocking from one side of the house where the brickwork is being repointed. I receive a very warm and friendly welcome from the married couple owners, who assure me that the noise will stop during the evening.

I am led to a small comfortable bedroom with wash basin and tea making facilities. An electric shaver socket is on the wall outside the bedroom. I am invited to use the lounge downstairs whenever I wish, and instructed how to operate the television set. When I ask what shows are at Blackpool during the evening a leaflet containing the information is given to me.

CENTRAL PIER SHOW

I choose the Central Pier show, as the performance commences at 7.00 pm., which allows me about half an hour to walk there. The main artists in the show are singer Ruby Murray, and comedian George Roper.

MORE WALL WORK

I am well pleased with the exceptional hospitality shown to me by the married couple at the guest house, which continues until I leave. Breakfast is ready when I come downstairs just before 9 a.m. It is of a high standard, and there is plenty to eat and drink.

When I pay the bill, which is a modest price, they invite me to return at any time in the future. As I am leaving, the owner has re-commenced work knocking out the soft cement between the bricks on his wall, as he has taken the opportunity of doing the necessary repairs during a quiet week of the season when he has no other guests.

I remark: "It sounds like the song in Snow White and the Seven Dwarfs – 'Hi ho, hi ho, it's off to work we go'."

WHAT IS AN APARTHOTEL?

The hotel where I originally booked a room is described as an "Aparthotel". I had never heard of this type of accommodation before seeing it advertised in the "COSTA NOTTA LOTTA" – 1985 Blackpool Holiday Guide – so arranged to stay there to find out what it was like.

An Aparthotel offers freedom to guests to decide what they wish to do. A modern bedroom with private facilities is provided, with shower or bath and toilet, colour television, central heating, and electric kettle for making tea and coffee. Breakfast can be taken either in the Dining Room or served in your own bedroom. The price for bed and breakfast, daily or weekly, includes everything.

NORTH PIER – THE "PHANTOM PRINT PINCHER" STRIKES AGAIN

The North Pier show is again advertised above the booking office and entrance: "Mike Hughes presents stars of the ALL LAUGHTER SHOW: Les Dennis, Dustin Gee, special guest star Vince Hill, Ray Cornell Dancers, Pavlov's Puppets, Greg Rogers . . . Nightly 6.10

p.m. & 8.40 p.m. BOOK HER."

I laugh at noticing another letter is missing and think, "This time it's the 'E' that's silent, as in '.. by gum'."

A notice is displayed outside the entrance: "BUSINESS AS USUAL". The Pier is still open after a fire caused some damage to the Pavilion earlier in the week, and the evening show is continuing as usual.

LIFEBOAT STATION

An Austin Metro car supplied by a local motor dealer is displayed at the Lifeboat Station. It is first prize in a draw, and I buy a book of tickets.

The lady who is selling tickets thanks me, and says that the grandmother of the missing boy who was swept out to sea in his plastic inflatable dinghy has just been in to thank the lifeboatmen for searching for him, and to look at the lifeboat.

TRANSPORT DEPOT BLUNDELL STREET

This year is the centenary of Blackpool's electric tramway, which commenced operation on 29th September 1885. A programme of special events is being arranged during the season. I visit the Transport depot at Blundell Street to find out whether any guided tours of the Works are being arranged, but am told that there are only tours for booked parties, and the next one is not due until a week next Saturday.

Thursday 6th June

I PUT MY FOOT ON IT AT THE TOWER

There are more changes at the Tower, open for thirteen hours of entertainment daily, seven days a week, all for the price of admission, which now costs £2 for adults. There are many different things to see on five floors. I remain for about three or four hours, taking refreshments at the buffet in Jungle Jim's Adventure

Playground for five to twelve-year-olds, between exploring and finding out what is going on.

After I have had a good look around I look for the way out. At the top of a flight of stairs leading to the main exit an attendant bars the way, and advises me to please use the stairs on the far side of the ballroom.

If there is a wrong way to perform any action which is obvious and simple to do the right way by anyone else, I will do it the wrong way, not because I am deliberately awkward; it just happens automatically.

Although I do find my way through the ballroom to the other staircase leading downwards, in the doorway a man is talking to two women, and rather than try to push past them unmannerly I decide to turn back instead. I return to the top of the first staircase, and as no one bars the way this time walk down the stairs towards the main exit on the ground floor.

An unusually large number of police are outside the Tower entrance, among a large crowd of people. I ask a policeman standing in the doorway what is happening.

"Princess Alice has just gone in", he replies.

I look down and discover that I have been walking on a long red plush carpet which extends from the staircase to the pavement outside. It has apparently been laid out specially for a Very Important Visitor, and I have put my feet on it!

PRINCESS ALICE'S VISIT

Later I discovered that eighty-three-year old Princess Alice, Duchess of Gloucester, had flown into Blackpool Airport for a visit to a St Anne's convalescent home which she had opened twenty-five years ago.

A SUPER CIRCUS AND A "FIVE AND A HALF'TH" BIRTHDAY

This year the world famous Tower Circus presented by Peter Jay is billed as "Super Circus '85". Animal acts include horses, camels, unrideable mules, performing budgerigars and sealions.

A high percentage of the audience at the evening performance are children. A row of disabled and handicapped people in the rear stalls thoroughly enjoy the show.

An additional delight for me is to watch the expressions of wonder on the faces of young children, many of them fascinated and spellbound at seeing live Circus acts of jugglers, clowns, tight rope walkers, trapeze artists, acrobats and performing animals for the first time.

During the Circus performance the Ringmaster invites any children in the audience who have a birthday today to come into the ring.

Five children run down from their seats into the ring. The band plays and the audience sing, "Happy Birthday to you", and the children receive small gifts from the Circus staff.

The Ringmaster interviews each child in turn, with the aid of a microphone.

"What's your name?"

"Sharon."

"How old are you?"

"Eight."

"Where do you come from?"

"St Anne's."

"That's a posh place. Where they eat their fish and chips out of plastic bags instead of newspapers!"

The Ringmaster comes to the last small boy and asks, "How old are you?"

"Five and a half" is the reply. Everyone laughs.

When he has finished laughing the Ringmaster says, "We haven't had anyone here before who had a five and a half'th birthday. When will you be six and a half?"

"Tomorrow!"

Friday 7th June

THE GREAT BRITISH FUN RUN

After tea I walk along the North promenade towards the North Pier. Near Butlin's Metropole Hotel there is a double-decker bus and marquee advertising the arrival in Blackpool of the Great British Fun Run. This is a twenty-eight day road relay around Britain organised by the Health Education Council, to encourage people to follow a healthier way of life – exercising, eating sensibly and relaxing more.

Samples of bread for visitors to taste are provided by the bread manufacturing companies sponsoring the health and fitness extravaganza. An information and fitness testing centre is inside a caravan nearby. Some of the advertising balloons tied to chairs outside the marquee are almost blown away by the strong breeze.

MORE MISFORTUNES AT THE NORTH PIER SHOW

There is disappointment at the North Pier: Dustin Gee, one of the stars, is ill in hospital. The show has to be completely re-arranged at short notice.

Those who have booked tickets for the "All Laughter Show" strive against the strong wind to reach the Pavilion and shelter at the end of the Pier. The first house starts at 6.10 p.m. The performance goes on in spite of difficulties, and the performers receive quite a good reception from the rather small number in the audience.

Saturday 8th June

STANLEY PARK

After lunch in the cafe at Stanley Park, I walk towards the six flat and crown bowling greens. Not all of the greens are being used by bowls players. Three mallards are sitting on the grass on one of the unoccupied greens. They remain there while I move nearer to take a photograph.

Stanley Park appears to have changed little in recent years, but there is something which I have not noticed before. Near the lake is the Round Table No.18 Wishing Well. An inscription states: "Drop coins in the bucket and make a wish:". The Wishing Well was opened by the Mayor of Blackpool, Councillor Robert Brierley, on September 3rd 1966 in aid of local charities. A list of those which have benefitted is printed on a notice board.

Sunday 9th June

END OF STAY AT APARTHOTEL

Before leaving the Aparthotel, I thank the manager and staff for their hospitality. I tell them I find this new idea very convenient and comfortable. The manager apologises again for any inconvenience, and explains that the reason why I could not stay there on my first night in Blackpool is because somebody who booked until Tuesday for a conference stopped for an extra day without telling him. As he was out during that day he could not be contacted until it was too late.

VERDICT ON APARTHOTEL – IT SUITS ME

My verdict is in favour of this type of accommodation. You can return to your room at any time you wish instead of at a fixed time for a meal. When the weather is unfavourable you can go back for shelter and warmth. You can make tea or coffee whenever you want a drink. If you prefer to take your meals other than breakfast outside, there are plenty of cafes and refreshment places in the town.

CHAPTER 12

18th – 21st OCTOBER 1985

A (N)ICE SURPRISE & LUCKY RETURN VISIT

The main reason for a second visit to Blackpool in the same year is because I was given two pairs of complimentary tickets for the Ice Show. I received them by post on the day after my arrival home from my June holidays, from Mr Geoffrey Thompson, after I had left a photograph of "The Ranger" at the Pleasure Beach for him during my visit.

Friday 18th October

ICEDROME

It is lucky that I have chosen this weekend instead of next weekend, which was offered as an alternative date by the hotel where I am staying. I find out from the Icedrome Box Office that there are no performances on Friday evenings, and as the free tickets are not valid on Saturdays and I will be returning home on Monday, the only show I can attend will be on Sunday afternoon.

The last performance of "Hot Ice 2" will be on Saturday 26th October. In the week commencing Sunday 27th October, Roberts Brothers Circus will be performing on ice.

IMMEDIATE WELCOME AT "PERFECT GUEST HOUSE"

Although I arrive at the small hotel about 5.15 pm. just as the hostess is busy serving dinner to the guests, this does not prevent her giving me a prompt and friendly welcome. She carries my case upstairs and shows me to my bedroom.

Everything is spotlessly clean and beautifully laid out, with every comfort. As well as the private bathroom with shower, toilet and wash basin, and other advertised facilities like tea and coffee making, telephone, radio and colour television, there are useful unexpected extras like a Phillips Hair Dryer, electric blanket, and needle and darning set in case of accidents to clothing.

MILLION POUND MARVEL

The Illuminations are claimed to be the greatest tourism attraction in the western hemisphere, hosting eight million visitors during autumn. About half of the estimated yearly total of sixteen million come during the Illuminations period; business is estimated at £100 million. No one else has anything like them on such a scale – on nearly six miles of promenade. They have universal appeal to all ages.

The cost of the Illuminations increases each year – in 1985 it was estimated at about a million pounds, with the total value of equipment over £2½ million. Over 75 miles of cable and wiring, 375,000 lamps of over 100 different types and sizes, 50 miles of festoon strip, over 1,500 floodlights and spotlights, more than 1,000 decorative designs and 60 animated tableaux, consuming 800,500 units of electricity off peak.

Most of the cost is met by the ratepayers, but in recent years collecting boxes have been introduced along the promenade for voluntary contributions from motorists and coaches.

Each year something new is added to the Illuminations, with glass fibre and electronic control units bringing them up to date and maintaining a high standard. A brilliant excuse for extending the holiday season on dates when many other resorts' main attractions may have closed down for the winter. No wonder the evening atmosphere along the promenade is electric.

OPERA HOUSE – LENA MARTELL

At the Opera House I book tickets for the evening theatre entertainment – Lena Martell in concert. The Glasgow born international star singer has recently returned from a tour of the U.S.A. In the second half of the show she gives a non-stop performance lasting over an hour, and receives a good reception from the audience.

Saturday19th October

BREAKFAST BANQUET

I have booked for only bed and breakfast, but the morning meal served contains such a tempting choice and quantity of food that it is as much as I can manage to eat, and during the rest of the day snacks are adequate.

I have two complimentary vouchers, each to be exchanged for two tickets for the best available seats at "Hot Ice 2", and offer them to the other guests at breakfast. One voucher is accepted by a married couple sitting at another table. I offer the remaining free seat to another guest who is on his own, but he declines.

NORTH SHORE CONSTRUCTION WORK & SAFETY MEASURES

I walk to the cliffs above the North Shore Boating Pool. A notice on the top promenade reads: "WARBRECK COASTAL PROTECTION SCHEME. RECONSTRUCTION OF SEA WALL AND N. SHORE BOATING POOL. MAIN CONTRACTORS DEW CIVIL ENGINEERING DIVISION, OLDHAM. PROJECT PARTLY FINANCED BY EUROPEAN REGIONAL DEVELOPMENT FUND."

Near Gynn Square and the lower promenade where the construction work is being carried out there are plenty of safety precautions in case of danger, lifebelts, lifesaving equipment, safety net harness and ropes. Warning notices are posted: "IN CASE OF ANY EMERGENCY DIAL 999 ASK FOR POLICE". And: "TIDE REACHES WALL. HIGH WATER LEVEL WALL".

A Land Rover patrols the lower promenade frequently. The driver has a "walkie-talkie" radio. His vehicle is full of all kinds of safety equipment both inside and outside – life lines, lifebelt, spare rubber tyre, ropes and poles.

DOG LEADS FOR INVISIBLE DOGS

Seen on a notice board outside a souvenir shop in Coronation Street: "ON SALE HERE – DOG LEADS FOR INVISIBLE DOGS".

I wonder: "Are they the dogs which belong to fairground barkers?"

FLUCTUATING FORTUNES FOR FOOTBALL CLUB

At Bloomfield Road football ground the cost of a ticket in the West Stand for the League match against Bury is £3. Blackpool F.C. are now in eleventh position in Division 3, after gaining promotion from Division 4 last season.

The attendance this afternoon is announced as 5,496 – above average for the season, but fewer spectators watch games than when their team was in the First Division.

The home side start off well, and are two goals ahead including a penalty after the first seven minutes. Early in the second half one of the Bury players is sent off for a foul. Blackpool take advantage of their opponents being one player short for the rest of the match, and score three more goals. The final result is 5-0, their best win of the season, and the team are applauded off the field by their supporters after the full time whistle.

Sunday 20th October

BRITISH LEGION PARADE

Walking along the North Promenade in the morning, I am attracted to Princess Parade by hearing bands playing in the distance.

A procession from the Cenotaph to Talbot Square is led by military bands. A smartly dressed kilted regiment with pipes and drums receives applause from the spectators. Next follow rows of marchers, including the Eighth Army Veterans Association, wearing their medals and poppies. Then comes another military band playing. More civilians, flag bearers and a St. John Ambulance follow at the rear.

Police control the traffic along the route to Talbot Square, where the parade ends among crowds across the street waiting to welcome the marchers. After the bands finish playing, their members disperse. Some enter waiting coaches, while others walk off in the direction of the Council offices.

ICE DROME – "HOT ICE 2"

After a light lunch, I make my way along the promenade to the Pleasure Beach, and arrive at the Ice Drome ten minutes before the show is due to commence.

At the Box Office I exchange the complimentary voucher for two tickets, and try to dispose of the spare ticket. All the people following who do not already have tickets seem to be in family groups, and decline when I ask if anyone wants one free ticket. I offer it to a man who enters on his own, but he turns out to be the Ice Drome Manager. As the show is due to start, I abandon further efforts to dispose of the ticket, and go inside to my seat.

"Hot Ice 2" is a spectacular, fast moving, modern family entertainment, with highly skilled ice skating and dancing by many international stars. The finale is a sumptuous Carnival on Ice. The costumes are particularly lavish and colourful.

I enjoy the show very much. It brings back memories of past visits to the Ice Drome.

TRAM TOUR OF ILLUMINATIONS

Every available tram is brought into service for evening tours of the Illuminations, including those on loan for the Tramway Centenary this year.

Blundell Street Tram Depot, 5th June 1985. Left, Sheffield no. 513, built 1950: Centre, Standard no. 40, on loan from Crich Tramway Museum: Right, one of Blackpool's streamlined "Balloons", built about 1935 by English Electric.

Long queues wait at the North Pier where the tours start. The tram service is frequent. A transport Inspector supervises operations, and as soon as one tram has filled up with passengers signals for it to move off, and the next tram waiting behind takes its place.

At 8.00 p.m. I board an open topped vintage double decker tram – Bolton No. 16. Most of the passengers choose to go onto the top deck to obtain a favourable position for viewing the Illuminations. "You'll be sorry", says the conductor cheerfully, as it is rather cold on top when the tram is moving.

We first head north towards Bispham, where the Illuminations end, then continue through comparative darkness to the next turning point at Little Bispham.

The tram returns southwards to more dazzling displays of set pieces with changing sequences and messages, some sponsored by well known advertisers. Along the crowded promenade, passing the Tower, three piers and Pleasure Beach, with a stop at the "Welcome" archway near the southern end at Starr Gate.

On the return journey towards the Pleasure Beach we stop again, owing to a power failure which brings every tram to a standstill for about twenty minutes. It is probably caused by the extremely high demand for electricity.

I take a flash photograph of the well known Muppet character, "Miss Piggy", whose features on a set piece change each time the lights go on and off.

When the electricity comes on again the tram resumes its journey. It is ten o'clock when it reaches the original starting point at the North Pier, and the passengers alight. The whole tour has taken two hours for a £1.70 fare. It is the best opportunity I have had of obtaining such a good view of the Illuminations.

Monday 21st October

"PERFECT GUEST HOUSE" MAKES WEEKEND MOST ENJOYABLE

I regret having to leave so soon after such a favourable weekend, but the guest house is fully booked up until after the Illuminations. In fact I am lucky to have been able to stay there at such a busy time when practically all available accommodation is fully booked, and "NO VACANCIES" notices are displayed in most hotel windows.

I thank my host and hostess very much for their exceptional standard of hospitality and personal attention, which could not have been better and really justifies their rating of number 1 guest house in Blackpool out of about 2,000. I feel treated not merely as an honoured guest, but almost like a member of the family.

SPECIAL AWARDS FROM AUTHORITIES

It is not only my own opinion that this is the best guest house, but also the British Tourist Authority's. It is the only guest house in Blackpool they give a special commendation for outstanding service and comfort. Special awards and approval by others whose inspectors visit the establishment include the English Tourist Board, the Automobile Association, Royal Automobile Club, Michelin Guide and "Guestaccom".

MAINTENANCE WORK ON ILLUMINATIONS

Before driving away from Blackpool I stop near the Pleasure Beach to take a photograph. I notice a yellow Dodge van parked on the promenade next to one of the Illuminations set pieces. Extended above the van is a long "Simon" arm, at the end of which is a bucket compartment. About half way up the fixture an electrician is working on electric lamps.

On looking closer, out of the thousands of Illuminations figures on the promenade it turns out to be "Miss Piggy", the one which I had photographed from the tram last night.

CHAPTER 13

1st – 5th JUNE 1987

Monday 1st June

NORTH PROMENADE, WATERED GARDENS

After arriving in Blackpool in the afternoon I walk past the Derby Baths to the North Promenade, and have a look at the sea. The weather is now fine after having been wet during most of my journey by road.

Near Gynn Square I notice a Council gardener at the North Promenade Gardens watering a flower bed with a hose pipe. I ask him if it has been raining in Blackpool today. He replies that there has been rain in the early morning, but not heavy, and it stopped in the afternoon.

I would not expect that the flower beds would need watering today, but the workman is giving them a good soaking. Another gardener is working in the rock gardens a short distance away.

WINTER GARDENS – CONFERENCE & EXHIBITION CENTRE SECOND TO NONE

There is always something to see at the Winter Gardens, even if nothing in particular seems to be going on, which was the case when I had about half an hour to spare, explore and wander around during my first evening. All kinds of conferences, exhibitions, dances, reunions, variety shows, dinners and special functions can be arranged in many halls, rooms and lounges. This particular week, I think some Trade Union conferences, including U.S.D.A.W. and the Engineering Group Sectional Conference are being held during the daytime.

The evening appeared to be the time for clearing up the mess left behind from the day's meetings. I looked into the magnificent Embassy Ballroom, which can seat up to 3,500 delegates or 1,000 at tables. Papers littered the floor – notices, magazines, leaflets. Delegates had obviously not taken much notice of the anti-litter laws. Attendants were making efforts to tidy up in time for tomorrow, but it would be a long and tedious job as there were other rooms in a similar state.

I was not the only one who remembered the Embassy Ballroom as one of the most famous dance halls of the past. A middle aged man who spoke to me remarked how it had changed since he last saw it. He said that he was in the R.A.F during the Second World War and was stationed near Blackpool. He used to come to dances here, as did lots of other servicemen.

Upstairs in the Spanish Hall tables were laid out, as if for a dinner or banquet. Behind a row of notice boards workmen were doing something to the floor.

The main Floral Hall contained a few stands, mainly advertisements: First Leisure Corporation, owners of the buildings, posters of their summer shows. C.N.D., the Campaign Against Nuclear Disarmament, you could help yourself to their leaflets.

GRAND THEATRE – HIGH LIGHTS OF THE EVENING

At the Grand Theatre a one night variety show commences at 8.00 p.m. The only seats available are in the gallery, very high up, for £2.50.

There are many stairs to the gallery. At last we climb to the top. Jokes are made about needing oxygen masks and being nearly as high as the top of the Tower. We look DOWN on to large chandeliers hanging from the ceiling and on two spotlights operated by electricians – the HIGH LIGHTS of the evening, by kind permission of the North Western Electricity Board?

Two of the stars in the show are well known comedians, Charlie Williams and Norman Collier, and the supporting acts include Irish recording singer, Rose Marie. The show is well received by the audience and generally up to Blackpool's high standards – we are certainly high up enough to appreciate it.

Tuesday 2nd June

WET DAY

It is one of those very wet days when rain continues non-stop throughout the daylight hours. However, there are compensations, and certainly no lack of interest, even without going outside the hotel. Plenty of good quality food and drink whenever required, both in the bedroom, where there are tea and coffee making facilities, and in the air-conditioned dining room and lounge bar, which is open from 11.00 a.m. until late at night; snacks can be ordered at any time while it is open.

The main activities during the day are eating and drinking, and sitting in the "sun lounge" looking through the windows.

I watch trams going along the promenade in the rain, and reckon how useful they are, not only as a means of transport but also for advertising purposes. What is written on trams and buses is seen and read by thousands of travellers every day, whereas yesterday's daily newspapers soon become thrown away and forgotten or used as today's fish and chips wrappings.

I count a total of about thirty different varieties of advertisements printed on trams and buses going past the hotel during the day.

There are people to talk with – other guests and the hotel staff – newspapers to read, postcards to write, television to watch and radio to listen to.

I remember once when I was waiting at a tram stop near the Tower, a lady in the queue grumbled after two trams passed without stopping, as they were only going as far as the next stop, Talbot Square. My thoughts were that one should not become impatient if kept waiting for a mere ten or fifteen minutes. After all, trams have been running at Blackpool for over a hundred years.

Wednesday 3rd June

"EVERYTHING UNDER THE SUN FOR A GREAT DAY OF FUN"

It is my first visit to the glass fronted Sandcastle. You can stay for as long as it remains open. I pay £2 for the entrance charge, which includes admission to everything inside. Food and drink costs extra, and there are numerous places where different kinds of refreshments can be bought.

Sandcastle Centre, 3rd June 1987

I walk around the four leisure pools, where people of all ages, most wearing only bathing costumes, are enjoying themselves. The indoor temperature is a constant computer controlled 84 degrees Fahrenheit, so there is no need to wear any more than the bare necessities.

There are water slides, water chutes, fountains, palm trees and tropical plants. Some of the pools are one metre or more deep, other parts shallow enough for tiny tots to sit or play in. Adults sit on the terraces, eating, drinking, watching their children and taking photographs.

Overhead are 3,000 coloured lamps, 155 miles of electric wiring, and 6½ miles of piping for beer – so I am told.

Plastic pink flamingoes suspended from wires float in mid air. In one of the pools are six large plastic blue balls on which swimmers can sit and climb. Children have great fun squirting anyone within range with a water cannon. Bathers stand underneath a fountain, taking a shower from it. A waterspout shoots high into the air and then disappears, to the wonder of young children watching.

In the 1.8 metre pool a wave machine causes groups of young swimmers to bob up and down in the water.

On one side a "Kiddies Harbour" supervised play area has activities for young children, with wooden houses, rope walks to climb on and swinging baskets.

A balcony above one of the pools provides a good view and vantage point for photographs. It leads to a veranda with white chairs and tables, some with blue umbrellas above them. There are more kiosks with refreshments and ice cream, and a games room with pool and snooker tables and amusement machines.

Another veranda higher up leads to the Crows Nest Pub, outside which are more tables and chairs. From the top I get a colourful view of the pools below, with different coloured electric light bulbs, and the greenery of palm trees and tropical plants.

Adequate facilities for disabled people are provided including a slope for wheelchairs from the main entrance, and separate toilets. I go into one of the "Gents" toilets and find it in a very clean condition.

So the Sandcastle is proving successful as a major attraction and indoor leisure and entertainment complex, and claims to be "The world's greatest inside seaside".

DERBY DAY

Today is Derby day at Epsom racecourse. In my hotel at lunch time, a turbaned resident collects money from diners who wish to place their bets. This year's race, the Ever Ready Derby, is reported to be the richest ever, worth £267,600 to the winner. I wonder what a racehorse would do with all that money?

RACEHORSE REVELRY

The answer to the author's flight of fancy about how the winning racehorse might celebrate with the prize money from the Derby is shown in Wrexham artist David Walker's drawing above.

Anyone who may be interested in this artist's work or would like to offer him a commission may write to him via the publisher, whose address is shown at the front of the book.

RIVAL ELECTRIC SIGNS – "THE TAVERN" AND "MAGGIE MAY'S SHOWBAR"

Electric signs issue messages as a method of advertising bars at some well known places. Across a wide frontage of the Tavern in the Town opposite the Central Pier : "THE TAVERN – PROBABLY THE BEST PUB IN TOWN."

Across the front of the Central Pier continuous moving signs flash out: "THE AMAZIN' MAGGIE MAY'S SHOWBAR – OPEN THIS LUNCHTIME – ADMISSION FREE". As a General Election was due on 11th June, I was reminded by the Central Pier sign of a topical reference to Margaret Thatcher, the Prime Minister. "Maggie MAY win the election." As it turned out, she did.

Welcome to Central Pier. Maggie Mays, the non-stop Pierhead Party

Thursday 4th June

INSIDE PROFESSOR PEABODY'S PLAY PLACE

At "Professor Peabody's Play Place" are over thirty fun-filled play activities all under one roof and on two floors. Fun for all ages from six months to twelve years. I arrive at the entrance, and enquire

123

whether I can go in to have a look around. To my delight I am allowed in free. The admission charge for children is £2.25.

Every conceivable kind of brightly coloured objects and activities are available to try out, and children wander from one to another as they wish: A "Junior Ballpond" filled with coloured plastic balls to creep among or throw about; "Turtle Cars" on wheels to sit in and move along with hands and feet are just two examples.

In the toddlers' soft play area upstairs, young children run about with no shoes on. In "Peabody's Building Site" brightly coloured blue, green and red brick blocks with holes in them can be joined together. Adults are helping children to build houses and other models.

Looking down from the balcony I see the Hoppit: chains from an overhead pulley allow children to glide through the air above an uneven green wooden floor. Above the ground a set of six or seven red plastic "Space Domes" with holes to climb through. The return journey is down a yellow slide.

Downstairs there are "Twizzle Ladders" to climb, "Bounceabouts" to jump up and down on, with a wobbly floor, "Rock-and-Roll Rocket" – a large plastic red and white tent to explore inside – and the "Cresta Run" – a ride down a slope in tray shaped sledges on caterpillar runners.

Remote controlled miniature electric cars on a circuit are operated by putting two 10p coins in a slot. While controlling them by a steering wheel, the operator sits in a larger model racing car with proper controls and electric lights.

The steepest and highest slide is the "Monster Drop". It is supervised by attendants at the top, where children sit with their legs over the edge and launch themselves downwards when the signal is given.

Children have to find their way through a "Box Maze" and can swing on motor tyres hanging from a rope on the "Swingalong". Another "Ballpond" to play in is filled with brightly coloured plastic balls. Some children sit on sacks and descend a giant green and yellow caterpillar slide.

There are steps leading to balconies, above which are more ropes to adventure on, pipes to slide through, and a row of blue linoleum shaped cylinders hanging from wires which sway about when the invitation to "Punch me" is accepted. A large revolving drum moves when it is pushed – no more than four children at one time are allowed inside it.

Food and drink is available for all whenever wanted. It is served at Peabody's Picnic Place: burgers, chips, soft drinks and other light refreshments.

OPERA HOUSE – "THE VOYAGE OF THE DAWN TREADER"

After lunch in the Palm Court Restaurant, I book a seat for the afternoon performance of "THE VOYAGE OF THE DAWN TREADER" at the Opera House. A friendly attendant in the booking office replies to my enquiry whether it is a children's play: "It's like "ALICE IN WONDERLAND" – very nice. Suitable for older people too. You'll enjoy it".

Coaches full of school children accompanied by teachers arrive outside the theatre before 2.00 p.m., when the performance is due to start.

The play is an adaptation of a children's novel by C.S.Lewis, a successor to "THE LION, THE WITCH AND THE WARDROBE", in the Narnia series. The stage performance is exciting, magical and spectacular, with specially effective special effects. Smoke from each side of the stage camouflages the entrance and exit of the ship, "The Dawn Treader".

One scene merges into the next on the revolving stage. The young audience react to the sequence of events with imagination, as they watch spellbound. During the interval there is a rush for ice cream.

Friday 5th June

A HELPING HAND FOR A BROKEN DOWN VAUXHALL

Before breakfast I am packing some luggage into the car when I hear a voice: "Have you got any jump leads?"

I turn, see a bearded young man from the hotel with another lad looking inside the bonnet of an old Vauxhall saloon car, and reply: "I've got a tow rope if you want a lift to a garage".

He says that they prefer to push it to the end of the road, hoping that the engine will start down the hill leading to Gynn Square. One lad commences pushing the car, while the other sits inside and steers.

I follow, adding an extra hand in assisting the vehicle to move forward. We push it in the opposite direction to the promenade along a road which is fairly flat, until we reach a junction.

We wait until the road is clear, then turn right and give the car a push down the hill towards Gynn Square. It gathers speed, with the lad who has been pushing running after it. They travel too fast for me to follow. They soon disappear out of sight, so I return to the hotel without finding out whether the car actually did start.

CHAPTER 14

19th – 23rd JUNE 1988.

"YOUNG AT HEART" HOLIDAYS

This year specially reduced terms for accommodation are offered to visitors aged 55 years and over staying for three nights or more. These offers are only valid during May and June, except for Bank Holiday weekends. The holidays were given a special name by Blackpool Borough Council: "Young at Heart". A number of entertainments also offer substantial reductions on production of a concession card, which is obtainable from the Tourist Information Centre and three local hotel, guest house and self-catering associations.

Sunday 19th June

AN UN-NAMED PARK

It is bright and sunny when I arrive by road at Central Drive, and stop by a small park about 1.00 p.m.

Inside the entrance gate are a bowling green, putting green, and covered area where children are playing table tennis. Adults sit on benches watching the bowls players.

At the rear are a children's playground and tennis courts without nets. There is a grassy area where children play, and adults lounge on the grass. Trees border a footpath near the road. Birds sing and aircraft buzz overhead.

Leaving the park I walk along Bloomfield Road past the football ground main entrance and come to a bridge. The large Central car and coach park is below, full of parked vehicles.

After walking to Lytham Road I find a small cafe, outside which are a few tables with umbrellas. I am soon served by a pleasant waitress, and finish a cheese sandwich, scones and pot of tea without delay.

PROCESSION

Outside a newsagents in Lytham Road I hear the distant sound of a band playing. The music becomes louder, and soon a procession marching along the road comes into view.

It appears to be a church parade. Some of the marchers carry flags, crosses or banners, one showing "St. Peter's Sunday School". At the front is a teenage girl wearing a long white dress, carrying a bouquet of flowers and accompanied by a group of younger children. A band follows, then a ladies' choir in uniform, and clergymen. More adults march behind another banner. A group of Brownies carrying flowers and a pack of Cub Scouts with their leaders and flagbearers follow behind.

The procession turns left into Trafalgar Road and marches past a row of parked cars towards the promenade, watched by people outside the hotels, guest houses and holiday flats.

The Transport Depot is nearby in Blundell Street, where I walk across to have a look at the tram shed. Inside are trams in service now and others mainly used during the Illuminations.

I cross to the bus shed, where a number of double decker buses are parked outside. Inside are some new yellow and navy coloured twenty-one-seater minibuses marked HANDY BUS.

A row of lorries are parked in the yard of the Council Health and Environment Department in Rigby Road. In the middle a large notice board is headed:

"STOP! NO RUBBISH TO BE LEFT IN THIS SET. L.C.C. PROVIDE TWO SITES FOR THE DISPOSAL OF RUBBISH AT BRISTOL AVE. BISPHAM, AND EVEREST ROAD, LYTHAM ST. ANNES. OPEN DAILY 9 a.m. – 5 p.m."

FROM RIGBY (ROAD) TO RUGBY (GROUND)

On the far side of the yard a pile of waste paper and rubbish has been blown against a wall by the wind. Scores of seagulls are scavenging among the refuse.

A noise coming from the direction of the former Rugby League ground behind a high brick wall on the other side of Rigby Road indicates that something is going on there. I find an entrance by the stand and discover that the ground is full of people, players and spectators. Many of the onlookers are drinking and watching five a side soccer being played on three pitches across the field.

The matches are keenly contested, generally played in a good spirit, and continue non-stop. Some players take their shirts off after they come off the field, as the weather has now become very warm. There are no announcements to indicate which teams are playing.

Underneath the stand are a bar and changing rooms. The interior is crowded and rather dark. I overhear footballers with Scottish accents discussing tactics for their next match.

"Are we playing with a sweeper?" one player asks his captain. I think: "If I were at home I could have offered them the loan of a HOOVER".

An ice cream van is doing good trade beside a row of stalls offering goods for sale. The sound of music is heard from the other side of the stand.

The noise amplified by microphones and loud speakers comes from the rooftop of a single-storey brick building beside the stand. A musical group of three electric guitarists and a drummer are playing Country music, accompanied by a blonde woman singer. An audience of mainly young people watch and listen, some sitting on the rooftop with their legs dangling over the edge.

A THUG'S GAME PLAYED BY GENTLEMEN

Later I found out that there is no longer a professional Rugby League Club in Blackpool. The former team moved from Borough Park Stadium in 1987 because they could not afford to carry out the safety work required. They first moved to Springfield Park, Wigan, and played as Springfield Borough. At present they play at Chorley.

Their supporters' club organizes coaches for travelling to matches on Sundays and helps to keep the sport alive in the resort. The Stix Social Club is now apparently under the same old stand at Borough Park. The rooftop music which I had heard may have originated from a group connected with this club.

Rugby League still generates interest, and on 8th December 1990 the supporters' club arranged a "Memorabilia Day" at the Borough Park Stadium to stimulate interest in the game on the Fylde Coast. Many fans, ex-players and officials came from further afield for a day of nostalgia.

I was told that the Rugby League supporter considers Rugby League to be a thug's game played by gentlemen, whereas Rugby Union is a gentlemen's game played by thugs.

Monday 20th June

BUILDING SOCIETY LIFEBOAT DISPLAY

In the window of the Britannia Building Society is a display about the Blackpool Lifeboats, with a notice that any donations to the R.N.L.I. would be accepted by the Society. It is reported that both sixteen-feet inflatable lifeboats were launched on 6th January 1988 in gale force conditions. With their boats awash two fishermen were rescued. One survived. Both lifeboat helmsmen were awarded bronze medals presented by H.R.H. Princess Alexandra in London. The other four crew members are to be presented with inscribed vellums in recognition of this outstanding service.

AN AFTERNOON ON THE CENTRAL PIER

After a visit to the Lifeboat Station I go onto the Central Pier for lunch at the Sea Chef Restaurant. Afterwards I have a look around the Pier.

Some of the children's activities are similar to those in Professor Peabody's Play Place, but there are also traditional fun fair amusements: miniature racing cars, Honda motor cycles around another track, a circular car ride around a large painted ball, a "Spotted Piggy" train – five brightly painted coaches shaped like pigs on rails – trampolines, a high yellow helter-skelter slide, a plastic play place on which children jump up and down, and rope

130

ladders to climb.

Trolleys on caterpillar rollers are carted up a slope, and children jump on and ride downhill. Near this enclosure lady supervisors are distributing sweets in bags to a long row of young dark-skinned children sitting together.

People sit on seats along both sides of the Pier enjoying the sunny afternoon. The tide is coming in and there is plenty of activity on the beach – donkeys, stalls and, of course, the sea for paddlers and bathers.

Tuesday 21st June

"THE AMAZEMENT PARK" BEFORE OPENING TIME

In the morning I return by tram to the Pleasure Beach, where the amusements do not open until 11 a.m. An hour before business is due to commence a few people are already going inside.

(Blackpool Pleasure Beach Company)

General view of the Pleasure Beach about 1987

I find out that tomorrow is the official opening by Eddie "The Eagle" Edwards, the Olympics skier, of "THE AVALANCHE", the first bobsleigh run in the U.K. which costs £2½ million. I walk around to look for this latest "white knuckle' ride.

I discover two more new features. A railway station for the Pleasure Beach has been opened recently by British Rail, and I look along the main line to see it in the distance.

Not far from the entrance near the Star Hotel and one of the Pleasure Beach railway stations are foundations of the new "WHISTLE STOP" pub planned to be opened this season.

I find the AVALANCHE station building, which is in the form of an Alpine Cottage. Workmen are painting and adding finishing touches to it. The surrounding area has been landscaped, and a marquee erected ready for tomorrow's opening.

Snake like steel structures for the ride spiral overhead, and an empty train of seven bobsleigh cars is being tested on the quarter mile winding steel chute with banks, curves and circles. Preparations which commenced over twelve months ago are reaching a climax, watched from vantage points by a few spectators.

At the White Tower Restaurant, about fifty tables are laid out as though for a lunch party. The reason is there for me to read on a window poster: "Manchester Taxi Drivers Outing to Blackpool for handicapped children, Tuesday 21st June".

Some of the previous names to catering units and bars have been changed. The former Magnolia Cafe is now Bourbon Street, offering quick snacks, American style Southern Fried Chicken, pizzas and Danish Open Sandwiches. Bean Street, a licensed courtyard, has corners for a Pancake House, ice cream bar, Thwaites family bar shaped like a double decker bus, fish and chips, and a sea food bar. A choice of a take-away service or sitting on chairs at tables inside is offered. The Sheriff's Family Bar specialises in giant hot dogs and roast beef sandwiches, and has a free children's show.

MORE CHANGES AT THE NORTH SHORE BOATING POOL

In the afternoon I walk down the cliff footpath to the North Shore Boating Pool. More alterations have been made, and there are now some amusements for children.

A small number of people are sitting on seats in the open by a kiosk, where snacks can be obtained.

A notice by a concrete floored area advertises: "MINI RACING CARS 35p", but there are none in sight.

There is still one boating pool for children. What used to be a second boating pool has been concreted over and is now a children's playground, with slides, swings, trampolines, table tennis and a large brightly coloured plastic giraffe.

I remark to a Council attendant who takes money from children wishing to use the playground, that it seems to be rather quiet. He replies that there are not many people here on weekdays until July, but they are busy during weekends.

END OF AN ERA AT DERBY POOL

The Derby Pool is being closed to the public by Blackpool Council after fifty years' service. A notice on the door reports that the sauna will be open until 16th July only.

A party of school children comes out of the baths. I walk through the main entrance, and meet three workmen. I say that it is a pity that the baths will be closed. One worker replies that the Pool is still being used by schools but will be closed altogether at the end of this term, in just over three weeks' time. They are hoping that a developer will take it over and convert it into a Leisure Centre, so that it can still be used as a swimming pool. Some of the staff have been made redundant, and others transferred or have obtained other jobs.

Wednesday 22nd June

OFFER OF HELP

In Dickson Road a woman trips and falls down onto the pavement. Immediately a friendly shopkeeper dashes out to offer help. He invites her into his shop to sit down, rest and have a cup of tea. However, she declines, and says she is all right. She is wearing trousers, does not appear to have suffered any injury, and on recovering is able to walk away with her husband.

DUTCH STREET ORGAN

Outside the Coral Social Club a De Harmonique Dutch Street Organ (built about 1930 by the Belgian firm of J. Verbeeck) plays music in aid of Cancer Research, and attracts a number of passing visitors.

CHINESE CIRCUS AT THE TOWER

It is a rare opportunity to see one of the world's finest acrobatic troupes from Chong Qing in the People's Republic of China performing live in the Tower circus ring. Their acts include the Classic Lion Dance and Dragon Dance. For the finale they have chosen the ancient Chinese Leather Straps, with the dancing coloured fountains of the world famous Blackpool Tower Water Spectacle in the background.

WHO'S THE BOSS?

Parked outside the hotel is a red saloon car marked on the front windscreen: "BOSS – SLAVE".

I mention this to one of the hotel staff. "Yes, it belongs to one of our chefs", he replies. I do not ask whether the driver is the husband or the wife.

FOREBEARS AMONG THE FOOD

I am tempted by a notice in a restaurant window advertising speciality ice cream dishes. "Go on, spoil yourself!" I think. I go inside and order a Strawberry Romanoff, which is strawberries with ice cream and a greenish-coloured flavouring served in a long glass.

While I am enjoying it, at about 9:30 pm, four young men come in through the door and give a loud cheer to attract the attention of diners and waitresses.

Suddenly, for no apparent reason, the intruders turn round and lower their trousers exposing a quartette of bare bottoms to all eyes which are already turned upon them.

Then they give another cheer, pull up their trousers again and disappear through the restaurant door before any of us have time to recover from our astonishment.

This unexpected disturbance brings the restaurant to life. Whereas it was previously quiet, now everybody starts talking at once. Some of the waitresses laugh about it. The manageress, however, is not amused. She goes to the doorway and looks outside, but she is too late. The offenders have escaped; there is little anyone can do about them now.

Thursday 23rd June

ADVANTAGES OF "YOUNG AT HEART" HOLIDAYS

Another fortunate and enjoyable holiday comes to an end. The hotel manager and his wife, assisted by their staff, work hard and long hours to attend to the needs of guests. The hotel is comfortable, with plenty of food and drink available whenever required, and is efficiently run.

In addition to favourable conditions at the hotel, I am also pleased with the concessions gained from the "YOUNG AT HEART HOLIDAYS", and think that this scheme is a good idea for welcoming over 55s to Blackpool. It is an improvement upon the former "pensioners' holidays". It makes me feel younger, and not forgotten.

HOW OLDER FOLK HAVE THE LAST LAUGH ON HOLIDAY

As we grow older, our opinions as well as our needs change. I used to think that Blackpool holidays were mainly for the young. This extract from my July 1951 diary proves it:

"Old people usually sit in the shelters on the promenade, smoke their pipes and talk. It is not a particularly popular place for old people. They are not very popular with landladies either, as many pensioners are very fussy about what they eat and what they do."

Eight years later my diary records different views on the subject:

"The popularity of Blackpool appeals to both young and old. Children can find plenty to do and lots of different things to eat —

sticky toffee apples, ice cream, rock, hamburgers, hot dogs and fish and chips. Old people can sit and watch the younger ones enjoying themselves, and remember that everything was less expensive in their younger days. As prices normally increase every year, older people have the last laugh by recollecting that their holidays in the past did not cost as much as their children and grandchildren have to pay today."

CHAPTER 15

1st – 7th JUNE 1990

THE CHANGING FACE OF BLACKPOOL

A significant visit, so much to see, so much to do. The main problem in Blackpool is finding time to fit everything in.

What is most noticeable is the large number of alterations which have been made since my last holiday only two years ago.

Friday 1st June

WINTER GARDENS FACELIFT

The first place visited in the evening is the Winter Gardens. It has had a multi-million pound facelift to improve its appearance and facilities as a major conference centre, but much of the original Victorian structure and detail is still retained.

On a wall near the Church Street entrance is a 1889-1989 Commemorative Roll of Honour, unveiled on July 26th 1989 by Lord Bernard Delfont to mark the century of the Opera House. It lists the stars who performed there each year, from Wilson Barnett in 1889 to Marti Webb in "CATS" in 1989.

Other new features in the Winter Gardens are decorated barrows selling personalized leather gifts, and Apple Annie's Drinking Emporium, a bar with disco music and flashing coloured electric lights.

GRAND THEATRE

The Grand is Blackpool's only all year round theatre. It was built in 1894 by architect Frank Matcham, saved from extinction in 1970, and is now administrated by a Trust.

Staged this week is the world premiere of a new comedy, "Seaside Romp", written by Mike Bennett and Dave Taggert, and starring Mollie Sugden and Jack Douglas. The fairly small number in the audience laugh frequently during this evening's performance, with the stage setting an antiques shop at a fictitious seaside resort.

Saturday 2nd June

TOWER SHOPPING CENTRE

Before 10 a.m. in the morning, I have a look inside the £14½ million Tower Shopping Centre, which opened last autumn. It is elegant and brightly lit, with black and white marble floors. Everything looks clean and new. An escalator leads to the first floor.

At an attractive confectionery and ice cream unit, exotic Belgian hand made chocolates are priced at £1.38 per quarter and £5.50 for a one-pound box. Upstairs the Gallery Coffee Shop's menu is displayed on a blackboard, and trays of mouth watering cream cakes revolve inside a glass case.

A number of uniformed Security Guards are on duty inside the building.

TOWER CERTAINLY IS ABOVE ALL!

I have an appointment at the Tower at 10.00 a.m. and go in through the staff entrance door in Bank Hey Street, directly opposite the Shopping Centre. I receive special attention from the staff of First Leisure Corporation, and gain some information about the past history of the Tower company.

I am escorted to a special viewpoint at the top of the Tower to take photographs. As we ascend in the lift, the reason for the Blackpool habit of writing on rooftops as well as on walls becomes plain. Names like "LEWIS'S" can be clearly seen from above.

The lift holds a maximum of twenty-six people, but I am elated as well as elevated to be allowed higher than the other passengers, who alight at the enclosed observation deck. Doors are unlocked so that I can follow the Tower staff up two flights of steps to an exposed platform.

From the top there is a magnificent view of the surrounding countryside, coastline and rough seas. At this height the wind is too strong for me to risk wearing a cap. I am as high above ground as anyone can venture, except the "stick-men" – the expert maintenance workers who actually work on the very top.

It is an exhilarating, gratifying and thrilling experience, like climbing the highest mountain. The Tower certainly is above everything. I take three quick photographs, then am glad to return down the steps to shelter and the less dizzy height of the observation deck.

After descending in the lift, I am given a conducted tour of other parts of the Tower, including "MEMORY LANE", the room where Blackpool's past history is shown in pictures and displays.

PLANS FOR MORE CHANGES AT THE TOWER

Since taking over the Tower, the three piers and winter Gardens in 1982, and more recently two major conference hotels – Savoy and Clifton – First Leisure Corporation has made many improvements to combine better quality and higher value facilities.

A scheme for extensive redevelopment of the Tower building costing over £17 million had been planned to start after the end of the 1990 season. Owing to delays in receiving consent from the Department of the Environment, it was decided that there would be insufficient time for the work to be completed by the beginning of next season, so the alterations would be postponed until the end of 1991.

The Tower continues to operate in its previous form in 1991, with the exception of the circus arena which will be preserved to provide some form of live entertainment, but with no animals and, in fact, no circus.

All the historic Victorian parts of the Grade 1 listed building are to be retained because of special historical and architectural interest.

The owners of the Tower recognize that changes must be made to keep up with keen international competition in the leisure industry, changing patterns of holidays and higher standards demanded by tourists today.

CENTRAL PIER

A prominent new attraction on the Central Pier is the 108 feet high Ferris Wheel, which cost £750,000 and can carry up to 216 passengers. Opened on Good Friday this year, it is at the centre of a number of other new or re-designed amusements and refreshment places, including the Wheel House Bar, Disco Super Waltzer, the Arcade, food bars and kiosks.

Sunday 3rd June

SUPERBOWL

Ten-pin bowling seems to be regaining popularity as a sporting pastime for families. One of two similar centres in Blackpool, the Superbowl, on the promenade near the North Pier, opened just over a year ago. I walk upstairs to the first floor which is open this morning.

In addition to the games area there are amusement machines, a pool table, light refreshment counter, tables and seats. The majority of players are young people, but there are also parents and older men and women using the ten lanes on this floor. Some physical effort is needed to play, as bowls for men weigh 14 or 16 lb., 10 and 12 lb. for ladies, and 8 lb. for children.

All the equipment and furniture look new and modern. Scores are recorded automatically on computer screens above each lane. Play continues non-stop until the end of each game. If anything goes wrong or needs attention a loudspeaker message from reception calls for a mechanic to attend instantly.

ALL NEW INTERNATIONAL TOWER CIRCUS

This year's Tower Circus presented by Peter Jay is expected to be the last in which animals will be included. Apparently animal rights campaigners have persuaded First Leisure Corporation to ban animal acts after the end of this season.

The Circus costs over £600,000 to stage, celebrates ringmaster

Norman Barrett's 25th year at the Tower, and is due to run until November 3rd. Every artist seems to make a special effort for their performance to be of the highest standard, in case it should be the final Circus at the Tower after 96 years.

Mr Geoffrey Thompson is arranging for the Pleasure Beach Company to take over the Tower Circus, including animals, from the 1991 season. Peter Jay is again to be the producer, but this time at the Pleasure Beach.

Monday 4th June

OCEAN BOULEVARD – A £6 MILLION SHOPPING DEVELOPMENT

The most important addition to the Pleasure Beach this year is the new £6 million Ocean Boulevard shopping development, scheduled for completion in August.

Shopping is considered to be an important leisure activity. In the 1950's Disneyland combined the addition of purposeful shops to a major leisure park. Ocean Boulevard carries on this trend into Europe. It aims to transform the Promenade into a kind of Covent Garden of the North, with decorated domes, tiled towers, and colourful cornices of elegant Edwardian terraced buildings.

Thirty-five prime shop units are to be let, including more cafes and restaurants to add to the almost endless variety of food and drink available at the Pleasure Beach.

MORNING AT THE PLEASURE BEACH

I spend an instructive and enjoyable morning at the Pleasure Beach, and find out more about what is going on there.

Rehearsals for the popular HOT ICE '90 show, which is due to commence on 16th June, are taking place today at the Ice Drome.

All the Pleasure Beach staff seem to be very busy. I take photographs of three of the rides, including the TIDAL WAVE, where passengers sail to and fro in a pirate ship suspended from forty feet.

MEMORIAL HALL SOLVES A PROBLEM

After lunch, I approach a church in Bond Street. Next to it is a Memorial Hall with a notice on the door: "SEQUENCE DANCING 2 p.m. – 4.30 p.m. – 65p INCLUDING TEA".

I open the door and hear dance music, but there is not a soul in sight. There are two doors on the right, one marked "LADIES" and the second "GENTS", where I enter, as it is just what I am looking for.

On a notice board in the hall I read: "TRINITY THEATRE GROUP PRESENT 'The Secret Diary of Adrian Mole aged 13 3/4.' 17th JUNE AT 2 p.m. and 19th-20th JUNE AT 7.30 p.m."

Who is this young upstart Adrian Mole? A rival diarist more than fifty years my junior?

"HOTELS LIKE LIQUORICE"?

I like looking at the different notices displayed outside numerous hotels to see if any are unusual or humorous. Like "LICENSED ..... CAR PARK". Do they drink unleaded petrol there?

At this part of the season the majority of hotels have "VACANCIES" notices in their windows. If any strangers wandering around appear as though they may be looking for somewhere to stay overnight, it is usually not long before someone asks if they want accommodation. So I am not surprised when one of the landladies sees me staring at notices outside her hotel and asks me if there is anything I want.

I tell her what I am thinking: Blackpool's hotels are like liquorice. There are ALL SORTS. Wherever you look. All shapes, colours and sizes. Every one different. Guest houses, hotels, flats, holiday flatlets. With different notices outside, like OPEN ALL YEAR, TEASMADES, HAIR DRYERS, LATE KEYS, SATELLITE TV. There are over 200,000 beds altogether. That's a lot of washing to be done: all those sheets, blankets and pillow cases!

DEMOLISHED DERBY BATHS

In the evening I walk along the North Promenade to find out what has happened to the Derby Baths. They are being demolished. The part facing the promenade is just a heap of rubble surrounded by a wooden fence, on which a comment is written: "BRING DOWN THE COUNCIL, NOT THE DERBY".

The Warley Road side part of the building is still standing, as it seems that the demolishers have not yet finished their work. On the fence another comment is written: "BACK STROKE, NOT BACKHANDERS".

£12 MILLION DEVELOPMENT AT DERBY BATHS – PEMBROKE HOTEL ALREADY EXTENDED

The Derby Baths have been sold by Blackpool Council to the owners of the Pembroke Hotel nearby, and a £12 million re-development scheme is planned to be carried out.

An £8 million extension scheme has already been carried out at the seven-year-old Pembroke Hotel, with a new bedroom wing added and the main building refurbished.

Blackpool Council plans to build a new £3 million swimming pool at Moor Park to replace the Derby Pool.

When the equipment from the Derby Baths was up for sale last year, some Tunisian business men wanted to buy the 1,700 plastic seats in the swimming baths to use in their soccer stadium. They offered five camels to Blackpool Council in exchange for the seats. The Council did not accept the offer. They already had plenty of camels, which had been bred at Blackpool Zoo.

Tuesday 5th June

"SIT THEE DOWN" FOR AN EVENING OF LANCASHIRE HUMOUR – HOUGHTON WEAVERS

At the Grand Theatre this evening the Houghton Weavers provide a generous helping of Lancashire humour. The well known musical quartette take their title from the town of Westhoughton, between Bolton and Wigan, and as Blackpool is in the same county, the performance is on their own doorstep.

There is no better place than a theatre for artists to communicate on the stage with the people they entertain. The "Weavers" get a good response from the audience, who join in choruses and enjoy the jokes. Both the "Weavers" and their audience show that Lancashire folk have a great sense of humour.

Wednesday 6th June

OCEAN BOULEVARD NEW BUILDINGS TAKING SHAPE

A tram ride in the morning brings me back to the Pleasure Beach for another look at the construction work on the Ocean Boulevard. Three cranes and rows of lorries are working, supplying asphalt, roofing, flooring, bricks, concrete and other materials, with helmeted workmen busy on the site.

NORTH SHORE METHODIST CHURCH – ST ANNE'S LADIES CHOIR

During the summer, an evening of "Midweek Merriment" is held at the North Shore Methodist Church on Wednesdays at 7.30 p.m. The admission charge is £1.

This evening St. Anne's Ladies Choir entertain a mainly middle aged audience of about a hundred people. The Choir give a varied programme in their 40th anniversary year, led by the same conductor who has been with them throughout their existence. A fourteen-year-old boy plays flute solos.

Thursday 7th June

THANKS TO APARTHOTEL AGAIN

Before leaving, I thank the manager and waitress at the Aparthotel for their hospitality and helpfulness. It has again proved very convenient for the freedom to decide what time of each day to return and as shelter during a certain amount of unsettled weather.

FIRST VISIT TO MODEL VILLAGE

Blackpool Model Village in East Park Drive has been open since 1972. It is the last visit of my holiday, and proves a worth while stop for about an hour before I drive homewards.

The Village borders Stanley Park, and has been landscaped in parkland against a background of waterfalls, lakes and running streams, among over 1,500 varieties of shrubs and plants. As I wander through footpaths like a giant, individually created miniatures of practically everything that might be found in a real English village come into view. Even blackbirds appear gigantic compared with the Lilliputian-sized figures.

Church in model village

Some of the models are based on real places, such as Fleetwood Pier, lighthouse and jetty, and Oswaldtwistle Village Institute. Most, however, are imaginary, with fictitious names like Mr. Fixout's Builders' Yard, Old Mac's Farm, Stoney Broke Quarry, Prop. Rock Hard, Steakaway Butchers, U.Stampem Post Office and I Suppem Outdoor Licence. I like the accompanying spectator sounds of the "Kop Choir" at the Seasiders F.C. soccer match. Wedding music and church bells are recorded beside one of the two churches, outside which the miniature bride, bridegroom and guests are having their photographs taken.

DISABLED BOYS TAKEN TO MODEL VILLAGE

As I return to the car park, four disabled boys in wheelchairs are being lowered from a van marked "FELDHEAD HOSPITAL SCHOOL" by girl attendants, and moved towards the Model Village entrance. A final thought is that physically and mentally handicapped, blind and infirm people like to go on holiday, but many need help from others to enable them to do so.

WELCOME AND HELP FOR THE HANDICAPPED

Blackpool Council welcomes handicapped visitors, and a guide to assist in planning their stay can be obtained from the Department of Tourism and Attractions. It gives information for the disabled visitor, and lists hotels and flats which have indicated that they are willing to accept guests in wheelchairs, and/or cater for the disabled.

7th – 9th DECEMBER 1990

CHRISTMAS SEASON AT BLACKPOOL

I decided to take a short break just before Christmas to combine both business and pleasure, and also because I had never seen Blackpool at that time of the year.

Saturday 8th December

CORAL ISLAND

The Coral Island Indoor Leisure Complex on the Golden Mile, opened eleven years ago, has been refurbished in 1990 at a cost of £3 million to include a monorail.

CORAL ISLAND.

Social Club, Bingo, Cabaret Bars, Sundowner, Kiddies' Amusements, Fun for the family. 7th June 1985.

During a short evening through the amusements I discover that they are quite extensive. On the ground floor flashing coloured lights of very up-to-date amusement machines, some computer controlled, can be seen everywhere, and kiosks where change for the machines can be obtained. Although it is a quiet period of the year a number of children and adults are taking advantage of what there is to see and do.

A Children's ADVENTURE PLAYLAND – admission £1 for up to one hour – provides activities for children like ropes to swing on and soft surfaces to bounce up and down on, similar to those at Professor Peabody's Play Place but on a smaller scale.

The ISLAND DINER RESTAURANT is open and advertises fish and chips on their menu for 99p. The FLAGSHIP BAR and SUNSET BAR and RESTAURANT are closed when I pass. Other attractions include the CORAL SOCIAL CLUB and SHADES DISCO.

Sunday 9th December

SHARKS AT SEA LIFE CENTRE

Blackpool Sea Life Centre on the Golden Mile is a new £5 million joint venture between Sea Life (Holdings) Ltd., a company specialising in marine biology, and First Leisure Corporation plc. The Centre was officially opened on 9th August 1990 by Bill Oddie, Patron of the British Trust of Conservation Volunteers and honorary Council Member of the World Wide Fund for Nature.

There are eight Sea Life Centres in Great Britain at present. The first opened at Oban in 1979. Each one has its own imaginative displays of all kinds of marine life in specially constructed tanks, which provide uninterrupted views and give a real insight into life beneath the seas. At Blackpool the huge eye-catching design outside the Centre entrance reads: SHARKS IN BLACKPOOL.

The most remarkable display at the Centre is Europe's largest aquarium tank, which houses a collection of large sharks. From a tunnel which runs underneath the tank, visitors can watch sharks swimming past only a few feet away. It is like the view of a deep sea diver walking on a sea bed, or from inside a glass-sided submarine.

Extensive information about sharks is displayed. Some of the 350 different kinds of sharks face the threat of extinction. A forty-minute video film screened in the cinema shows fascinating underwater scenes of a team of divers carrying out experiments to test the strength of shark bites, including feeding blue sharks by hand.

Caring, inspiring and pioneering, the Sea Life Centre aims at increasing understanding and respect for the sea to ensure a safer future. My own view is that the Centre is educational, and well worth seeing, for it provides a complete contrast to the many other amusements and attractions nearby.

CAROLS FESTIVAL

The North Shore Methodist Church in Dickson Road is already full when I arrive about fifteen minutes before the Festival of Carols is about to start at 3:00 pm. A number of disabled, elderly and blind people are helped from ambulances and motor vehicles by church members and volunteers to seats.

A kind lady member takes my bag and overcoat, says she will look after them, and shows me to an upstairs seat. The whole church is beautifully decorated.

The Warbreck High School Band accompanies children's choirs from Devonshire, Moor Park, Anchorsholme and Baines Endowed Schools. The offering is to help build a clinic in Zambia, where there have been riots in an area hit by hunger, and a number of children have died owing to lack of food.

The minister welcomes everyone to the church and introduces the programme. He says: "Our worship seeks to unwrap the true meaning of Christmas, and you are invited to share with us." He points to a notice board which sums up the real message of Christmas: "Jesus is the Reason for the Season", something that may easily be forgotten in this modern world.

Children take an important part in church activities at this season. So many want to contribute to the carol service that another similar festival is arranged for next Sunday, with a different High School Band and children's choirs from another four schools.

After the end of the service, the lady who has looked after my coat tells me to have a look at the pictures, drawings, models and gifts which have been donated by children, and are displayed around the windows and spaces downstairs.

GRAND THEATRE

At the Grand Theatre in the evening I attend another carol concert arranged by the Blackpool Citadel Corps of the Salvation Army in their fifth annual visit to the theatre.

The programme is introduced by the local Salvation Army captain and his wife in a natural and entertaining manner, and with a sense of humour. The main theme of "Christmas Unwrapped" is similar to that of the North Shore Methodist Church, although in a different setting and in a full theatre.

Music is provided by the Silver Band, Timbrels, the Songsters choir, Young People's Corps Singing Company and two solo singers. The audience join in singing some of the well-known carols. Instead of an interval halfway through the programme, a collection is taken in aid of local charities which are helping the homeless at Christmas.

The importance of the real message of Christmas is again emphasized, that it is centred on the birth of a baby boy around two thousand years ago, which originated a new faith: Christianity.

CHRISTMAS CONCLUSIONS

From what happened to me during the weekend I believe that there is no better time of the year to be at Blackpool than Christmas. The friendliness, kindness and hospitality from almost everyone I met seemed to be even greater than ever, especially at the small family-run hotel where I stayed. People who although busy with their normal daily life and work were willing to help others less fortunate than themselves – such as the elderly, ill and disabled – and could still spare the time to give practical help and advice to

150

visitors on holiday.

I received a warm welcome, although the weather was very cold outside. However, the snow and blizzards which swept through other parts of the country missed Blackpool.

Although not on the same scale as the autumn Illuminations, the coloured lights, Christmas trees, decorations and illuminated festive figures around the main shopping centres and Tower brightened up the place and added to the normal frills and thrills.

Blackpool will always be a very special place to me. I have only to follow my nose and something new or surprising happens, fresh surroundings are discovered and people met in different circumstances. There is more than meets the eye of the casual day tripper who may drive through the town, or conference delegate staying for a short time only.

The desire to return next season for another holiday is strong. There will be more new discoveries to make, more entertainment to enjoy. The fun is contagious.

What is more, next time I will actually be an old age pensioner. I have already noted with glee the amount of Retirement Pension which the Department of Social Security notified will be payable weekly from the Monday after my sixty fifth birthday. So I will be highly delighted to qualify for financial benefits and discounts like free prescriptions, reduced rates for entertainments, sports and hotel accommodation.

Any excuse for another visit to Blackpool and making whoopee. Let yourself go! Go for it!

CONCLUSION

LOOKING BACKWARD AND FORWARD

COAT OF ARMS

Blackpool's Coat of Arms pictures some of the Borough's past history in heraldic symbols.

Borough of Blackpool Heraldic Significance of Arms
(Blackpool Borough Council)

The resort's name was derived from a pool or stream which formerly ran from Marton Mere into the sea near the present day Manchester Square. The peat lands it flowed through discoloured the water, hence the name Black Poole.

On the shield there are eight wavy bars alternately coloured black and gold, representing waves. The black bars stand for the "Black Pool", and the gold bars represent the sands on the seashore. A herring gull is pictured in the act of flying.

A thunderbolt which is shown as two flashes of electricity surmounted by a pair of wings alludes to the early use of electricity. Blackpool was the first Public Authority to introduce electric

152

lighting and an electric Tramway system on a permanent basis.

Two families associated with the early history of Blackpool, Banks and Cocker, have distinguishing charges of a red fleur-de-lis and lion from their Coats of Arms on the Borough shield.

The crest is composed of the battlements of a tower, the sails of a windmill and a red rose. The tower is believed to refer to Blackpool Tower. There are many windmills in the Fylde, which comes from a Danish word meaning "field" or "flat area." The red rose is the badge of the city of Lancaster.

The helmet and mantling in arms, the decorative ornament attached to the helmet, are appropriate as a crest for a Corporation.

The motto, "PROGRESS", indicates that Blackpool looks to the future, and recognises that it is necessary to move forward, continually make improvements and advance in knowledge.

PLANS FOR THE FUTURE – MOUNTING MULTI MILLION POUND INVESTMENTS

With the mounting growth of millions of pounds being invested in tourism and leisure, prospects for the future appear to be bright. Blackpool is becoming known as the Number One holiday resort in the whole of Europe. According to a survey, over 16 million individual visits were made to the resort in 1989, and a mammoth £400 million spent by visitors.

If all the schemes for developments go ahead, the total investments in Blackpool over the next few years will amount to hundreds of millions of pounds. As most of the investment plans are by private companies, the fact that so many are prepared to spend such vast sums of money indicates their great confidence in the future of the resort.

A million is a very large number, whether it is money or visitors. But people are more important than statistics, and every one is different. It all depends upon people, and people depend upon one another. The visitors rely upon local people to provide their holiday attractions, services and accommodation, and their hosts and hostesses rely upon visitors for their income and living.

Every individual has different ideas about holidays, and everyone needs to be considered. Finding out what they want and knowing how to treat them is not easy. If visitors are made to feel welcome, their main needs attended to, and treated in a helpful, friendly and hospitable way, they will want to return.

If you give your customers what they want and they like it, they will be pleased and tell others about it. Whatever kind and size of business you may run, from a multi million pound leisure centre, amusement park. entertainments complex or luxury hotel, to a small self-catering establishment, guest house, restaurant, cafe or fish and chip shop, if they enjoy what is offered and consider it to be good value for money they will be satisfied.

Providing entertainment that children like, and keeping them amused and occupied, is important. Not only because the young people of today will grow up to be the adults of the future, but also if a lot of them enjoy anything very much they will be attracted to it in large numbers, and their parents will naturally accompany them.

Is this one reason for Blackpool's popularity – offering such a variety of amusements where children and the rest of the family can all enjoy themselves? Entertainment for all ages, mother, father, grandparents and children?

With the Illuminations the major attraction in autumn, Blackpool can certainly claim to be one of the country's LEADING LIGHTS in leisure and tourism.

SOME TOURIST INFORMATION ADDRESSES

Some addresses where more details about holidays in Blackpool and elsewhere can be obtained are shown below:

Association of British Travel Agents, 55-57 Newman Street, London W1P 4AH. Tel: (071) 637 2444.

Blackpool Borough Council, Tourism and Attractions Department, 1 Clifton Street, Blackpool FY1 1 LY. Tel: (0253) 25212 or 21623.

Blackpool Hotel & Guest House Association, 87a Coronation Street, Blackpool. Tel: (0253) 21891.

Blackpool Private Hoteliers Association, 281a Clifton Drive South, Lytham St. Annes. Tel: St. Annes 711628.

Blackpool Self Catering Holiday Association, 2c Caunce Street, Blackpool. Tel: (0253) 22771.

Blackpool Transport, Rigby Road, Blackpool. FY1 5DD. Tel: (0253) 23931.

English Tourist Board, Thames Tower, Black's Road, Hammersmith, London W6 9EL. Tel: 081 846 9000.

Lancashire County Council, County Information Centre, Talbot Road, Blackpool. Tel: (0253) 751485.

North West Tourist Board, The Last Drop Village, Bromley Cross, Bolton, Lancashire. BL7 9PZ. Tel: (0204) 591511.

In memoriam
LAURENCE POLLINGER
1898–1976

N D

New Directions in Prose and Poetry 34

Edited by J. Laughlin

with Peter Glassgold and Frederick R. Martin

 A New Directions Book

ACKNOWLEDGMENTS
Grateful acknowledgment is made to the editors and publishers of books and magazines where some of the selections in this volume first appeared: for Peter Blue Cloud, *Akwesasne Notes;* for Octavio Paz, *Poetry Nation V* (Carcanet Press, Ltd., Manchester, England).

James Purdy's "True," Copyright © 1976 by James Purdy

For Henry Elinson's "Eight Drawings," special thanks are given to the Yale University Art Gallery and Joseph Szaszfai, photographer.

Manufactured in the United States of America
First published clothbound (ISBN: 0-8112-0634-3) and as New Directions Paperbook 427 (ISBN: 0-8112-0635-1) in 1977
Published simultaneously in Canada by McClelland & Stewart, Ltd.

New Directions Books are published for James Laughlin
by New Directions Publishing Corporation,
333 Sixth Avenue, New York 10014

CONTENTS

TWO PASSAGES

ROBERT DUNCAN

EMPEDOKLEAN REVERIES

Dread Love   that
 remorseless Aphrodite raises   to drive home   her   offended
                Pow'r,
I've been your battlefield
where lovely Hate   alone   men call κακαὶ 'ἔριδες
      defended me
 contending there ever   with would-be over-powering
             Adhesion
  severing the Bond   dispelling   the Word
    Eros demands,   keeping the Heart of Things
     at loose ends.

I have tamed the Lion Roar.
It will no longer use me.

Orlando, felix, my little household   relative of the Lion,
I will remember to pet you;
 Death takes his time with us.

Long the sexual uproar dies away in me.

 Lighting a cigarette.   Coming to ourselves.
 From long ago   ceremonies of burning and smoking.

1

I have burnd the Lion in his own fire.
The Lioness rages in the hunting field
    far from where we are.

Because of what we love   we are   increasingly at War.
    That Sphere of all Attractions   draws us from what we are—

    In this place
    I make my stand
    and a Line appears
    or I have drawn a Line
    where resolute
    or in my fear compounded
    I face
    the rapt Sphere
    of a dissolving Pain.

There is no kindness here,   no one I would draw into this.

Love that would dissolve all boundaries,
    so that Blake is outraged by the first dissolve of outline
    and rages out at Titian, Rubens, Rembrandt,
        for the in-mixing of light and dark,   the color in turmoil,
    resolving in him an undying Hatred

that would annihilate all kindness,   not
        his kind
    not like him   I am   to be
                        Being Isolate

    Even wiving must offend.
        Don't wife me   you arouse

that animus   the wrathful knight   who upholds
the honor of the Lady Anima,   her token,   that
handkerchief
to be stolen by her handmaiden,   her confidence

bridles at the touch   in touch   music
the wedding ground of Harmony   and Discordia

melody ever upon the point of   leaving   returning
a turmoil of sound the center and surrounding

begins:

Love ever contending with Hate

Hate ever contending with Love

"never, I think, shall infinite Time be emptied of these two"

Never being the name of what is infinite.

In bright confusion.   White,   the interpresence of all colors,
shining back on us—
Black, taking all back into itself.

They never cease their continuous exchange.

The eye imitates Seeing   particular from particular,
cell from cell,   searches
for what it's thought to see—
this week the track of a monopole   previous to a field of gravity—

The Sun as if It were an infinite fire, infinitely hot beyond our
heat;
The Earth turning from summer into cold and dark,
ice widening over   the sea's reaches

But in Wrath they are all different.   They dance in differing.
     There is a field of random energies from which we come,
     or in such myriad disorganization   *"field"* rises as a dream,
          the real   this projection of many dreamers,
daimones, the Greeks named them,   still to be realized   Here

          this demon comes into Being   as a mote

             temporarily   needs

     higher organizations to reveal himself,

          Man so organized   the woman seems taken out of him

               returning to his side   admires—

—Darwin comments: *"The deity effect of organization"*

                         The two
                         contending Spheres

     (Il combattimento di Tancredi e Clorinda)

                         dazzling,   darkening,

                         come into
                         come in order to

                              each other

                              sing

(Nothing in the libretto is for the moment
not embarrassing: enemies in love?)

"O tu che porte, correndo si?"

Risponde:

He: *"E guerra e morte"*

       Life's an organization of time to allow
       the suspension of an order out of order,
       longing then ever to come into order it yet
       avoids   prolonging the exchange

     "It is by avoiding the rapid decay into the
     inert state of equilibrium, that an
     organism appears so enigmatic," Schrödinger writes:
     "so much so, that from the earliest times
     of human thought some special non-physical
     or supernatural force was claimed to be
     operative in the organism, and in some quarters
     is still claimed."

       "Guerra e morte avrai"

disse

she answers—

thruout the Contest, the Musical Ground
      where they contend

Colei di gioia   forth in enmity
    transmutossi e rise

     enter Song's opera

       a smile

As if in the distance   arriving or departing

the dying or arising of a roar—

    the Arrival or Departure

        animal laughter

        advancing

        thematic

to all that's gone "before"

JAMAIS

(homage to the youthful Zukofsky, leading toward "A"–23 of his old age)

must   extend   beyond the throw of the dice   "a" just now, yet

    no throw of the dice may   chance IT.

        Let us take the excellence of the style to be

                LUCIDITY—

    Clearly, there is no last chance

whether a certain word is to be taken with what precedes or with
                        what follows

hard to punctuate
as in Herakleitos: *"Reason being such always*

men fail to understand"

All ways   men fail to understand.

Lovely, the Dreams and Chance encounters

but Now   is wedded thruout to   the Intention of a
                                                    Universe.

Verse   linkt to the Idea of that Governance

moves "beyond";

not forever on earth   NEVER

only an interval   HERE   entire   given a life
                                                     takes

—the octave the first and most

powerful overtone:

given in the Nature of Sound
        which is God's Art,   the principle of recognition—
Man's Art   an other   arbitration   of the Whole

"Nature of Sound"   in which
the "sameness" of the note is   dismisst.

In the flicker   shutter/ or shudder   ancient, absent-minded,
    the granite massif   is was?   PRESENT   in Mind

disrupting the pervasive   overtones of Universe

—so taking place

in the particular   NOW,

following,   is haunted,   a unique moment   taking over,

the Demon of Incident   *"hugeness"* reorganizes

the insistent beating of the moth's wings at the screen

where panic tears apart

SILENCE   THE ETERNAL   INERTIA

thunderous outweigh

"the stability of the central triad"

in which the impression of a "key" wavers.

What!   I do not "know" what I see?

entirely in C   all feel of "home" abolisht   Love flings itself
forward

at sea   in its Work   harmony   dark-winged

creature of the air

"THE"

A PARABLE OF GUERRILLAS

An excerpt from the novel *Mesmer Facing Algiers*

ROBERT STEINER

Our women do not collaborate horizontally with aliens. Our men agonize laterally over the wisdom of cooking fish in ass's milk, of eating garlic blessed with urine. We sterilize women by burying them in heaps of dung and we fertilize virgins through the mouth. In our myth we are born of the swallowed brain of a magpie; once, we were two-headed and ripped the hearts of enemies with the eagle talons that were our hands.

Violinists and dancers, singers who celebrate Black Sara and Our Lady of Rags, pray for the death of the reticulate snake, which will mean luck, fertility, eternity. Our eternity is constructed. Our chiefs are fat as rabbits, our women bloated with fever from giving birth by the river. The river spavines our people like an ax. From the stringy throats of witches dangle amulets with a tricon of stars, of mystery and magic; and when they are witches our women will speak nonsense to the sick so that the sick die glimpsing eternal unreality. Our king will steal a bicycle and curse children who shame him in the public square. He will tell us how the toad loved the tarantula beside the road. For us an eye is a balcony, water is a net: like the bird we know that if it were not for air we would be free. There are red mice in our thoughts and the tears of the snotty-nosed worm in our prayers.

But I do not care for their suffering, just as I do not cheat the

local merchant or wax a mustache. I do not savor the nose on their face, the sauce of their heart, the crab in their trousers.

Imagine a cartload of my people being drawn along a muddy road by a swayback, a nightmare cob porting the crimes of his masters. In his yellow moist eyes the pleading of my people can be seen, in his broken back their defeat travels. They travel, brace of rabbits in a torn sack, wooden black madonnas carved to sell, fleas, lice, the horse pissing near their pillows. What I abide—and offer as an emblem in the tradition of my race—is our law that he who stares at one who is not one of his own must return to the place where he stared and, in the presence of an undressed woman, spit in the alien eyes. Spit is sex, water a net, a stare is a curse. Sex, net, curse. Good good good. We undo history: that is what I want you to imagine. And the sight outside my villa door of fierce ants descending from a hot sand hill to a drying sumptuous fig.

This is only a whisper before the dead of dawn, citizen. Think of me not as whisperer but as the whispered or even alluded to, neither sinking nor rising but the stillness before the dog wakes, snaps his yawning jaw, before he pisses, before the laws prowl. I see the laws from the window through a shutter slice, and the dog is booted out half-pissing along his leg to finish in the wilderness of my garden.

But before this it is the fear that today it will happen and there will be no fear any more. This whisper is my paralysis of tension, with fingers rigidly balancing a cigar, waiting for the loam at dawn to lift me from fear. There is no grin where there is no fear. The tyranny of another day to manage keeps fear on the move, makes the whispered necessary and desirable. And when I don't have to whisper and the setter has smelled the villa with piss and the laws are roaming with their Sten guns, the idea that I have been awake and whispering is as delightful as the hatpin searing the base of the copper's skull. Yet these ideas are whispers too, nothing more, allusions to something loved during the dead before dawn. That I am uncaptured has me in grins but only after the knowledge that not being captured means I will be, and I am frightened. It is the fright of the previous day, exhaustive and a trifle foppish, that has me whispering and, on the following dawn, makes me the whispered.

Here then are the rules of this house: the setter is always

parallel to me, at the foot or under the foot of the cot, one ear falling back, lagging, demonstrating the pink vulnerability of his flesh: the she-goat nibbles straw in the parlor, dropping olives onto her bed of sack: the broad-hipped radio tunes to Cairo, its frequency hums through the headset: I strike a match and mine is the only light for miles around, or if there are other lights there is no way to know because everyone keeps shutters drawn and doors bolted. These days our nation is awash with truth. It has given brain fog, this myth of our truth, this wave of plotting; and unless my earsight fails I will continue to hear the bullets promoted in our square and the rapes acomplished along our beach. The setter howls, we overhear the stutter from the village, we whisper, grin and whisper. A dog's grin is the sweetest.

My buzzing voicebox, crouching black screamer, reveals that the king has been active, reveals that he knows something he does not want revealed. Cairo will try to reveal it. Perhaps it is an explanation of our earthquakes, perhaps the king is capturing the guilty ones in simultaneous night raids throughout the country. We have had opportunity to ruminate on the rumors of new natural phenomena. Voices say that the king has slept ill; no one, unless he has grave personal doubts, could help but sleep soundly as a lamb behind the king's electric gates. Cairo says the man has nightmares which wake him screaming; he has had disgusting visions and shares their content with no one; he will leave a room when his wife enters; his bowels, Cairo insists, give way in conference; he has bewilderment. They have sent forth a leech-gather, Cairo says. When I decode such a message, such a communique borne under the legal frequency, the thrushes commence to sing, day burns wistfully, and the flowers of my garden, though they are dying, lean with sovereignty and aroma toward my open window.

In the transparent sense I am dropping my cover, stepping out bald and podgy, full of health and overwrought. I had tossed off my felony shoes clotted with mud, breathing deeply the veranda mist, and had surveyed the quiet coast of our promontory through the binocs. There are enemies and there are allies, that is for certain. Having seen much, the citizen must jot a heavy dark illegal and meticulous period to his amorphous nature. He must tear the citizenry into sixteenths to be certain they will flush. I held Mother's false teeth in my palm. Like tourism, the future could rot you with diversions. The future—I was kicking sand from the

veranda with my toes—was there before the travelers and the laws, in every murder of a messenger, in each mapmaker's compass, in the slime and mortar of the first wall, the whitest wall of the village. In Mother's teeth I saw the bowed head of a villain facing camera lights, the sign of a screaming sky. I witnessed a blizzard of para- chutes floating deep into the mountain. Putting myself at rest until the sun was agleam as a wounded lion's eye, I stalked my way again toward the walls of the village.

My first was a native face, an exotic thing limp and napping on his father's porch. There was a light at the back of the flat, a bare dull bulb under which parents were sorting diapers from socks. Breathless as a shoplifter I scooped the dark bundle up and dropped it into my fruit basket among the bananas and cool limes. A child of lustrous sexless eyes, drooling lips poised in humble puzzlement, an unself-conscious face. The curve of a dwarfish hand fixed him for life, and the play of foot against mouth. This was not an intellectual babe, the ones from cold countries with wizening philosophers' frowns. The first fellow was the type you see endors- ing apple sauce in magazines. I set him on a pillow and ordered the setter to keep him in his place. That was evening.

The night would not stop growing, brooding, sending me to the garden with demon cramps and with lizards clawing into the light of the moon. Near sunrise I felt tremors.

The piper came forth, a bandit dropping from a tree. Baby prints in the sand, the cup of a rump, the leaf of a hand. A mother stood speaking to a crater on the beach out of which toys flew one at a time; she was going for an ice and would leave his sister with the child to keep him from an angry sea. I watched her struggle away; I watched as yet another piper stepped from the woods, startling me when he leaned forward to study the terrain toward the village. He flung pebbles. Together we caught sight of the sister when she poured lotion onto herself. Where the crater was a hand felt along the rim, found a tiny shovel and dragged it into the pit. Sand flew. By now the intruder had shown himself, flicking the kinch of a spring knife at the sister's thin brassiere. I reconnoitered when her brassiere landed at my feet.

He dropped his rubber trunks and straddled the girl's chest, while she in her shyness and virginity made a cradle for his penis with her breasts. Much as I thought how oafish it was I was not to

be distracted or interfered with, neither misled nor delayed. I too spoke to the sand and, following the reckless prints of an unstable body that was, after all, only new in the world, found the little squirt in a shallow hole, a pool in which he sat safe and regal in the rubber life preserver with a duck's feathered head. How many tiny pails of water had had to be lugged to that grave only to arrive half empty, to the baby's amazement? This one was a gritty swart urchin who I feared might cry out when I lifted him from his muddy paradise. He stared at me, seemed to protest silently, struck my head with the heart of his shovel, looked then in panic at his inundated sister and seemed to say, yes, you're right, this is no place for the likes of me. And that was afternoon.

The egg, this little egg is round, all is round, now go to sleep god damn you. No sooner did I have my pair of sprawling boys than the entire point, the pointlessness that was to be the pattern, disappeared. How productive was destruction, I thought, studying their useless feet which seemed, as did their bodies, to be randomly stuffed with down, a bit like sandbags though light as muffins. So outward was my gesture, so rugged the optimism I must have had that it was impossible for me to commit an antisocial action. There is no accounting for genius in some men. So social was I, in fact, that the merest glance down the throat of the law let me know instantly where infection lay and what compress or what surgery would serve to cure. I felt I could not help but have meaning. Thus the nappings themselves were not the important matter, and because of this fact I decided to do it some more.

Had there been, the citizen ought rightly to ask, any method of selection to the sneak thief's work? Did I know whom I was lifting from whom, or why those whom I did lift were chosen? I did not and there was no reason. I am no elitist, you understand, which means I am not by nature suspicious; there was nothing in the appearance of these boys to serve as proof to me that they should be taken above any others. I took them, and they were cute as fudge to me only because they had been available.

Now however, having concluded that the stealing of children was not in itself enough, I had to make some selection in the next crime. I huddled in the armchair with the radio tuned to Cairo, hummed into the ears of the babes, one in each cradled arm, as they slept peacefully and hotly against my bare chest. I would take a child of blonde blood, and the child would be a girl.

With my ear to the pillow I hear into the depths of invisibility, see the last fluffy donkey on our estuary. Then the propeller beats of the warplanes are only cuffs against silence. If it is in the village square that I die I will take the quiet with me, drain it from the noise of pushcarts and Sten guns, and at the moment I fall there will be stillness in the air. And when the blindfold is removed and the bullet is pried from my head only the shreds of noise will be left them. I will take the fissures of silence, smoky and stinking, and leave them chatter, rumor, libel, sobs.

Words will come unheard from my mouth, and imaginings unsnap from my riddled skull. They will seal their fate. I will have been an explosion splitting a flash of corrupt silence, the second before the dynamite blows, the breath held before the shot is fired. I have come to be quiet in their ghost of noise. There is a phantom, they will say, dead in the square from a bullet, who soundless, almost motionless, went about his task of fragmenting the noise of the sick and the lying, bore the quiet breath of a pickpocket and the touch of a finger that leaves no print. Yes, I hear the catacomb footsteps where they hatch plots and where still more plots are dug. Where there is sickness, after a time, it is only as if noiselessness has settled and the illness itself dissolved. I have come to think, ear to the pillow, that crime is the only objectivity I can know. It is to be held in a cup of thought as a weapon against their confusion. This life of nonparlance day and night is refreshing in its truth and terrifying in its separation of myself from fellow villains. I think then, that however you see it, my whispering is the coward's way. So much for the melodrama of waking at three in the morning in a befouled bed. Give me a minute. *They* are responsible for the condition of my bedsheets.

I awoke to find teeth marks along my arm, blood dots on the meaty underwidth where there are watery veins slightly within a baby's skin. I swung the arm close to my face, parting the shutters for the cool new light with the other. Autos streamed down the road to the beach. My teeth fit perfectly into the bruise marks. This is what comes from eating raisins and bad cheese; I ran the risk of doing something ridiculous and so stood fearful lest I lose the basic fear. I could afford to think negatively; it was an affair of patience, which remained to be plucked, unlike however the sucking of blood from my own arm. It was my calm versus their calm.

To the snoring babies I padded. They seemed to offer their arms to my mouth, and quashing their cries in my hand I bit indelible tattoos into them.

Would I prefer the laws to annihilate me despite their liking me, in the unblanching face of their duty? Or out of a sincere disgust for what I had done? The days of tortuous interrogation can be dreary or not, regardless of pain, and irrevocable ties are known to have been made between the cop and the criminal: the spiller of blood who does not see it as blood may not see the killer as killer but as a brother instead, strapped to a chair, face welted black, nose crushed to a porridge, eyes closed but eyelids swollen as mountains. There is opportunity yet for the doer of heinous crime, once he is changed from beast to object. Do they not give us a glass of water to slosh out the blood? Are we not isolated from lunatics and forgers? I may yet have a cousin who in slitting my throat will feel he is making a contact. That will be enough.

It is not different from being at sea in full view of a storm. You are expecting to drown but not planning on it. You are sick when the gale begins but soon it passes and keeping the ship off her side is all you can consider. The brill in your stomach, the smell of fart in the wind are suddenly just accouterments, parts of a description and not the subject at all. After the storm has been weathered they may be important again, but there is a kind of smugness about them this time, a superfluousness, even indulgence, as if they are rewards for a job well done. Truth is floating around on the surface where you spit. The meek stink as bad as the rich, and both of them make a lousy soup.

The voices of Cairo said the cabinet is in chaos, resignations abound, they are holding their noses in the king's presence. The man himself mopes and rushes from rooms when his wife appears; he makes speeches after coming from the royal toilet and drinks what smells suspiciously like pabulum. Some of this may be propaganda. Yet I make speeches too, and if my comparison is correct no one is listening to what the king says except his enemies. The voices got me to dress and the static of the scrambled frequency drove me back into my felony shoes. The sudden painful whistle as the channel vanished forced me, I say, to jam a fig between my teeth and bite into the ancient gummy fruit.

This one I took while she slept in the rear seat of an automobile that was the color of mercury. I took her without breaking

or disturbing the oatmeal cookie in her hand. It was just about the time, breezy time, noted by all who pass this way for its infinite quiet and solace. The child had palm-green eyes.

Imagine the change in the sea when I saw it from the roof of my villa between the fragrant banana trees. I was crouching down to the tiles, binocs strapped to my neck. Unbroken waves tumbled beyond the black leg of the coast; a blue calm drifting into an oily fester-green fish run was mapped inside our promontory. A series of chopped foaming crests made by a passing steamer that fumed at the horizon. Squid boats nested in coves or motored gently out from shore, the only beasts to have broken the ocean glass.

I was satisfied because the law could never take me by surprise. I had wired my land with barbs and traps, desperately practical yet subtle, and despite the expected disappointment, I felt secret. Imagine the joy in finding at the first daylight view from the chimney that village, sky, sea, mountains, the very tree tops not ten feet away, had been transformed and stood majestically before me at one eyefull. The short stretch of beach crowded with bathers who lay sunning over tank tracks in the sand; the surrounding dark and green-dark peaks of rare clarity, the one rare moment. Those who would say that at the top of the world is an oppressive or defiant expansiveness have never been there. At the top of the world everything is riven into deliberate points, is reduced until what is set before you as on a breakfast plate seems as easy to pull into yourself as do the young squid to our piscators; or if you are a gambler, and who is not, it is the same sweeping motion of rounded arms and fingertips touching as you win all the chips, big and little, and shuffle them to your apron. Proportion, imagine.

Change is abrupt in crisis. Space, time, the fluid continuum, continuous creation, expand, expanding, exploded. The spliced and pied, the visible at a glance, even a furtive one: natives and gunmen, boats and angry planes, workers and bathers, the shepherd in his hill. I conclude beyond all expectations: bananas ripening, the howl of creatures and wind in echoes under me. What else? All this oxygen.

The search for me was frantic and insistent. You do not forget such deeds. Here the criminal watched them uncover garbage lids, prowl through stores, open oversize handbags, bending in his sneakers and blasé in his whistle near the woods and gullies scoured by

their hunting dogs. I was nonetheless planning seriously and well. In truth there was no time, there were no roses, no lovers or haters, just the gratuitous shock that I was intending to survive; feeling the heart flap madly in its sac and realizing it only does so lest you forget. I would walk in circles on the roof, chew a sandwich lazily behind the chimney, shine my torch into its mouth to see if it could hide a body large as mine. We were, as a family, together after all, and in the villa within view of each other constantly. Goat's milk not twenty feet from the children, veggies ten feet from the goat, shelves and cubicles built with plywood and bricks, and peepholes in the shuttered windows. The setter, my loyal toothless mute, rehearsed protecting me, hurled himself at the door with all his canine fury, unaware that the law would surely shoot him first.

Nonetheless, I was charmed. And lest this picture seem bleak to those who are not waiting for arrest, imagine, citizen, what a world the fugitive rejected! Do dogs piss on everyone's shoes, or only on mine? How wrong could my wife have been to accuse me of thinking of people as if they were peaches? I made no comment to her in return. What could I resent? Charm, I tell you, charm.

Sun against the white walls from off the sea, the solid squareness of each building drawn in kelp-green and violet. Doves, swallows swooping and hovering. Vendors in big voice before the café where at night you could dance and drink, dance and drink. The foreigners landed in armies, their low sporty autos and creaking buses parked like bullets waiting to enter the chamber. Men in white boaters and porcelain-faced women in blowing mushroom hats. No, I repeat, no flowers. Up one side, down the other, along the alley toward the law, no flowers on anyone anywhere. I was terribly touched. I was touched to the threshold of agony. A life of garlic and rubies, a productive life in the ringing joy of doomed mountaineering. The totality of the sight from the rooftop was crushing. The village, I thought, the world, I thought, living as if there were a reason to go on—there is no reason unless you are waiting to die. And the babes in repose, sleeping on their sides, hands pillowed under one ear each, lying there like bananas.

I was never very good with the children; and worse, they weren't doing much for me. They lay dumb most of the time, lined up in crates for cribs, looking boredly at the ceiling, examining their toes, trying unsuccessfully to blurt out their first overwhelming

questions. Here, I had thought, I was doing what I did best: hoarding and cultivating as much of the country's livestock as I could grab with hardened freckled hands. Sporting with the children was exhilarating for a time. I learned to wag my index finger like a tail, learned to roll my eyes and wiggle my ears. They in turn managed to grip my fingers like delicate birds learning to perch, or they cuffed each other in play when I brought them together after the afternoon nap. But the she-goat suffered mange and the setter's eczema irritated his disposition; the babies grew sullener, depressed, unlikable. In their cribs they would learn the limits of the planet: a mobile cut from lemon rinds fashioned over their heads into dangling sailors the size of animal crackers: the smooth inflexible rails too small for their bodies, yet just wide enough in which to trap a pudgy unseemly foot.

O, it was different at the top of the world, but not better; quieter, but not more peaceful. Family snorting in sleep while I made coffee and separated pellets from the oats and hay. The violent rise of subsequent dawns during which my animals brayed and shat, babes wailed and wet, foliage soaked in the roaring sun. I was still being expected, grinning malignantly at the hideousness I had departed and the horror I had replaced it with.

I took up binocs again and looked again along the road into the village. A glint of metal struck my eye, a rise of dust halfway down the mountain, the tattle of gunburst. This time they were for me. I could not risk the family I didn't need. I slid from the chimney to a rainspout and from there shimmied down, thinking of the weapon trunk in the woods, of the cellar and the fetid plumbing, of simply nuzzling myself into the pink flanks of the she-goat. I planted the setter at the door, telling him, this is it, so long puppy, I know you will do the doggy's duty; and then I left the villa so I might meet the other villains before they burned the innocents along with the monster in the castle.

They have to get me precisely because I am average. I am moderate, do you see, in all of my ways, stealing rarely and then with affection, scribbling no letters with the blood of my palm. Somehow calm even in my intensity, friendly in my crimes, willing to admit error. Yes, they are determined in my case because I suffer no greatness, no madness or genius and so am far less likely to reveal myself than the really cunning ones, the characteristic outlaws.

A dead burro bleeding in the road. I was walking toward it, hands clasped behind my head in the gesture of absolute capitulation wearing a face as innocent and inhuman as a Pinocchio. I searched the camouflage of the woods for the gunmen, the tree-tops lined with snipers like anxious crows, the roadside gully jammed like a mass gravesite with trigger-mad young natives. I halted in the midst of them, letting dust kiss my shoes and listening to the flies that swarmed the burro's carcass. I always knew I would just stand one day, remaining waiting while I squinted with one eye because of the gleam of metal against the sun.

They will come, I thought, and with such confidence they won't bother to come sneaking, but rather arrive as if delivering groceries. I looked for them to march from the village, to light from their hidings, their Sten guns on hipbones, skeletal gunbutts like leaden nooses. And I will beg, childishly, with dog trust that they will hear me before they shoot. I knew, above all, it would be a tasteful capture, and that is what had to be spoiled. The neighbors ought to gossip that they suspected me all along, my shady private ways, my unclean fingernails, a native who finally seemed and felt foreign to every other native. I am only getting what I have asked for, living that way.

Yes, I thought, I will not make it easy. I was prepared only to be unprepared. No spectacle of pride, no come-and-get-it fervor— only the same dull ordeal as the arrest of any hoodlum caught brandishing a pair of knuckle-dusters. The kidnapper without mercy. the criminal who refuses to give them their day: there will be lugubrious sobbing, citizen, even a spitting up or two, the offer of a deal, informing on innocent friends I've had, the burning of all personal papers that might exonerate me. I would be the snitch who pulls fatal messages out of toilets. I tell you, I will suck every uniformed ass, cop into my throat every stale beer fart, gladly choke on the semen from their smoking barrels. I will vote if they wish; I will run for office if they wish.

I do not think it a great test of mettle or conviction that while standing in the hot sickening road near the stench of dead flesh, with arms strained to remain together so there could be no mistake about the surrender, I rolled all such original thoughts in my brain, wobbled in surprise at the actual event. I had rehearsed everything: how I would be startled out of a nightmare by their assault on doors and windows: how I would drop immediately to my

knees beside my blanket, fumble with the fly of my pajamas while they were looking with astonishment and disgust at my filled spaces, my jars and beakers and reeking livestock. And I would beg instantly, offer them the pleasure of being generous, of a moment's mercy to a silly vain ruffian who holds beliefs no more deeply than his victims, than the she-goat, than his poor dumpy mother who had beached herself, I will add, on just such a scorcher, like a ghost ship. I wanted to be submissive, I made every cowering gesture, but I was not repentant and especially not vengeful. They were merely doing what it is they do, and I the same.

By the time, citizen, this drama had curtained my eyes it was pure imagination. With cautious certainty I stared from limb to ditch, bush to high grass, and lowered my arms. I walked to the burro, saw that it had indeed been shot dead, and then saw below it, in a weeded moist ravine, the wheels of a motorbike still spinning. The spokes of chrome were bent and shining. Abandoned in the ravine and injured beyond repair, a bullet hole in its proud chest, the machine lay riderless. My crimes themselves were unimportant, the private pain of children does not amount to a fig in the infamy. What remained important was the nearly explainable element, the shattered torso of the motorbike, the puddles of blood under the burro, the astonished villain gathering bugs and dirt in the empty road.

In fury at the villa I wrapped my human livestock into three sweet bundles of straw and strolled with them down the mountain to the deserted rocky end of the beach. There I deposited and unleashed them. There they crawled out of my hands one at a time back into the luminous gaping world. I returned the darlings not to their doorstep, though not for cowardice, but to a spot where they would choose a direction in which to slither. I watched impassively. Village left, dense deadly woods full of hungry dogs right, the wide huffing sea straight on. Sex, death, water. They moved with reluctance, with pathetic discernable grins on rubbery faces. They went with teeth marks in them, my stain of poison. I did not remain to see their decisions; they scudded to instinctive places, feeling their way past pierres and shells like diapered crabs. Strong limbs got them to the middle of the beach, and there they sat digging holes, digging and pondering. They bore my saliva. The needs of even a child must be met if he is not to be found dead behind a door.

I was standing at the motorbike—I have pieced it together a thousand times since—weak in the knees and bladder. The motorbike was leaking fuel, wheels informed a gyroid image of stillness, the rider's chain belt was tangled about the headlamp. I had always hated that motorbike. It had got what it deserved. It would not get up again. Like all machines, I thought, it is human.

This one is the bloodiest: toppling verandas, ripping sportscars like a knife rips the stomach. Burros have collapsed on the roadside, trapped under grain sacks with the bodies of their masters. The countryside will ooze like sludge over the village to bury laws, thugs, piscators, all. Geologists will be coming, bespectacled men to slowly pump our veins. Force bowels reluctantly to churn. These aliens will connive to start our heart thumping by blasting rock, digging bodies, raising warships, erecting derricks on the seashore. They will film newsreels.

There is a new mountain, citizen, on the other side of the village, making a sultry crater of the obsidian promontory. We heard it quaking in the night, in a roar of ocean spittle, the spray of history. It is monstrous; it is foreboding. The washerwomen, picking twigs from linens, can pound rock against blood in its lusty shadow. At sunset it will brood, make us moody, fill our gullets thick with beer while it smolders hard and dark as a bull's pizzle. Sun will corrode the whitest wall, no planting will be planned, no harvest; we will not bear olives or pomegranates or figs. From the freak of the mountain and the rubble of our earthquakes we will go blind. Our myth will have its ictus. The tourists totter lamely, legs in steel braces singing like piano keys on our cobbled streets. They sense our hell. Where there is no allegorical dahlia.

In our hell they breathe rooty barreled heaves that trail them in the ferrous hallow of our cathedral door as it booms shut safely behind. Touch gently as a moth the peacock blue of the statues' robes, hard solferino noses, the albino features of death masks. Our horror stories in each stained glass.

FIVE POEMS

PETER BLUE CLOUD

1   O-NA-NO-RON

you
    swamp root
who drink the sun through steam
and in your night mirror
gather stars about you.
your feet in warm decay
the black, wet mud
a multitude of new
      born creatures
swim beneath your head.
you
    sacred plant
as you hang to dry
we feel the power
      reaching out.

2   MILKWEED

your blood mixed with air
holds the world together,
with your fiber sinews
the bowstring hums
to slightest wind,
your grey-green leaves
are signals of a friendly camp,
and then your seedlings
float gently
like first flakes of snow,
and your empty pods are fashioned
into rattles,
or taken by children
to become canoes
with pebbles for passengers
taken to far away lands,
and now your yellowed leaves
rustle the music
of another snow
and your seedlings
lie sleeping.

3

your mother combs your hair
and stars fall at your feet,
hair like the cool night river
dark blue with droplets of moon,
fat little fingers dance and curl
their very own playful stories
        and grandmother's eyes are filled,
and when you sit alone to play
humming your baby song
to wildflowers and tiny bugs
        there is a far away playing
of an elderberry flute
        brought by the wind.

4   YELLOWJACKET

for Coyote

He rode into town upon a wild-eyed mountain horse
his hat pulled low, and down his back and shoulders
swaying and blowing in wind, long black and grey hair,
and no one saw the eyes, but even the soldiers felt
themselves being studied, maybe as coldly as the wind
        blowing downriver,
man and horse, passing through town in silent watching
stirring only small puffs of dust and leaving behind
the strong odors of buckskin and cedar smoke,
"he carries a pistol besides that rifle," someone said,
and a young and respectful voice said, "a real bad one, too,
        I hear."
an old man, a healer, who still dared perform the rituals
of curing, but in hiding from the eyes of soldier and missionary,
hummed and muttered an old mountain song under his breath
and whispered, "a spirit rides with him and he carries
a whole tribe; he is what remains of a tribe, and we,
        the ghosts,"
"yes," said the sergeant, "another godamn fence has been
ripped down and dragged until tangled and useless. We give
the heathens a whole valley to live in, but it ain't good
enough for them. Should round them up and shoot the lot,
like we was doing before; or at least the real bad ones,
        especially Yellowjacket!"
with half a butchered steer tied to his horse
he approached his sister's tiny shack at the edge of town,
"the deer are moved to the high mountains like me, don't like
the smell of oiled leather and iron stoves. Here is meat
of a kind best left for the buzzards, but meat at least
        to eat."
another fence was torn down and three head of cattle
slaughtered, and the meat left at the edge of town, as a dare
to the hungry to take, and to eat and to live a while longer,
and a soldier, too, found with slit throat, a quick and
clean kill and no signs of cruelty or anger, a hunter killed by
        the hunted.

and mounted, the soldiers rode through town
and the people watched and knew a longing,
a feeling for a something lost, just out of reach,
but not a one of them mounted a horse or reached for a rifle,
but merely watched and waited, ashamed to raise their eyes to
      one another,
and they saw him, hatless and riding slowly, so slowly
into town, and the clean upriver mountain air wildly
blew his hair about, and as he passed he stared into
the eyes of each with no reproach, and each of them saw
the holes and streaming blood as he rode through
      their midst.
and was never seen again, and the talking, too, stopped
when his sister said to a crowd of them, "don't speak
of him again, you don't deserve his name." And they
watched her saddle up and take up her child and
turn her back upon her husband and home and never
      look back,
and on that same evening a few youngsters, too, saddled
up and for the first time in many seasons, openly
showed their rifles, and some old people joined them
and they rode upriver, up toward the clean air and
naked stone, and the soldiers saw them pass, and dared
      not interfere.

5 COMPOSITION

there was the buffalo blowing
blood and steam from throat wound
and even the smell of gore and
of fear mingling hate anger,
the sound of the great heart
                                        thumping,
        and a leg convulsively pawing
a furrow, and already
                        the first flies,
the hunters desperate pull
upon the short thrusting spear,
                                        ashamed
of his poor aim causing
        such pain to his brother,
        desperately
wanting to plunge again
                                true,
to end mutual pain,
and the horse standing trembling
and frothing from the wild
        ecstasy of the chase,
        and a plain,
and mountains and glorious clouds,

all such a rich canvas,
and beyond the easel a bare
                                white wall
and the inner image of a composition
        beyond manipulation

Those rain trombones gulping the wind!
Those giants climbing back from their defrosted morgues!

By hair of rain
By roots of rain
The earth attracts me

Stricken with rainsickness
I weep I weep

When will you come to sleep, small rain?
When are you going to dry, small tear?

HAILING THE EVENING

To have been only a thallus
Providently masked in chlorophyll
Bearer of fruit as marble is of thought
And hailing the evening
With my inflorescent song

I shall bless the trees that patiently grow old
Near the sensual fountains
I shall think of the sea-lettuce
The red-eyed dancer who with her four whips
Will make the Marly horses whinny
On a day of flood tide

Consenting dust
Near the Pompeian atoms of the Tuileries
I will have my orange-colored look
I too
One who lives on Paris

MARINE ARCHITECT

The stickleback in its credulous water
Descending as far as Notre Dame

The stickleback builds a nest of algae
In the running water of our heart

With the green needle of its body
It sews the walls of its house

And turns blue and gold and red with happiness
As it devours nocturnal meats

NATIONAL GEORGIC

The Clichy virgins draped in songs
Carry sheaves of lilac
As they walk down to a Paris encamped
On the Concorde in marshes of rain

But they need only a spring of wormwood
For diadem and in the wild herbal
The lover recognizes their subtle power

A flurry of crows released from the bells
In all directions pulls up stones
In readiness for the coming insurrection

So we will wait no more for some decayed July
Before we root in the sky the trees of the Flood
And launch corrosive hearts
In the charnel houses of Saint-Paul

In clandestine night
The national Georgics are printed
On the molds of the flaming Seine

THE FISHERMAN BY THE SEINE

I fish not for carp
But for the supple-hipped wave
That gives birth to the universe

The migrating tench
Lays its eggs in the rainbow
The plover's arrows
Pierce the rock of Notre Dame
To reach the west

And I have not changed since the reindeer's time
My weedy beard floats on the willow's branches
My skull is shinier than flying pebbles
Between absolute reigns
My mist
Endures

Following the stream
Halved and double
Head down and kicking the clouds
Do I fish for pike or swallow?
I fish only for my heart
Fallen into charming darkness

Servant of desires and echoes
Friend of feathered fish

From time to time I kill the blue fly
And beg pure pardon
Of the occult grass

THE VISUAL POEMS OF THE VOU GROUP

Introduced by Shimizu Toshihiko

INTRODUCTION

Shimizu Toshihiko

This is the second time for the Vou group to contribute to the *New Directions in Prose and Poetry* anthology. The first, in 1938, the poems (previsual) of fourteen members were published with the introduction by James Laughlin.

The experiments in visual poetry in the Vou group were started in the late 1950s. Most of them took the form of photo poems and were based on the idea that in order to present a poetic impact exactly, a poet can utilize figurative space as a means to amplify or control it.

It is, however, through the effort of Kitasono Katue that the direction was clearly defined. In the note to his plastic poems *Moonlight Night in a Bag* (1965), he declared: "Words are the most uncertain signals severally devised by human beings for communication. . . . Plastic poem is the figure of poem itself, in other words, it is an 'apparatus' of poem in which rhythm and meaning are not essential factors. . . . I will play new poetry, in the viewfinder of my camera, with a handful of paper scraps, boards or glasses etc."

Under the influence of Kitasono's conception and method, Vou poets began to fix the poetic impacts in various ways: Shimizu

32

Masato, Tsuji Setsuko, and Sawada Shin'ichi investigate the plastic poems from their own standpoints. Takahashi Shohachiro, Itoh Motoyuki, and Shimizu Toshihiko make book-poems, object-poems, and conceptual texts, as well as visual texts where words and images collide, change energies. On the one hand, Torii Ryozen, Fukuda Kazuhiko, Okazaki Katsuhiko and Hibino Fumiko produce poetries in pure photogenic images, while Kiyohara Etsushi seeks a new visual language in making plastic poems.

As for the relation to the international movement, Kitasono is the first Japanese poet who came into contact with concrete poetry, and the other poets (especially Takahashi, Itoh, and Shimizu) followed him. It is no wonder that they did not move toward the pure concrete but a totally free visual mode of writing, invigorating the tendency to break away from it.

In this sense, the following statement by Jean-François Bory (*Once Again*, New Directions, 1968) may appropriately summarize the essence of the visual poems of the Vou group: "Most of the Japanese visual poems are photographic works and this is important. For these photographs are not represented or thought of as final (or finished) works, and in that they go beyond what constitutes the essential element of language or what it could be by concentrating attention (the action + the tool) on the PROVISIONAL ELEMENT OF THE PROCESS OF COGNITION rather than on what is perceived."

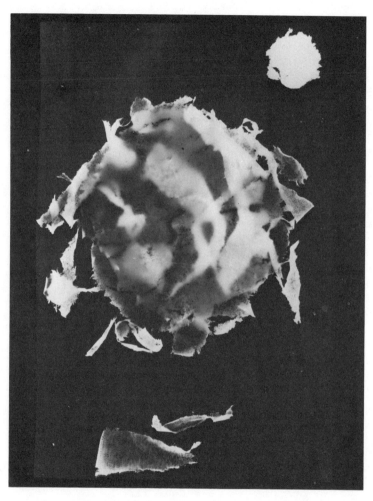

Fukuda Kazuhiko. *Paper poem. Op. 75-2*. 1975

Hibino Fumiko. *Graffiti-A.* 1975

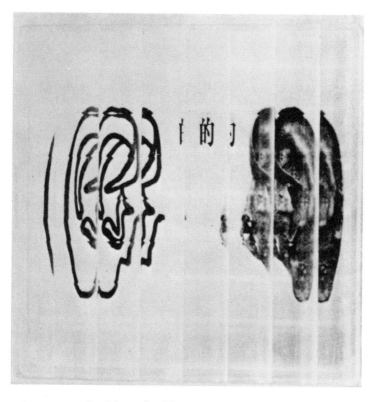

Ito Motoyuki, *Plastic poem 11.* 1970

Kitasono Katue. *Plastic poem.* 1973

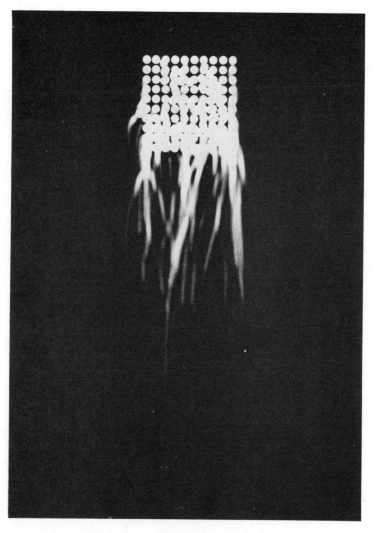

Kiyohara Etsushi. *Op.–A–152.* 1975

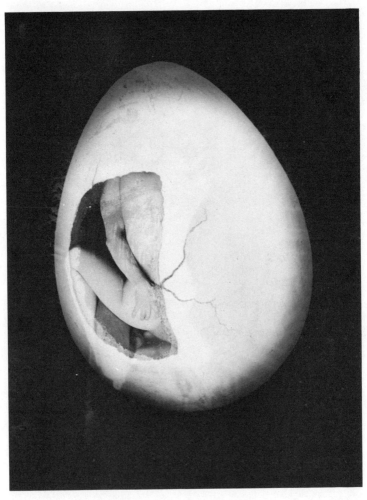

Okazaki Katsuhiko. *Lovely vomit 4.* 1973

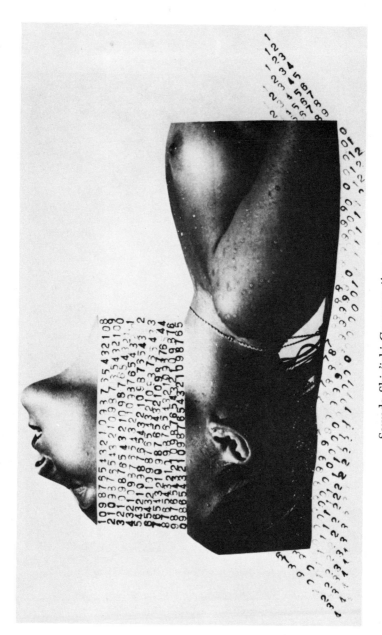

Sawada Shin'ichi *Generous time* 1. 1974

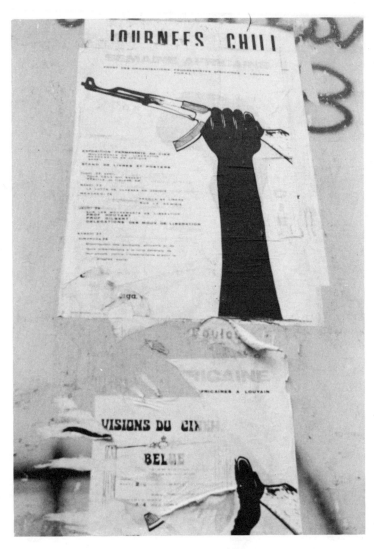

Shimizu Masato. *In memory of Leuven 2. 1974*

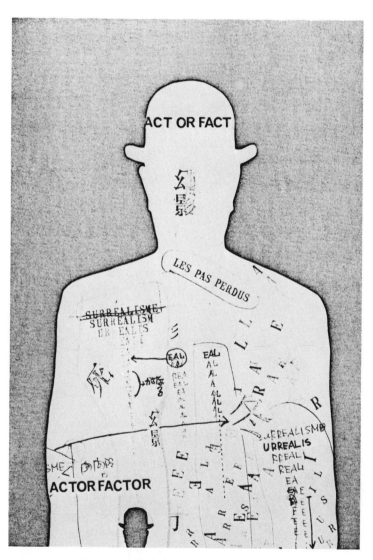

Shimizu Toshihiko. *Anti-illusion 2.* 1971

Takahashi Shohachiro. *Block poem for endless A.* 1973

Torii Ryozen. *Katachi.* 1975

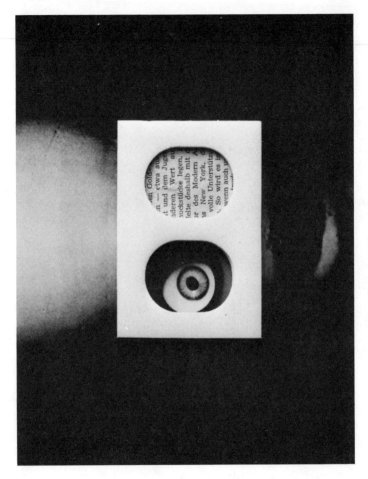

Tsuji Setsuko. *Photo poem.* 1971

TWO POEMS

GUILLEVIC

Translated from the French by Mary Feeney

OBOE

1. Seeing it was
   Surrounded by poppies,

   Red became
   The bluet's favorite color.

2. The weather's beautiful. The earth
   Goes up flights of stairs.

3. In all the ballads
   That came through open windows,

   The grass
   Heard the trees.

4. There's a rough agreement, here
   With space.

5. Far off in time,
   The well sauntered.

6. A man goes by

He has the feeling
He's important.

The tree does too.

7.   The clouds had taken me
     For a friend.

     But I
     Had no need of them.

8.   Dialogue between the blackbird
     And the nightingale.

     Let's imagine.

9.   A wind that knew
     Every leaf in the park.

10. The earthworm,
     Happy
     In its civic duties.

11. In every shadow there's
     A sun to drink.

12. Between the sea and the salt flats
     The wind

     Gave us our dimensions.

13. The oak tree isn't the only one
     To know

     How a balance
     Can endure.

14. No use, basswood tree,
     Trying to hide in yourself.

     I know you.

15.   The colt is taken aback
      At the cry of the hoot owl.

16.   In the orchard,

      The stones in the walls,
      The plums

      Counted by centuries.

17.   You can fall.
      Of course.

      Otherwise
      Why keep going?

18.   He died standing up
      The way things burst.

19.   Nothing.

      It's because
      Of the light.

      In the fall, everything's possible
      On a level with the sky.

20.   Eyes that say that
      In spite of everything

      They'll wait.

21.   Light on the way
      To knowing light's clear.

22.   Because
      Of the ash tree branch

      The hour is won.

23. This light

     That was sometimes able
     To seem our very own.

24. For want of an ocean,

     There is your palm
     To look at.

THE PLANTS OF BRITTANY

1. Everywhere plants
    Grow among the dead,

    Dig their roots
    Into cadavers
    From all the kingdoms.

2. Are the grasses
    In cemeteries

    Different from
    Those in parks

    When you see them
    But don't place them?

3. In fact, Brittany
    Is no more a cemetery

    Than any
    Other spot on earth.

4. But in Brittany, it's true
    That something ends,

That you're there on the edge
Of a space where living
Would be different.

5.   Elsewhere, plants
Are willed to fill up
Verticality.

Here, the sky
Is a neighbor
That takes an interest.

6.   The same height as man,
The sky.

The same height as man
Dreaming.

Here, space
Is a ground floor.

7.   Here plants
Seem taller.

Govern space
Just as houses do.

The moors
Touch the sky.

8.   Here, plants are far
From having settled matters.

Horsetail ferns as
Well as gorse and furze.
The wind must have something
To do with it.

9.   A wind that knows the sea,
That comes from it
Or comes back to it

And that never
Forgets their wedding.

10.   So, of course,
The wild grass here

Cannot be the same
As elsewhere

Even if
It bears

The same names.

11.   Here, wild grass is not
The same rest as elsewhere.

It too
Calls to you.

It too will say:
Grow.

12.   It says:

Do as I do,
Leave and stay.

Know the far off
To know the more what's here.

13.   Says the grass
The wind

Has told me
Much about the elsewhere.

So that it can
Be fed with here.

14. I know that the wind
    Carries me.

    Even when it comes from afar
    It tastes of me.

    I'm sure I am in it
    Among its resources.

15. The ferns
    Are more modest.

    They close tight
    Around their secrets,

    The oldest
    On the old earth.

    They do not look
    Toward the horizon.

16. Yes,
    There's water.

    Water
    Always present.

    As long as against the rain
    The furze bares its spikes.

17. Sun, also.

    Nowhere is the sun
    The same as here,

    All the day long,
    Morning sun.

    And that is why plants,
    Even ferns,

Speak of the birth of the wind
And stay young.

18. Brittany
     Carries its dead
     Toward the future.

     A carpet
     For this ceremony,
     The grasses

     Of meadows, embankments,
     Pathways.

19. The grasses ring
     With sounds of bells.

     Will not accept
     Just any sounds.

20. Gorse
     Is like the poor,
     It goes with them,

     Signifies
     They must go on,

     That it is worth
     The trouble.

     It sings
     As the poor do,
     Sometimes,

     When the weather's fair.

21. The oak records
     What all the plants speak,

     Keeps it
     As testimony.

22. Never, afterwards,
    Could fruit

    Taste half so much
    Of earth.

    There was sap of roofslates
    In the blackberries.

23. The houses wanted to be
    Right next to plants,

    Belong to plants
    But in a lighter shade.

    Hear their voices.

    With them take part
    In the hopes of the ocean.

24. There was no lack
    Of danger.

    Kelp
    Could stranglehold.

    Beneath the ferns
    Lay vipers,
    In wait for us.

    Briars
    Tore at eyes.

25. A mere scrape at
    An embankment

    Uncovered roots
    Sizeable roots
    Of things unknown.

One day, one of them
Turned out to be a viper.
Was killed.

26.   Nothing
      Was less foreign
      Than violets.

      They promised us no more
      Than the possible.

27.   The lichen
      On the grey stone.

      Which had
      Secreted the other?

      Which
      Was the rider?

      You could tell
      That their story
      Was endless,

      Met at some point
      The saga of kelp.

28.   We had enemies
      Without knowing why.

      Among them,
      Nettles

      Seemed to sleep
      As nettles will.

29.   These enemies.
      Were a whole world

      Apparently it could not
      Be explained,
      And we endured it.

Wild lilies
Would heel bad wounds.

30.   There were some leaves,
Some grasses

That we could tell
Everything.

Even our fear
Of night, our fear of people.

31.   With ivy
We made ourselves houses.

It too knew

That the earth
Rose up in each thing,

That everywhere
We were in the earth.

32.   Nothing perhaps was so sweet

As crushing a leaf, a wild plant
Between the palms

And cupping them, breathing in, stroking
Them with the lips a long time.

33.   Flagrant and commonplace
The leaf and flower
And their revelation

Of what the earth
Makes of the universe,

The thing that in woman
Finds outlet.

34.   I named you softly:
Heather, heather—

As if I knew that later
I would miss you

And the sunset
That crowns you

Empress who ranks with the poor.

35. Between the saxifrage and the heather,
Between the moss and the periwinkle,

Between the dandelion and the gorse,
Between the forget-me-not and the honeysuckle,

As between the azure and the cloud,
Between the sky and the rowboat,
Between the oak and the slate roof,

I existed. I was there.
I served as place.

36. If you know
Something of the universe,

It means you've looked deep,
As if in your self,

Into the rock,
Into the unknown plant
Growing against it,

It means the lichen
Has felt your cheek's touch.

Then the sky and the ocean
Did not reject you.

37. Where else can there be
In any atlas

A region where all has the weave
Of a blade of grass?

ANATOMY LESSON, ETC.

ANTONIS SAMARAKIS

Translated from the Greek by Andrew Horton

A thirteen-minute delay is a thirteen-minute delay. In other words, an eternity. Because if you have stood and waited impatiently someplace for someone, time takes on another dimension. And if you are waiting not simply impatiently but with unrestrained passion, with great yearning, then that's exactly how he was waiting for her.

As usual, he had been the first to arrive for their rendezvous. Usually, she would have arrived in three, at the most, four minutes. But she had not yet arrived. Meanwhile, standing on the freezing tiles, he felt bad. High on the wall above the broken oil heater pipe, the two large familiar spiders and the third smaller one have gathered as usual to watch their erotic scuffle; to the left and right, in large bottles filled with formaldehyde, are a variety of long-dead objects: livers, frogs, chameleons, and something else—all of which seemed to come to life and twist around nervously because of this unusual delay. The curtains over the only window, which had nailed shutters, loaded with dust and memories of the good old days, shook with anxiety. As for the one-handed skeleton in the corner, he thought it smiled ironically at him. The Great Napoleon seemed to smile in the same ironic way; he doesn't know why the autocrat is on his stomach but he doesn't dare pull him up to see if he smiles or not because of his rheumatism and also because he feels as if he is beginning to slip a disk.

Finally! The door opens violently and she enters panting and with her brand new military styled yellow raincoat making a crackling sound (or something like that). In order not to lose precious time, he begins at once to unbutton the raincoat, and as soon as he has undone two of the five buttons, as playful as ever, she takes his glasses with masterly finesse (he has myopia, astigmatism, and is long-sighted) and not only makes them disappear like lightning, but she disappears as well. He just had time to see her figure, to see her—without glasses—somewhat fuzzily, open the door again and go into the dark corridor of the basement.

It isn't the first time she has played her tricks; either she hid from him his lighter, his pen, a glove, or both gloves, or she hid his undershirt, which had a melancholy lion embroidered on it with mauve thread; often she played these kinds of tricks on him and ran to hide everything from him inside the closet or in the eternally empty corridor. She liked to kid him, to sadistically choose moments and hours when she was greatly excited, burning all over with passion. After all, he deserves it.

Tonight, enraged by the entirely unpleasant suspense of the scuffle, he stumbles into the corridor feeling his way; he takes a few steps in the dark with his arms extended.

"My glasses! Where are my glasses? I can't see a thing. . ."

He steps forward two or three meters, goes on a few more meters, and turns left.

"Where are my glasses? I can't see without them."

Ah! He grabbed her! His hand clutches her raincoat while he leans on her left breast, which is unusually hard; he immediately grabs the right one.

"Do you find it necessary to touch me like this? I'm ticklish, you know . . . !"

A hard voice, a completely unknown voice, it was just as hard as the one breast he had had time to grab, it isn't her soothing voice, no, it's a man who speaks to him once again with the same bluntness, the same implacable way!

"I'm sorry, professor . . . but you are under arrest."

"You see, it's the environment that affects me. It sets off my fantasies. It provokes my sexuality. It is really 'something else' inside here. It's the so-called 'atmosphere.' Do you agree, my little corpse?"

Almost every time they had a scuffle, he did not miss the chance

to repeat the concrete details of the situation. Always, the dark truth was that the "little corpse"—for that's how she used to call him, tenderly—not only does not agree but also feels the root of "fear and horror" each Monday, Wednesday, and Friday at six-thirty . . . (of course the outcome varies according to the circumstances), when for her pleasure because the environment affects her, he is shut in together with that nightmarish decor. A decor which seems as if it had been taken from a vampire film, for example, *The Dracula of the Carpathian Mountains* of Polanski or something else with the same formula. How to discover a way with women and what moves them in sex today and tomorrow.

Once again the truth is that he knows by heart the skeletons, one-armed or not, and the various creatures in the glass jars of formaldehyde are playthings for the professor of anatomy. But he shouldn't have them as decor for a passionate love.

The truth, however, is something more: the shock he always felt entering the room, evaporates in five or five and a half seconds, when he double-locks the wormeaten wooden door, when she quickly falls on her back on the "dissecting table" with the spring of a deer and he rushes to meet her after he has climbed the bronze bust of the Great Napoleon—it is a mystery why the autocrat is in the closet of the anatomy laboratory—where with great force he has rolled it from the corner and turned it on its stomach in order to use it as a step so he can mount up, trying to jump with his little paunch, rheumatism, and the rest . . . Because she is thirty-four Mays or Junes old while the "little corpse" is fifty-five cloudy Novembers.

The essential point is this: the frigid and immobile "dissecting table" immediately warms up like a pressure cooker, and the erotic chill which produces the steamy universe of his fifty-five Novembers destroys the remaining barriers of "fear and horror."

Who would suspect that "the little corpse," with his paunch, rheumatism, and general arthriits, his cholesterol, myopia, astigmatism, and long-sightedness, not to mention some high blood pressure, but with the title of tenured professor of anatomy at the medical school of the university in the capital, who would suspect that he had such illegal flings during his daily routine. Illegal because he was a bachelor; she, however, married with two children.

The seventh in a row, this illegal fling today, Friday, December 20th. Tomorrow at noon the university would close for vacation.

The new year was fast approaching. About three months ago, the middle of September, she first appeared in the medical school, a newly appointed employee in the administrative office. She immediately caught his eye. He wouldn't dare, however, declare this unless she took the initiative; it was her decision to begin. It happened that one afternoon they both went into the basement to take inventory of the unneeded supplies in the storeroom of the anatomy laboratory. He kept the key in his office. There were two other rooms in the basement, storerooms, for what he didn't exactly know.

From the first moment she appeared in the medical school, she impressed him, not only with her very "sexy" manner, but with the "air" she had about her. Her "sexiness" could not be explained by the usual logic because she was far from "beautiful," she would have to be classified as "ugly," or "rather ugly," mysterious anyway, the driving power which she gave off and imprisoned others with. The "air," however, the "appearance" which she had, the unlikely snob, was not at all mysterious; it was known that she had "important connections," more specifically, a second cousin in an important and dynamic part of the System.

"I repeat, professor, that you're under arrest . . . and that you're under arrest for reasons you know very well."

The second time that this ticklish character spoke to him, and he stood listening to him petrified. Then this character quickly frisks the professor, his hand holds something in his right pocket of his jacket and he pulls it out.

"Here are your glasses! You had them in your pocket, professor . . ."

He takes his glasses, puts them on and for the first time sees the other: the Black Trenchcoat. Or rather, one of the Black Trenchcoats. That's how the general public called the agents of the System's secret service, whose power conceals everyone and everything from condemnation of penal law, for example, ethical crimes, adultery, and such, or subversive activities of the System.

The Black Trenchcoat also wears a dark smirk, no doubt remains about its meaning. The husband had suspected her, he had suspected them, he had hired them to follow them, she had already been caught as she entered the corridor to play with him, to make him hunt for her after she had first taken his glasses and at the

same time as she had hid them in his pocket as a trick, they nabbed her and who knows where they have taken her and disgraced her, it's not impossible that she saw the Black Trenchcoat and tried to escape, but they had seized him now and he was in a tight spot since he had been caught in adultery.

These are the fears which he is unable to verbalize, he only manages to see another Black Trenchcoat at the end of the corridor, he also sees seven students, his own students, he recognizes them, among the seven are two girls, and he becomes embarrassed in front of them, they stand and stare at him eye to eye. Eye to eye.

"Psstt . . . Psssttt . . ."

Two very mysterious "Psstt's" come—where do they come from? —and destroy the total silence of the anatomy laboratory storeroom. That's something! Could it be a mouse gnawing? Is it a piece of wood that made that noise? Or is it a person? But who? It's possible that he's fooling himself and that the noise didn't exist, only in his imagination.

A little while ago, his own Black Trenchcoat, that is, the one who arrested him, had taken him into the storeroom again, locked him in the familiar psychedelic decor:

"A little patience, professor. You will be taken in the special car we use in such cases. The students are still having classes above, preparatory classes, better not make a spectacle of yourself, gossip doesn't help matters."

Then the Black Trenchcoat left him alone.

So they would enclose him in the depressing "special car." They would take him directly from the basement; the small door at the end of the corridor leads to the garage of the university where one sees the road below.

He should not have accepted his arrest without some resistance, not like a chicken ready for slaughter. He must say something, shout . . . However, the unexpected was so very unexpected that he lost his tongue; how did it happen?

He worries about her struggle for her own fate, he didn't know what to think first. He closes his eyes to calm himself a bit, he uses this trick whenever, for one reason or another, he is psychologically upset.

". . . for the same purpose. Yes, professor. We came to the basement for the same cause you came. Can you hear us? Psstt . . . psstt . . ."

So, it's a man and he speaks, speaks to the professor, the voice of an invisible man is heard as if through a telephone receiver, that's yet another mystery!

"Psstt . . . psstt . . . psstt . . . We are your students, professor, you saw us in the corridor."

He got up enough strength to reach for the corridor where the voice of the other—of the others was coming, because the second time it wasn't the same voice: the old broken oil heater pipe, high on the wall, there where the two large spiders and the third smaller one exist. They spoke to him from the other end of the pipe in the adjoining room. And the various "psstt's" were necessary to clear the pipe in case it was blocked.

"And we're all for the same cause. Can you hear us?"

Of course he hears them, is he deaf? He knows what's going on! The students are in the basement "for the same cause": an orgy. Gang bang! So the second Black Trenchcoat was not standing by the students by chance, no, he had arrested them, and now they all wait, he in this room, they in the next room, for the "special car."

"We feel great comfort having you near us since you are with us for the same cause . . ."

Can you imagine! Can you imagine! They say his own public disgrace gives them "great comfort." It's not enough that he has his own worries about what will happen; now he has the students' too. But what do they really mean? This is no time for joking.

"You are the only one of our professors who is with us. Can you hear us . . . ? Can't you hear us . . . ?"

The same old tune! Okay, kids. The only one of your professors who is with you because he is the only one who is disgraced.

"You give us great comfort by coming for the declaration . . . That you have the courage to stand with us. Can't you hear us . . . ? We have to speak softly so that the others won't hear, they are in the corridor and are pacing up and down, we can see them through the keyhole. Can you hear us . . . ? The declaration is here, professor . . . They frisked us, just as they searched you when they arrested you, they frisked us but they didn't find it . . . We have the declaration for the new year right here . . . The declaration with wishes for peace and freedom."

"What? What's that again? No more of this, please . . . no more! Freedom is . . . is . . . how do they say? Freedom is "a joke." It exists only in yellowing encyclopedias and dusty dictionaries . . . Yes, and in freshly made speeches of the supporters of the System

. . . and of various other Systems throughout the world . . . because only these, the supporters of the Systems have the freedom to speak about freedom . . .

"You give us great comfort . . . you give us courage. You were notified that we would meet in the basement to discuss the declaration . . . you were notified and you came immediately. So, we're not alone, no, we're not completely alone! Because one professor dared . . . dared to support us. But why don't you speak . . . ? Aren't you in the storeroom . . . ? Can't you hear us?"

No, no! He shouldn't give them a sign of life. He should play dumb. All of this talk of freedom is not a joking matter, the situation is dangerous, explosive . . . Some stories came into his mind, circumstances which occurred and reoccurred; two or three wrote about freedom, three or four spoke for freedom, four or five heard about freedom, but did not rush to block their ears with wax, and here's the result: the Black Trenchcoats intervened, always ready to perform such services, then the supporters or the semiofficials of the System became interested and finally . . .

"What's the matter, professor . . . ?"

The pipe carried their questions to him, it is one of the two girls who spoke with touching anxiety. A warm voice, so warmly as if the heater had added a well-kept mysterious warmth. But his heart was frozen. Frozen? Eh, not one hundred per cent. But that is "top secret" . . .

"What's the matter, professor . . .? Don't you hear us? Just say a word to us!"

He was almost tricked into saying:

"No, I don't have a thing to say!"

He restrained himself and didn't answer her . . . but how can you hold yourself back when you have to sneeze? Because he feels he must sneeze twice. Then the students will hear that he can hear as well.

"At last! Finally you heard us, professor! And we were beginning to worry what was was going on. What could have happened. We'll read the declaration to you . . . it's short but to the point . . . if you have any suggestions, please let us know . . . maybe you won't find it forceful enough . . . For us to add your own name . . . next to our names . . . of course you can't sign in person by reaching your hand through the pipe . . . We have a way to smuggle out the declaration. So, listen to what we've written . . ."

With his fingers stuck in his ears, he presses hard, no, he isn't crazy enough yet to allow himself the dangerous luxury of sitting and listening to a declaration of freedom.

For a long time he covers his ears; the youths said the declaration was short but what can you do to be sure. It's better to be deaf for a few minutes.

Such an uproar suddenly comes from the next room that it destroys even this primitive gesture. What's the sense of trying not to hear since he hears anyway. Here the world is falling apart, the Black Trenchcoats have entered the storeroom containing the students; the voices are different now, voices of hard steel, implacable, and now and again some deafening sounds, sounds that make him shiver. They are beating the students . . .

He catches a few phrases from the Black Trenchcoats as it comes to a climax.

"So you make declarations, eh? For freedom, eh? So we have this sort of thing, eh? So the professor is on your side, eh? Eh?"

He is lost, weakened, collapses, dissolves, evaporates . . . And he who thought they arrested him because her husband suspected them and . . . His heart beats like a ping-pong ball, his blood pressure goes haywire. There's another "crack" in his vertebrae, that's the slipped disk he expected to happen. It chose the right moment to slip.

He feels such a collapse inside himself that he needs to bend, to lie down on his back, he faints, loses consciousness . . . Yes, the "anatomy table," is the only possibility for lying down except for the tile floor. You have my blessing, Oh Great Napoleon, because you lend a hand so I can climb . . . and he climbs. He lies on his back on the marble, he closes his eyes again, stops up his ears again; he doesn't want to see anything, no, he doesn't want to hear anything, no, he doesn't want to think about anything, no and again no! But the last wish is the only one he can realize.

His heart is with the students, yes . . . How could it be otherwise? He too has the same thirst and hunger for freedom, secretly, of course . . . He too feels the same choking lack of freedom, secretly, of course . . . He too is saved by the same hope for freedom, secretly, of course . . . The same dream of freedom warms him, secretly of course . . . But how many others, how many are there who secretly, of course, who . . . secretly, of course . . . only the students are not secret, only the young ones are not

secret . . . If he were young, if he were twenty years old! . . . If he were young . . . and if he was not a university professor, that is, a corpse . . . not a corpse, but he is a corpse, a corpse, a corpse, a corpse, a corpse, corpse, corpse, corpse . . .

But why such despair? Perhaps his situation isn't so tragic. It's a misunderstanding, he agrees. It occurred with the protest of the students in the basement. In other words, a misunderstanding is human. However, if they happen to catch you for matters concerning freedom, then try to prove you aren't *an elephant* but just a corpse. Certainly she would not have kept so cool, damn it! There's also the second cousin with "important connections" . . . who is personally the one with "important connections." Something will happen, it's not possible for the misunderstanding not to be cleared up, they will drop charges concerning the declaration, and they will charge him with adultery. Can the two be compared with each other? It's one thousand times better to be condemned for adultery than for matters concerning freedom.

As if it comforted him, his heart warms up, but his stomach is frozen from being on his front. He gives a push and rolls over onto his back. Another nightmare now: The students are around the "anatomy table," the seven youths, the seven including the two girls, they bend over him, they dissect him and give him an anatomy lesson at the same time . . . a bitter, harsh, relentless anatomy lesson . . . They open his conscience wide, fire into his subconscious, discover his deepest part, his essence . . . and they stare into his eyes . . . they stare . . . a bitter, harsh, relentless anatomy lesson but also something else . . . but also something else . . .

"An anatomy lesson and . . ."

He says these words out loud; he is ready to add "freedom," to add the prohibited word, the unique, precious, and cherished word, but fear grips him, he doesn't dare say "Anatomy and freedom lesson," but he doesn't resist not saying anything, something, at least to say this word in secret, in his own cryptic code and now he says more loudly:

"Anatomy lesson, etc."

"What is going on, professor?"

As soon as the Black Trenchcoat opens the door, always his own, and sees the professor standing on the "anatomy table" looking

high on the wall where the broken oil heater pipe is located. The
total silence from the next room made him extremely uneasy, what's
happening to the students . . . ? Perhaps something is stuck in
the pipe or he hears something, a whisper . . .

"What's going on . . . ? Nothing's going on. I'm staring at three
spiders . . ."

"I don't like spiders at all. They have a hardness, a cruelty . . .
Have you noticed how they 'take care' of their victims?"

"Has the 'special car' come?"

"It came. But it wasn't for you . . . professor, it was a misunderstanding. They telephoned 'from above,' understand me? . . . I'm
sorry . . . Your case has been taken care of, it was a misunderstanding . . . you don't have any connection with the declaration . . ."

He didn't say a word, he comes crawling down from the
"anatomy table." They both go toward the door.

"You may leave, professor. Just walk out."

"What declaration do you mean?"

"It doesn't matter really . . . just a declaration . . . You know
the way, professor. Turn left in the corridor and take the elevator
up, and . . . and that's it."

The moment he tripped on the threshold, the Black Trenchcoat
came behind to begin taking the students from the other room.
Four Black Trenchcoats push them against the wall, with their
foreheads toward the right, toward a small door that leads to
the garage and from there . . . He stops at the threshold, half in
the storeroom, half out, the Black Trenchcoat behind him, all of
the students, all seven including the two girls, in line against
the wall as if they have been lined up for execution, he looks from
one to another, he wants to be sure to see each face well, eye to
eye, and the students gaze at him too.

"Go on, professor," whispers the Black Trenchcoat behind him.
"Go on to the elevator. You're free."

How is he free? Free to take the elevator upstairs, yes . . . but
is he free inside himself . . . ?

"Move on to the elevator. Don't you hear me?"

He hears, he takes a half step forward, all the students watch
him, all seven including the two girls. They watch him not only
eye to eye but also with that great pride, a look which a child has
when he faces a man who is truly a man, a man who is straight,

they gaze at him with pride until he can't take it anymore and is ready to run with all of his strength, ready to run with all of his strength to the elevator to flee from those fourteen eyes which burn him, the seven students are seven professors, seven implacable incompatible indifferent professors who examine him on "The anatomy lesson, etc." . . . If only the "etc." didn't exist, he would handle only "the anatomy lesson," he would manage to pass it, and perhaps with a high mark, but the "etc." . . . but the "etc." . . . he did not complete the half step forward that he had made, he froze on the spot petrified, now the seven students not only stare at him eye to eye but without a word as if by lightning they shared a secret understanding and they create an empty spot among them, his own spot, his own place, now the universe inside him swirls, tears, overturns, if this concrete space among the students which magnetizes him didn't exist, if among the students there did not exist this concrete position which is offered him . . .

"The elevator is here, professor. I said, let's go!"

And so he goes forward, but not in that direction, no, he goes there, there to his own space and his own position among the students, with his head high he goes straight there where the seven students are and also the one and only, unique and beloved "etc."

NARRATIVE OF THE GREAT ANIMAL

NATHANIEL TARN/JANET RODNEY

Denali was our greatest animal.
We might   never have seen it, doubted
all reports, never realized
                         why it was unmistakably
lord of America.
                         It rose, when it rose,
two whole days
         out of surrounding mountains
                         like the sun's ghost
after a burial at sea,
                         like the white whale
out of the sea
         defining all else immediately.

Almost a painting.
   That unreal: as when they say: postcards,
                                           etc.
                  (or travel poster).
Archetype of all mountains,
                  behind the mind, lurking,
no, they say of a beast *lurking* / animal-negative
   and we talk of gods.
Always there: against, the epiphany.

White ship of space, rootless,
suspended from the clouds.
Sometimes, the whole sky grey,
the crown, floating by itself in the skies / or /
clouds on its face: recessing it,
into immeasurable farness,
or lifting it (the mountain) / depressing it,
according to the play of cloud, the *lila*.

A RESURRECTION.

de mortuis,
from the death of our senses, in its shroud,
which is also a wedding gown:
bride/bridegroom
in one plenitude.
Knowing, or not, the plenitude: there is
no other question.
(That we could have been, again, encamped,
with most of humanity at the foot, and spent,   days,   days,
weeks even;   and not seen it /   as so many, coming all this way,
these thousand miles, for a short time, on little money, their
poor lives spent, at the gates now, and, *still*, not seen it:
this   beats   all   matters   of   election, and Mallarmé's
absence, or Kafka's gatekeepers.)
When, thus, it rose,
and the traveler, disbelieving, who had said, all along the way:
"Is *this* Denali,
and then this, and this, and this—there being no end to
the mountains
but, patient: there being always a step below
perfection
until, at road-curve,
"Oh My God," hushed, and the other not seeing yet, and then:
the other, also:
"oh my god," in a still greater hush, because, now, there was,
no possible mistaking.

GREAT STAR OF SPACE

de mortuis
complete,

in its motionless travels,
even then: at its destination, never yet gone
from earth, its
mother. We might not
have seen it, never
have looked on god's face
and lived (so far) to tell tales.
Had we not,

seen it,
the world
would have always,
forever thereafter,
and its word, *logos,*
seemed smaller   because,
after the moon, after all,
it is never the same again:
an earthly thing has to be great indeed, perfect indeed,
to give that plenitude /that lack
of argument, tells us we have
looked on god's face
and lived (so far) to tell tales.

And, had we not seen this,
would not have seen, either,
in any sense of the word "seen,"
since, only this mountain gave the world eyes
and senses,
to apprehend it with: (catalogue / world model)
oh, the cinnamon mountains,
all, all, the other mountains,
in all their varied glory,
the heaving bears, with the earth,
like Atlas, on their shoulders,
the wolves, running as fast as cars,
the idiot ptarmigan, posing at roadside,
the payroll animals, bowing at each bus,
the tourists screaming . . .
(continue: at own leisure),

my, minute, pre-occupations,
under Denali,
  horned lark (American first)
  eagle (repeat); eagle (repeat, but immature)
  wheatear (American first)
  ptarmigan (American first)
  (continue, as per notebook)
  list climbing, x% of total record.
         but the invisibles:
                 harlequin duck, (later: St. Paul)
                 arctic warbler (later: Pt. Hope)
                 golden plover (later: Shishmaref)
                 all these,
                 waiting for the next time,
                 the world being in place,
                 no problem.
                 And seen, then, again, & again,
                 from: Turnagain arm, from
                 the plane, back from the Pribilofs,
                 from the roadside, back from Fairbanks,
                 as if, it were friend now,
                 and reluctant to leave . . .

              and the great animal,
              even greater than *this* animal
              Denali god-beast
              god-animal, with
              hips of stone and
              rock haunches,
              waiting for the next time also
              to get us before another sighting,
               another chance at the vicinity,
              but we have seen it
              and then, by implication, also the other
              as black as it is white . . .

Cloud of mosquitoes.
Splat: blood on hands, and face, and clothes:
wolf blood / moose blood / bear blood / bird blood, perhaps,
John Doe from Texas or Oklahoma blood,

("the animals")

What a merger in the sight of the whole!

Outside the park, every signpost in Alashka is
riddled with bullet holes
the land should have never seen people
this blight on it:

back into civilization . . .

FIFTEEN POEMS

CID CORMAN

1

Gathering
the rain. The
task of the

poet keeps
coming down
in buckets.

2

One's
already
one
too many.

3

A gust
rattles
the pane

A toy
for the
unborn.

4

Help me
even
if you
cant—and
you cant.

5

Death impresses—
is efficient:

every breath
brought to account

6

A flower
in a vase—
a tree at

the window—
your hand in
mine—the sense

If there werent
this—dear—what
would there be?

7

Wherever I look
the mirror looks past
my outstretched eyes. What

sort of a prayer
is this reflected
world? Who or what is

this trembling shadow
hardly concealing
its hungry blindness?

8

As though mountains existed
for valleys to persist in—
as though the silence lifted

underneath a music of
articulate soundings. We
may reach summits and plant flags—

but come back down to live where
word of it matters. We have
to die in order to die.

9 TAO

Not only unknown
and unknowable—
but given to us

beyond evasion—
as the body is—
as wisdom. Slowly

the trembling settles
to the terrible
equilibrium.

10

You say God—I say nothing.
What's there to argue about?
Out of need of touch to touch

we came into our own cry.
There are things that are silent.
What can communicate tries.

11

As if—in the woods
and no one around—
a pond—the day stopped

No question of time—
but a sense of in-
terdependency—

as if the sky had
waited for water
and this eye to be

taken into by—
as if each breath were
shared of the same heart.

12

Problems? What
problems? A
walk in the

hills: nothing
to solve and
all resolved.

13

I listen
at the night
but no sound

comes from the
fields out there—
not even

the sound of
wind. This is
the winter.

14

To stand at the edge
of circumference
and realize there

how within one is
all circumference—
always at its edge.

15

On the page
all these words
to read the
whiteness by.

EIGHT DRAWINGS

HENRY ELINSON

Introduced by Aleksis Rannit

Henry Elinson, A New Artist of the Surreal

Aleksis Rannit

Some three years ago, a Russian artist bearing the Western name of Henry Elinson was exiled from the Soviet Union. After a brief stay in Italy, he arrived in the United States. Rejected by the Soviets as a decadent bourgeois modernist poisoned by "Westernisms," he could not exhibit his work in his native country. Happily enough, he was educated as a philologist and could at least earn his living as a speech therapist. However, when Elinson tried to take his pictures out of the country, he was informed that he could not remove works of Russian national art without payment of a very high customs duty. Unable to pay this duty for his own pictures, he left most of his artistic production behind, taking but a few pieces to the West.

In the first period of his work abroad, Elinson expressed strong anger and anxiety fraught with nightmares and hallucinations, in a protest of sometimes excessive emotionality and brutal force. An intense treatment of line-tone-volume texture and choice of Expressionist and Surrealist visions (with almost no Surrealist pictorial objects, however, and without the Surreal handling of space) ren-

dered his creations provocative and soulfully demonstrative. Elinson's work of that time could be described by the untranslatable Italian word *terribilità*. The occasional overpowering of form by message is perceived in these pieces, along with an occasional antiaesthetic abuse of picture-space, overcrowded with figures and objects. Elinson's bitterness, however, was often profound, and his dense, refined, and vigorous penwork (he operates almost exclusively with a felt-tip pen), featured successfully the juxtaposition of unbroken lines. His distinguished graphical gift led him to improve on the technique of some previous modernist masters in handling reflected light. As his work progressed in the United States, form-conscious arrangement assumed an increasingly significant role, with a greater equilibrium of design and emotional power, the result being the justice of form and the punishment of content. Terrifying traits and macabre details will probably, nonetheless, continue to appear in Elinson's drawings, for his work in general seems to be rooted in magic and dark forces of life.

If sexual drive and imagination have always shared a direct connection with art, then Elinson's works clearly portray the struggle between masculine and feminine elements, with the masculine being the stronger force. In the artist's recent iconography, this compelling sexual inspiration transcends its original and frequently too exuberantly developed relation to mythological sources. It transcends, furthermore, certain conscious and unconscious psychological impulses, in an expression of great intimacy. The man himself does not appear often in Elinson's imagistic work; it may be that he blends allegorically with the horse, bull, or abstract, quasi-geometrical phallic figures. Throughout the work the image of the adult woman pervades the scene, sometimes simply appearing in the allegorical ovals of the female genitalia. In the artist's formalistically best drawings, however, the "evil of sensuality" is largely expressed by the innermost aestheticism of the surface, especially by the subtle texture of lines, yielding both linear and painterly effects. Consequently, in Elinson's vision, the sexual (as wrongly equated with "pornographic") is, as a matter of fact, not explicitly sexual; in his more expressly symbolic works, the nude figure becomes in effect the metaphor of pure form. The conflict is further resolved in the more tranquil, slow-moving compositions, in which many small forms are "melted" into one great form-block of bodies, sometimes of almost early Romanesque solidity.

Although Elinson does not consider himself a religious man, there is in his work an ever-perceptible mythico-religious background; thus, his thaumaturgic intentions cannot be disregarded. There is also a sense of *tremendum,* and of the eclipsing *maiestas* in some of his drawings, two sentiments capable of shocking the spirit of this believer, upon finding himself in their presence, and inspiring the terror of the sacred—a strange word, indeed, to apply to the work of an artist who has been educated in an aggressively atheistic society.

It is not easy to characterize Henry Elinson's highly inventive work in the context of already existing stylistic categories or to find for him a precise place in twentieth-century art. Occasionally I see him as standing somewhere between Max Ernst and Ives Tanguy. To the integrity of their calmer vision, Elinson brings his evident speed and fire. In an undefined, white, open space he obsessively creates the ensembles of pregnant images within images. However great his fascination with the unconscious, his aim is to build a new alternative artistic reality. A virtuoso of tonal texture, Elinson achieves with his large-size drawings a variety of multi-dimensional sculptured effects. His work manifests organic talent, a quick mind, original vision, and broad technical erudition.

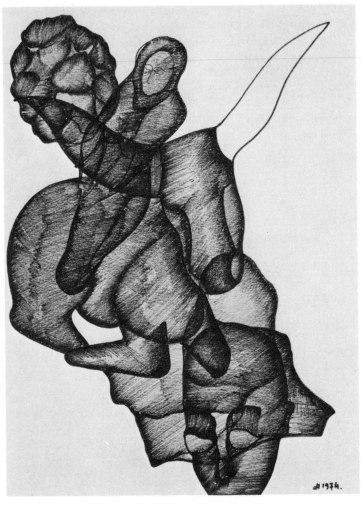

Untitled. Black-and-white felt-tip pen drawing, 14″ × 10″. (Private collection) 1974

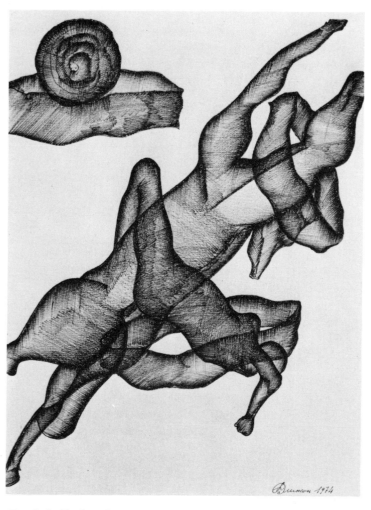

Untitled. Black-and-white felt-tip pen drawing, 14″ × 10″. (Private collection) 1974

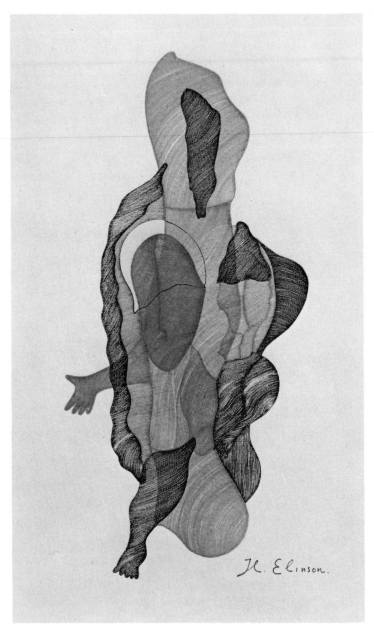

Untitled. Felt-tip pen drawing on beige paper; the colors used: black, reddish brown, green, and yellow; 18″ × 9″. (Private collection)

Let Islands Drawn. Illustration to the poem by Henry Lyman. Black-and-white felt-tip pen drawing, 22″ × 13″. (Private collection)

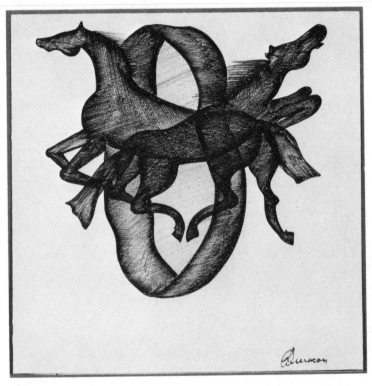

Untitled. Black-and-white felt-tip pen drawing, 8″ × 9″. (Private collection)

Church of St. Olev, Tallinn, Estonia. Felt-tip drawing on greenish gray paper; the colors used: bluish black and brown; 25″ × 19″. (Private collection) 1974

Untitled. Black-and-white felt-tip pen drawing, 15″ × 19″. (Private collection)

Untitled. Black-and-white felt-tip pen drawing, 21″ × 15″. (Yale University Art Gallery) 1975

THE STYLE OF OUR COWARDICE

A Sequence of Psalms

ANDRE LEFEVERE

AUTHOR'S NOTE. *These "psalms" are part of a larger, as yet unpublished sequence. They are modeled after a few little-known poems by Brecht. Other influences are shown in the epigraphs:*
—Irony is the style of our cowardice. (John Updike)
—And wit depends on dilatory time. (Othello, II, iii, 373)
—And David danced before the LORD with all his might; and David was girded with a linen ephod. (II Samuel 6:14)

The psalms are, on one level, a meditation on Gödel's second theorem, "which showed that it was pointless to try to discuss the consistency of a language in that language itself" (cf. Popper, Conjectures, 269). In other words the consistency of life can only be discussed in terms of death. Its presence provides meaning and motivation for the two basic human activities which are, in reality, one: love and creation, which are always shaped by words, even if they go beyond them in the end. So does death.

On another level these psalms are an experiment in form. I wanted to try to say something in a more discursive way about things transcendental without (necessarily) becoming (too) hermetic, mystical, bombastic, abstruse, sentimental. I also wanted to emphasize the transcendental power of the comic, which is so much more than a temporary shift from the norm. Hence the shifts in diction. I hope they are disturbing.

The aim of these psalms is summed up most concisely in Psalm X:

>   *The promise of deliverance.*
>   *Eye to eye in the stark and final knowledge of killer*
> *and victim before the blow.*
>   *Emboldens our waiting as You stalk Your prey,*
> *hunter of hours, irrevocably Yours and rejoicing in the very heart-*
> *beat that marks Your progress.*

—A.L.

PSALM I

There is so little left to say that only poets can be trusted not to.

Words are when death conceives in us, low and halting, but steady too, barely but clearly louder than our anticipation.

We listen half entranced and half in fear and almost confident.

Pull on the thread with infinite care, unravel a life as they phrase it towards You.

PSALM II

Our dubious calling is to remember, articulate the limbs and joints of time.

In words smooth as the hands of Isis that brought form back, and name, to the scattered dead.

Praise the sacred agony, the ransom paid for days assembled to a final shape unchanging.

Free.

PSALM III

We know we should wait, in the patient silence of belief, until Your word comes to us.

Nurse it inside and teach ourselves to speak it in the slow stammer of the child.

It has meaning only when it has grown ours to share, a power only in submission, a learning only in defeat.

PSALM IV

But our ears turn inward in time unworded, and the hollow grows inside.

Until we ring our anguish shrill and brazen like a bell and when the string of pathos snaps we are left behind.

Wizened and almost sober in the clear, cold, cruel silence of faint ridicule.

And sit fragile among things loud now in their power.

PSALM VII

The rites of revelation, rehearsed, rephrased, for ever re-enacted as our hands move over them and our tongue in desire.

We fashion them from hope and shame and limpid in delight they dance for us the secret, sacred figures of fulfillment.

Do not weigh them: they have no center but in You.

And forgive us our posturings: truth will bear silence only, fear breeds words in us.

The fierce and flawed pathos of revolt that rises up against You, half-unbelieving, splendid and futile in self-intoxication and soon shriveled in bland embarrassment.

And the thin, cool, defiant, dissecting voice that speaks from gangrene fascination.

We have been delivered unto Your presence from our mother's womb.

And Your presence has split our soul. There are many now, in the mansions of our mind, Your creatures that will speak to You in different tongues, and speak by Your leave only.

In our lease of days our words are at Your mercy: the smallest of all mercies: speech.

PSALM XI

The worst is in the waiting, when day speaks all and night Your word grows light unheeded.

Like a child its toy You give us back our brain at every dawn, scarred with Your seed, the womb sleep swells with Your power.

Cauterized in the red reprieve of waking, hours of flaccid reason and far-off voices.

A gentler world behind the veil that is Yours alone to lift, dark lover.

Master of Illuminations.

PSALM XIV

Only when the knife is in and blood drawn will the dying gather all their self, and renounce.

Only when pierced through the mortal slit, pared down to the bone, one for ever and never more in the ghost-white flame of knowing.

And gone the marvel in simpler light full-bodied and uncaring that gently joined their softer selves.

Will lovers shudder, and withdraw.

PSALM XV

The day a simple love has run its course and will begin to haunt the memory and breed pretense between light seen and light remembered.

The sore, always expiatory smile, the frail and awkward tenderness of the defeated, the fierce and vain attempts to forge lust back into the mold of innocence.

When the simple time is past You have either set us free and stripped us for Your labor:

To break the grip of fear that stifles us in pretense of possession, and shape our giving towards Your liberty.

Or we stand naked, captive, despoiled, condemned to stage our sorry fight unto the death to disculpate the trapped, the bitter, the bound, the beholden.

Or the simply lost in harsher confidence that used to call down gods and will not be undeceived.

PSALM XVI

In submission of the flesh we pray to her, Your Lady of the avid arms.

Praise her in the toil of tongues antiphonous, Your Lady of the broken cries.

Who pries on our desire imperious, Your Lady of the halcyon eyes.

Prizes us, Your game well-kept, Your Lady of the scathing smile.

Preys on us, Your Lady of the shackle-thighs, plays us to Your tune unending, whoremaster eternal and virgin bridegroom of her wiles.

PSALM XVII

In fear of You he acts his share of the pretense, Your beast of death, Coyote, knows she doesn't know and soulfully prepares to play the part again, honest and faithful, the pendant virtuous to his more fashionable emanation:

Passionately adulterous, dazzlingly virile, touchingly childlike, conscience-panged, even guilt-ridden, if need be, and full of deep post-coyotal philosophy.

The blessings of cliché afterwards, when the great mystery dissolves in tired mascara and we are alone, naked under our goose-bumps.

The glorious sin perfunctory and procreative.

He knows she's crying now, aimless until time in his mercy shall fill her life again, until he suspends time again.

But for him time Your henchman has no mercy, Coyote mute and quite convincing in his dumb-show, in the long ambush of months a lone survivor.

PSALM XXI

It's the Hoover.

Coyote's irredeemably naked answer when she, too, insists on trivializing the superanimal mystery with the apparently ineluctable:

Why do you love me?

The Hoover and his tongue adjustable moves gently over and over every inch of the skin newly acquired.

The ultimate charm against technology's discreetly lethal instrument of domestication.

And when she does not understand he sucks from her harsh and unrelenting the bittersweet pleasures the mind erects defiant on the flesh resigned.

PSALM XXVIII

The Aztecs, she says, rolling over, it's fascinating what you read about them, especially the sacrifices, these people willing to die that the sun might live, this almost erotic attitude, *Liebestod*-like if you see what I mean, these young women watching the sun rise, all white and gold like a young prince coming for his bride, their bodies washed and anointed as if for love, shuddering under the touch of his rays as they climb the stairs, and pearls of glistening sweat strung around their nakedness as they stretch out on the altar, waiting for the knife.

But Coyote merely pats her by now well-oiled rump with the mechanical tenderness that is a tribute to passing years.

Then trundles off to get the cold beer that alone bloats the ego of a man.

Waiting for the knife.

PSALM XXX

At times we think unaccounted they uncoil, lean under our hands, the women we prize.

We proceed to possess them with great economy of words wizened and caresses worn thin and sharp like the seducer's floret that could draw blood at every stroke.

Test our strength in stealth against an abrupt thigh until stiffened brittle, firm under pressure in glorious diffidence we enter the time-governed spasm towards the half-life-drained moment.

Nearer to Thee?

But from the peace You resurrect a hand half apologetic to sketch the shapes of absence on the skin they shed with us.

The women we prize, smooth and coiled to kill as time runs empty in their eyes.

PSALM XXXII

As soon as she closes the door behind him, brave as nails.

(They will, he hopes, fade from his flesh in time.)

The web of feeling opens wide as the city Coyote tries to escape in, but every footstep sets a thread vibrating back to the neutral place.

Not allowed to grow in their imagining.

To be kept blank by mutual consent and safe, they half expect to hope, from the heart.

PSALM XXXVI

Her body on the stretcher in the corridor outside the emergency ward.

A sheet thrown over it with the lighthearted efficiency we lavish on those who will go on, after all.

A foot sticks out and on the toenails the color of dried blood.

Later, when she comes back to him, desperately cheerful and adamantly unapologetic.

What does he give her, what does he tell her?

You would not smile on her and the earth would not close over the body he would not touch and the world that would not release her fills her mind he would not enter.

A life for a life he knows as she forces his arms around her.

Cruel suppliant she will not rest until she drinks the love she was no part of, eats the life he lived without her, breaks the faith.

Coyote opens his arms to her and his legs in defeat and she comes to rest on him, spreadeagled.

The nails that tore her flesh tear his, the highly fashionable color of dried blood.

She screams triumphant, reinstated in their pain.

PSALM XXXVII

The body knows, of course, long before, in its blind and stubborn way.

Then the slow bending of the mind, the knife-edge rites of delusion and desire.

Until the need is done, distant in guilt and glib in passion.

Never, quips Coyote unflinching from the hollow of his soul, is the help of a loving spouse more sorely missed than in the smooth and spotless making of adulterous beds.

Coyote philanderous impaled in dubious decorum on the blind and stubborn spike fear plants between piteous male thighs.

Not alone in the blood red light under the eyelids, he feels You moving towards him as he stumbles, blind and bitter in the small white cries of passion.

Captive and conqueror deep in trust and frenzy, pain and power in Your moist hollow that holds, anoints, absolves his red root.

No more helpless, endless to the hunt and eaten by Your quarry, but the body healing, of flesh Your promise and Your praise beyond.

Under the eyelids and behind in Your white, silent, unwavering light arcane, light inviolate.

In the still rounded radiance untouched keep the faces of love.

Crystal and whole at the root of sight.

PSALM XXXIX

My shaping, my smooth, my subtle, my smitten, my sleek, my stealthy, my silken, my soft, my secret, my shameless, my supple, my shining.

Love of my blood, my beginning always.

Redeemed from the froth of time in holy mid-point mating.

Mortal and marble as the great vaults we build to circumscribe Your mystery:

The craven desire, the fearful delight, the bond enduring, secure, beyond all deeds and their dying enshrined.

PSALM XL

Let me run my poor love softly through your sorrow and hold you.

In the fitful whispering of the defeated, still.

Not attuned to lips that feasted loud on laughter in our predatory days.

Dazzled. Let their shadow be our shelter now, our bold words humbled. But the rites of passion endure.

As always cast in the sting of Death the matrix, the great womb of all our loving.

PSALM XLI

Love is each lethal time we dare usurp Your powers.

Have others entrust us with their days and live them at our mercy.

While we slowly mold towards them the self precarious with the impassioned patience that is the craftsman's.

Until with his quiet pride we can lay it down, ours.

To be ravished in the receiving that ends all things known and husbands us in wonder.

PSALM XLII

We must not speak in anger of Your savage loving, the awesome glory of Your claiming her unyielding in the rape of blood and final paroxysm of hands that close around the throat.

For Your harsher peace in fear and redemption consummated.

These are poor words of ransom for what must be saved from all this gloating, pain and squalor:

Her crystal loveliness translucent now in our days of genteel impotence and slow surrender.

(The peace that rots in shrivelled expectations.)

The smooth grace of her limbs, the bright and conquering joy of her unfolding mind.

May Your earth rest lightly on her: her body left her soul behind.

PSALM XLVII

By Your leave a subsidized practitioner of verbal homeopathy, a doctorer of words, slightly bored in academic corridors and sparingly bestowing a wicked avuncular nod.

Epitome of centuries, footnote to a period.

Coyote prescribes the painless cure of jargon for those infected with belief.

Teaches others the self- and state-preserving use of sacred platitudes.

Serves all comers now and prostitutes—frigid in gaudy robes—the books that beat their power in his blood.

Sets exams and signs degrees, an agent in this troubled world of social prophylaxis.

Titled and mitred and dispensing to all and sundry the dubious and decisive honors of the certified mind.

There is a sad similarity between teaching and sharpening pencils: both essentially pointless and subject to the law of diminishing returns.

PSALM LII

Not really like a summer's day nor does she walk in beauty all that much.

More like a duck, in fact, paddling hectic on the surface of our sullen days.

Half awkward, half in earnest, trying to make up in movement what she lacks in grace.

Busy getting busy.

Her face a thousand changing shapes on running water.

Careless in generosity and with the short and hollow daring of bravado ruffling every feather in a world of whitened swans sedate.

A mildly irritating, mildly moving presence.

Rather lovable, after all, and no doubt radiant in the passion that has been lasting up to now only in the books she reads with half a mind.

As soon as she can find the long dull courage to orchestrate in patience the sparkling cacophony of all her safe discordants:

The endless blackmail of promise unredeemed in voracious submission that absolves of all responsibility.

And be sound.

PSALM LIV

Words break on her eyes transparent, luminous with the cold sparkle of too many things seen through.

Touchstones untouchable that seal the fragment world behind.

Bits of it break through the looking glass sometimes and she tastes them on her tongue until they vanish again into that world of divine ennui where great Achilles, among others, leans for ever on his broken shield.

PSALM LX

This night he nurses it on his tongue, his unbelief, the word the bombs have sprung on him.

Coyote tries to soothe it back from blood and mangled death to white sheets antiseptic.

His hand can move still to write and fear is whole still in his limbs and anger still alive and stringing lines in horror and in pain.

A charm around his sanity.

The paper gauze-blood-soaked and patient still absorbs impartially the outrage and the indignation: the bombs, the bullets and the words we wear against them, razor-thin.

PSALM LXIII

If they don't make too much fuss I give them a drink, or a cigarette, even though it's against regulations:

Identify target, gain admission to target's dwelling, subdue and eliminate.

It's pitiful how fast their words disintegrate.

Threaten, cajole, offer, plead.

Then raw animal sounds and silence after the last ludicrous contortions.

The unfreed You catch self-blinded in the gap between fear and faith Your coming closes.

PSALM LXVII

For Rembrandt a Dutch peasant girl, appropriately potato-bellied, or a prostitute maybe, mildly bored with meaning.

The ropes an afterthought.

Languid and long-legged for Delacroix and from the way she wears her chains obviously trained to cater for the less obvious taste.

Or in Hopkins chastely disembodied.

Sonnets only for the victims, or sketches allegorized, a footnote to the Perseus myth, a waste of canvas space.

We have seen her so often, walking through our streets, and today for the last time, Andromeda.

The perfect martyr: body and mind bound by the spell of fear, the good the mighty conjure up for us in their image, and the evil.

No chains for her, no ropes, her will is theirs, her body resplendent, empty, the shell of state the arrogant in power fashion with great care and without a thought abandon.

The fatal bait for monsters, for princes the perfect prize.

We could shatter it so easily, if we dared live outside the pretense of its protection:

The high deeds of our heroes, who did not stir when she was claimed.

The courage of our soldiers—the king her father used to count them for her, and they roared her name in anger when he drew his sword.

Our holy priests—and smooth their words that lower the heads of kings, and their swords.

The king her father in his wisdom and her mother the queen counting the children of ripening years.

The wine on our tongue and the coins we break our teeth on in the market place when the sun warms our bones as well as theirs.

PSALM LXIX

The days grow drier as he counts them, and shrink

The sun's red rim around them is the margin that widens between time reclaimed and time left fallow

In it Coyote writes his words shrunk to their just measure, one by one, the days we cede to the rhythm of the heart

And it will be as when we lie still, love, our life all spent and conceived again, recast in the perfect white moment, the mold Your chisel breaks

Open and we stand revealed again in time a presence, in pain a witness, and a pledge of joy

We are as raw silk stretched on Your loom, dyed in Your colors, fashioned on bodies to strengthen their beauty or shore up their decay, torn into rags and discarded, transformed

Let our words be like water running through a valley; it sustains the plants, and the trees, the animals that drink from it and men who draw from it

Let our lives be like water running through a valley, now and in the hour of our death.

LA BUENA FORTUNA

IPPY GIZZI

Señor Ramon Idalguez lived on the fourth road of the town Portales just outside of the aluminum mine with a bright light hanging over his tin house, which he had to perpetually reinstall. The front of the house was incomplete yet terminated, as though the burnt smell of a dog exuded from it, with dilapidated, shutterless windows that seemed once to have danced all night, but now danced no longer. A brief interlude with the track car system had once changed his life, but it was a momentary flame that moved out as quickly as he had wanted it to move in.

When the tracks of the system were abandoned after four years Señor Ramon grew the national flower between the rails and he took down a small gray bell which read "welcome travelers" from his door and he pressed it to his heart. The distance of his life from the real world frightened him and he lived in a continuous frenzy to secure an area of life before it had gone entirely out of his way. He could only understand the most rudimentary relations; and he had once spent several years trying to induce an affair.

What Señor Idalguez appeared to think was real reached him over a great space and he appreciated every idea which he received, understanding the distance it had to travel to reach his own poor, bent house. The way the sun rose and set aroused him, and he hung a silver charm over his bed to stimulate his nerves. At night he prayed for the liberation of his country, for the health of the poor, the patriotic, and the face of God.

There was only one prayer of Señor Idalguez's that stood apart from the others, although he never recognized anything indiscreet in the prayer or the rejoicing thereafter. Señor Ramon had devoted one or two weeks to the construction of the prayer during which he weeded between the two rails of the track and watched his hands bleed impulsively at the cemetery where his mother had died. There was one particular verb in the prayer which meant the most to him, and on the night that he chose it he clasped his hands together very tightly with no intention of ever opening them again, as though a small bird had lived and died inside. The prayer had twelve words in it and each word was pure. At the end of the prayer he said "Ramon Idalguez" with somewhat the same purpose as autographing one's name on a dark wall in the world in a city where one wants to be respected and liked, but fears the impossibility of both.

Ramon Idalguez was frightened of how long his body was, and of how prostitutes walked. He preferred to receive the ideas of the world, which he so much wanted, while he was sitting down. Several years passed without the collection of anything new. He prayed that Marta Torres would come crawling back to him like a worm.

Ramon Idalguez was born during a partial solar eclipse in 1913 at the edge of a local vineyard, seventy miles south of the town Portales. There had been an abrupt shift in winds and the main vines turned a color which the local peasants claimed did not exist anywhere else naturally. For several days afterwards Ramon Idalguez's mother wore the same lavender dress she had given birth in and held her suspicion that Ramon would die. His father put a shrine at the edge of his third of the vineyard and urged his wife to plant geraniums around it. Inside the shrine was a letter to the heavens that requested Ramon's life. Ramon lived and grew and went away.

When Ramon was thirty-five he worked in the aluminum mine in the town Portales and voted for the track car system and met hundreds of men and women and eventually introduced himself to Marta Torres. She was wearing an aqua dress and shoes with open toes but that was three years ago. Now he had only one photograph of Marta and he kept it in a drawer of linen in a cardboard folder. The folder was smaller than the photograph, and the bottom half of the photograph, which was of Marta's legs, extended beyond the cover. Ramon sometimes felt inclined to look at her legs, which

he could see immediately when he opened the drawer. He was devoted to memories of the past, and to the idea that it was bound to happen again. His life had the direction of a man looking at a map to relocate a small, joyous road he had once taken during a brief holiday.

Marta Torres was not a physically young woman when they met but she had the youthfulness of women too simple and too good to deviate from the delicate, conventional form. She had three years of primary education and some natural gift as a hairdresser, unless, she said, the hair was too coarse and resistant to curl. Curly hair was, she felt, an essential facet of beauty. Her own hair was curled constantly. It was a gift she expressed freely, especially to Ramon, after they met. Ramon first saw Marta when she was thirty-six, holding uncertainly to her place in the track car, in 1951. No matter how abruptly the car stopped or started he felt compelled to watch her. He thought of this large, clean woman transported in the car over tracks which seemed at times so thin, so unprepared, but were, he knew, industrially sound, far past the hovel of the mine where he would disembark, and on to the hair salon, which, he imagined, was filled with rows of imported rubber flowers and gels. He was, he thought, certainly accomplished in this way. In one way or another he always triumphed over the mundane. He was always able to perceive a ritual.

Ramon Idalguez could always remember Marta's hair, for whatever it was worth, on whatever night of his life. Her hair was thick and red and she wore a calico scarf that sometimes fell down and blew around and around her neck. Her neck was thick and proud in a way that suggested an ability to horde conversations. On most of the occasions that Ramon could remember she had worn red shoes and a red florentine belt also. Their infatuation increased daily, long after the sun had set on the aluminum mine. Marta Torres was a Catholic woman with exaggerated lips.

Ramon and Marta had only kissed three times, but Ramon had a mental diagram of each kiss. The first had been slow and slight in any romantic aspiration. It was the second kiss that was the most successful. It lasted for a long, intense time near a vegetable stand in the summer. In the larger context of Ramon's life now it had become an anomaly. It was something he respected with the awe that one reserves for events in another person's life. To keep moments like this alive, Ramon re-enacted the kiss as though it were a scene from a film he had once seen. Marta was not a flirtatious woman then, and she had been simpler, with an acute sensibility of guilt and a desire to learn obliquely just like Ramon. In fact,

they had so many things in common they were overwhelmed not to have met before.

Marta was stronger now, and quite beyond what she had once been for Ramon. She had a revulsion for the commonness of her last name now, and a duplicitous way of receiving two men at the same time at opposite ends of her house. She developed a habitual sympathy for burlesque and a problem of overweight that increased proportionately to the men in her life. In short, she fancied she was an unusual woman who had blossomed out of an ordinary lot. Certain kinds of men encouraged her to believe this, and she sought them out.

The town Portales had eleven streets which ran vaguely from east to west. They were unpaved and uneven but arranged according to some borrowed municipal plan; the streets exposed rather than connected lots of space. There was one theater in the town Portales and one club, one post office, two markets, a pharmacy, and a picnic area situated in the hollow of a dead volcano which could only be reached by bus. There were three other volcanoes which rose over the town, all of them dead.

One morning Ramon went to the post office to mail a letter to a second cousin twice removed. She was a bland person, whose nephews were purported to have started a lacquer factory overseas. When he reached the post office after several minutes of walking he found a boy loitering in front selling eels. A few flat domestic flounder had been mixed in. "Eel!" he shouted into Ramon's face as if Ramon's face were a long alleyway with palm fronds that made the travel of sound impossible.

"No fish today," Ramon said. When he came out of the post office he saw that the boy was lying on his back in the gold dirt holding in his stomach so that it made a hollow the size of a soup bowl. "You see how hungry I am," he said. "Buy my fish."

"Let out your breath," Ramon said, "it's a waste of time. Some days, I'm always hungry." He turned around to walk away. Around the post office the dirt was gold and there were pepper trees that dropped spots of shade.

The boy ran in front of him and lay down and made the hole in his stomach again. He left his fish cart standing under a tree. "God, can't you see how hungry I am!" he said.

"Well, eat your fish."

"But I'm hungry for something else. For the love of God I'm hungry."

"Well, we're all hungry for that. One is always hungry for that."

The boy stood up and began to wander around Ramon slowly in what seemed a necessary dance to relieve a certain source of pain. He had a tiny pinched waist lassoed by a yellow bandana and miniature hands and feet. The boy said his name was Jalisco de la Frontera. The edges of his eyes were round to a voluptuous point, with a black globular hesitancy. His lips were very thin and sweet and plain.

"Señor," he said, "there are so many fish there under that tree. How many do you want? Do you know the love of God?"

"Well," Ramon said, "that is something I do know." He looked up at the high breach of sky where there was a full moon placed in the daylight. "I'll take one or two," he said.

"The love of God," the boy said, and he took Ramon by the hand over to the cart under the pepper tree where it was very moist and green and shaded as if they had moved under water. He held a large eel up in front of Ramon. "The meat is very white," he said, smiling, "like chicken."

"That's a good eel."

"This is a splendid eel. Two eels in one!"

"Here," Ramon said, and he dropped several coins into the cart. "A very good eel."

Jalisco de la Frontera put the coins into his bandana. "Thank you very much. You're very kind," he said, his face exuding a strange earnestness.

"Thank you," Ramon said. He walked out from the humidity of the tree. "It is my pleasure." The insides of his legs did not touch as he walked away. The fish was in a small paper cradle and Ramon pushed it affectionately into his side. The town was very quiet, and the walk home would be short and well lit with nothing to cast a shadow. Water from the fish began to drip down his leg. When Ramon saw his house in the distance, and how pushed to the side it looked, he glanced over his shoulder to find that Jalisco de la Frontera was following him.

"My house is not very good," he said.

"Better than the one that's mine."

"I suppose, I suppose in the eyes of God, our houses are the same."

"Yes," the boy said, "I suppose."

"Do you suppose that, in the same manner, you and I are the same?" He was still holding the fish.

"The same," the boy said, turning his eyes to keep them from reflecting too much light.

The boy Jalisco ran back and pulled his cart out of the shade

and wandered like a flower through the light, through the sprays of artillery fern, until he reached Ramon. "I'm very obliged," he said, "I think this is my first invitation to lunch."

They shared the weight of the fish cart on the way home.

"The first invitation to lunch," Ramon said, when he got to his door, lifting his arms into the sky to embrace the shyness with which so many situations could enter a man's life.

The lunch was very short although Ramon Idalguez thought of every way he could to make it longer. He delayed the time it took to cook the fish because he wanted to absorb all of Jalisco's compliments without being distracted by the flavor of food. Jalisco admired the tablecloth and the plates and the legs of the chair he sat on. He confessed that he already had a sentimental feeling about the way Ramon arranged furniture, and that he would probably have a picture of the house in his mind all his life. After a little while he said that he had, in effect, composed a poem about Ramon's kitchen which he would recite to Ramon later.

Several hours passed and Ramon took a box of chocolates down from a drawer and offered them to Jalisco de la Frontera but he told Jalisco it was a certain kind of chocolate one might find oppressively sweet. Ramon himself felt this was absurd because he thought it was impossible that intense sweetness would ever avail itself to complaint or to one's disadvantage.

"I never had a sin," Ramon said, still wishing that it was lunch time, "that I didn't remember. And you? How is your life?"

"Too short and too long," the boy said, masticating the last chocolate.

"Aren't there some sweet pleasures?"

"This chocolate," Jalisco said, "is sweet enough."

"I see. But your mother, your father, God, your sweetheart. How about them?"

"No family," he said, "no sweetheart either. I have a seat saved for me in the pews."

"I see. No family. But then, what do I have? You might," Ramon said, "live here."

The boys eyes lit up and began to water.

"Impossible to be so kind!" he said, breaking the sentence in several places. "So kind, God!" he whispered, turning his head to show Ramon the number of tears.

"For the love of God," Ramon said. He pinned a small carnation to the boy's shirt. "And your fish cart, should we leave it outside?"

The boy knelt down and kissed Ramon's feet. Ramon had to control a desire to give him a silver chalice he had hung in another room.

"Of course the fish cart isn't mine any longer," the boy said, "it's yours."

"So many eels," Ramon said, and he began to count them with his hands.

"What room will I have?" Jalisco asked.

"This room," and they went into a room to the left of the kitchen which opened on a long hall. The silver chalice hung over the bed, but since it had never been polished it gave only a dull unpleasant glow. "I'm so obliged," Jalisco said, and he kept running his hands over and over the cloth of the old bed.

"I must rest now and thank God," he said, and he climbed into the bed with his clothes on except for the bandana which he took off, letting several moist chocolates fall to the floor.

"Well, we'll say good night then, until later?" It was not yet four o'clock in the afternoon.

"Good night," said Jalisco de la Frontera, "this is very nice."

The boy slept for several hours during which at even intervals Ramon Idalguez peeped into the room so that he could admire how well Jalisco slept. He noticed that the boy had put the carnation through the chain of the chalice so that the chalice supported it, but hung gently towards the bed.

That night Ramon Idalguez could not sleep. He rolled over on his thin bed so that he could face the wall which joined their two rooms. The wall was painted violet and it had no pictures on it. "My little Jalisco," he said, feeling himself float towards the future. He had the idea suddenly to go out into the yard and choose some flowers for the table at breakfast. "Good night Jalisco de la Frontera," he said into the wall.

When Ramon Idalguez stepped out into the night Marta Torres was standing in his yard. She seemed to be humming or singing, and he realized that she must have mistaken the window of Jalisco de la Frontera's room for his own.

"Marta," he called, smelling a disagreeable cloud of fish. He thought to advise her to stop singing under that window because he had company there, but he did not.

"You see how long I've waited for you, Marta. You look nice tonight. Your hair, is it still red? It's just the way it used to be. How nice. I haven't forgotten you, Marta." Ramon did not know if he wanted Marta Torres back any more. He did not feel any

external flame or urge directing him, and he trembled to see the powder that covered the details of her face.

"Ramon," she called, "I've come back." Her voice was vague, as if Ramon had brought her out of a distraction. Her eyes were very bright and high in her head and the skin around them perspired.

"But so much has changed, Marta. You'd better go away." He noticed her looking up at the window of Jalisco's room.

"You don't even remember my own window."

"My jewel," she said.

"I'm no jewel Marta, not any more."

"Oh no," she said, "Ramon is my jewel. It's what I always say. If there were more jewels like Ramon."

"Your dress is too tight, Marta."

"But it's silk, Ramon."

"And your hair—is it still red? I can't believe it!"

"They still call it red," she said, and she pulled off a calico scarf that showed how her hair had been curled many times and that her forehead was slightly foreshortened.

Marta walked several paces closer to Ramon and screwed up her face. "Don't you want me any more, Ramon?" she said. Behind his house, on a slant, there was an orchard from which a tin can began to roll. He had planted the trees there himself in rings of plaster.

"Now I can see that I hate unexpected visits," he said.

"I'll come back tomorrow, Ramon."

"Yes, come back tomorrow around twelve o'clock. There is some eel we can eat."

He went into the house, but he could not sit down anywhere because Jalisco had gotten up and moved all of the furniture into his room, and the only rug, and the two tables, and the few books. There were not even the religious portraits hanging on the walls.

"What is happening?" he said to himself. He held his head up and he went into Jalisco de la Frontera's room. "Do you see me, Jalisco," he said, "I have a great decision to make." He looked around the room and saw how it had been stuffed clumsily with all the objects of his house. "Help me," he said.

Jalisco de la Frontera held out a small perspiring hand to Ramon. In the twilight the zone around his mouth was illuminated with the light of his large teeth. The sheets were twisted around his body where he had turned and turned several times never alternating direction. Under the sheet Ramon saw the two dark

mounds of Jalisco de la Frontera's shoes. "La buena fortuna,"
Jalisco said. With his index finger he began to rub the enamel on
his front teeth. "Does good fortune always run out? I must yield
to the will of God. Have mercy! Have mercy!"

Ramon Idalguez told Jalisco to be very still so that he could hear
the mysteries that were traveling along the bittersweet bloom of
Ramon's life. A long way up on the exterior walls a bird was singing even though it was the middle of the night. "This is so hard,"
Ramon said. He felt through the obscurity for Jalisco's hand. His
hands bobbed for a while in the darkness and then drew back,
unaccompanied. "Hard, hard. Do you know what I'll have to do?"
He went over to the wall and turned on the light. "I'll have to
break a woman's heart! Ave Maria!" He fell down on his knees and
the light in the bulb flickered. "I'm so low," he whispered, "so
low down." His old suit crumpled into a shapeless mass that bore
no resemblance to himself and, even in the light, had no pattern
to divulge. Jalisco de la Frontera stretched out his hand which
was very still, always, and moist and solid, and tapped Ramon on
the head. "Tomorrow morning, you can tell me anything," he said,
"but right now, at this moment, I'm still thanking God." He folded
his arms and locked his fingers together on his chest as if he had
half shuffled a deck of cards but suddenly thrown them down.
"Will you put out the light, Ramon?" he said, pulling the sheet up
to his throat.

•

Señor Ramon Idalguez had once had several hundred escudos,
to be exact, E°800 during the spring that he was thirty-nine. A
large portion of the sum had dwindled in the direction of the
younger sister who was studying to be a seamstress in a remote
city. There had been an exaggerated filial pride in supporting this
sister, who drew on every letter she sent the elaborate pattern
of her life in the shape of a gentleman's clothes. Every letter she
sent to Ramon included a blessing and a sketch of Ramon standing
in a tailored suit with tassels and a vest and a pointed handkerchief
in the jacket pocket that made Ramon feel at once young and
old. That was in 1952 when the sister's letters were able to be
oppressively grateful and sweet. But Esmeralda Idalguez had never
gone on to become a seamstress, and Ramon had not been able
to continue sending her money, and she sent Ramon only one
shirt which was poorly sewn and exaggerated his posture in the
worst way.

It was that shirt that Ramon chose to wear in the morning for breakfast with Jalisco. He pinned it in the back at daybreak in the shadows of a platina mirror that hung in the hall. The buttons on the shirt were chintz, with embossed locomotives.

When the emptiness of the house began to gnaw at Ramon he wondered if Jalisco would ever wake up. He arranged the table in several different ways until he was convinced he had found the best one. Jalisco had slept, as far as Ramon could tell, some fifteen or sixteen hours.

The windows of Ramon Idalguez's house faced southeast and there were no windows on any of the other sides. There were twelve windows in all, two for every room. Certain of the walls in each room were perpetually dark. They were a dark cement brick painted a multitude of pastel colors that had been popular from 1950 to 1954, when the track car had operated. The window sills were lacquered with the same paints in a darker hue and while the paint was still wet small items of religious worth had been glued on. There was a statue of the Virgin in Ramon's room on the window sill and a smaller one in Jalisco's room and an almost imperceptible one in a third room. The uneven distribution of light was unforeseen, and Ramon sometimes struck a match to study what he had hung on a wall years ago and by now forgotten. The outside of the house was tin and concrete. Inside, all the floors were cement, or dirt. When Ramon was in love with Marta Torres he had watered the dirt floors with a hose and pounded them down with his feet. Possibly Ramon was still in love with Marta Torres, although now that Jalisco had been introduced into his life he did not know how it could be the same.

When Jalisco de la Frontera came to the table he bowed three times in different directions before commencing to eat. He salted his eggs and flounder so heavily that Ramon had to refill the shaker in the middle of the meal.

"God sent me a vision of the woman whose heart I have to break," Ramon said, looking at the piles of salt on Jalisco's plate. "God sent," he continued, noticing the way Jalisco speared bits of egg and fish through the salt, "a terrible confusion."

"Am I confusion?" Jalisco said.

"No!" Ramon said. "Such congenial lips! An angel!"

"Then we understand one another!"

"My little Jalisco," Ramon folded and unfolded his napkin. "Ramon understands you so well."

"How nice," Jalisco said. "What else is there—to eat?"

"Some sausage? Some bread? Some milk, Jalisco, to drink?"

"A little of everything," Jalisco said, "my stomach is a hole."

Ramon Idalguez put these things on the table with an elongated bowl of fruit. "Some fruit similar to this will one day grow on my trees," he said, "you will be here for that day, God willing."

"Oh, I won't ever leave! I might plant a few trees myself, now and then." Jalisco said the last words parenthetically while he broke a piece of bread in two and glanced at the wall between the two windows where there was a spot of grease. "A dull life is so happy!" he said. "What will we do today?"

"We might go to the matinee. Would you like that? Of course, the cinema could never become a regular habit."

"I see," Jalisco said, "money."

"Oh no," Ramon said, "there must be—some other meaning to my life!"

"Whatever you say and however you say it, there is always love." He looked at Ramon and blinked with a prolonged emphasis. "Have you got some cigarettes," he said, making a tactile gesture with his lips.

"I have never indulged, in my life. In my whole life," Ramon began, clearing off some plates of food, "I just never wanted to indulge."

"Well! I see!" Jalisco said. There was a yellow band of oil around his lips. "Well I call that fate! I'm sixteen," he said, looking at the ceiling, "I must have cigarettes. Now and then, I mean. I don't, how did you say it, indulge in so many other areas myself. Mostly I concentrate on human relationships and love."

"Sixteen! So young! I feel so much older than you. But I agree with you completely. You can get a cigarette at the matinee, anyway."

"What shall I wear? Really! Nothing to wear! Better to dress myself in a sheet, I just realized! What I'm wearing now is just a rag!" Jalisco de la Frontera slumped down from his chair onto the floor. "You don't see me as a boy in rags, do you?" he whispered, holding Ramon's hands by the wrists.

"I see your heart, Jalisco, no matter what you wear. I saw your heart the first time I saw you."

"That was just yesterday," Jalisco said. He turned his face to the side to suppress a yawn. "It was the best day of my life."

"Oh my God, I'm so lucky!" Ramon said. He went over to the window which was over the sink and lifted out a pane of glass. The air blew in slowly, without disturbing anything, but without failing

to arouse in Ramon an image of himself standing in a bright stream of momentary life.

On the way to the theater Jalisco de la Frontera's eyes were black and reminiscent of nocturnal life. The walk was speckled with blank lots of dust and dull ruby-colored signs that advertised the coming of the archbishop. Jalisco sang, with an arm around Ramon's waist. It was a warbling song with a precise message. The message was that a first love is not forgotten. The matinee showing began at twelve-fifteen. In the back of Ramon's mind it occurred to him that he was avoiding something else.

Inside the Teatro Portal were lavender and maroon seats seldom matching from top to bottom, mounted on cylinders of cement with a free odor of urine about them. A fraternity of younger men monopolized the frontmost rows, with their arms slung over the sides. The men were reading magazines they had pilfered at the stand outside. When Ramon walked in with Jalisco's arm around him they turned around in their seats and hooted. Then Jalisco de la Frontera broke off from Ramon, as if suddenly he did not know him or could not place their acquaintance, and hurried through the aisles until he was out of sight.

Ramon felt that a disaster had come over him, in the form of a stunt, and he began to shake. Although it was unbearably hot he buttoned up his jacket. He moved somewhat unconsciously into the first seat he found. When he sank back into the chair the pins in his shirt pricked him in the back.

After awhile he felt that someone was near him, with the intention of talking to him, but who did not seem to be Jalisco de la Frontera. As he turned about he saw that it was Marta.

"I seem to run into you so frequently now, Marta."

"Well, Ramon, I plan it that way."

"Some plans don't work," he said, dulling the shine of his armrest with his thumb.

"God knows," she said, "I have my heart in this plan. May I sit down? Thank you," she said, breathing fast, "I already feel more comfortable."

"Do I encourage you like this?"

"Ramon, I don't need encouraging. It's like this: life comes in, and it goes out. It leaves a strange flower with a man in the middle of it. My Ramon."

"My little Jalisco," Ramon was thinking. "I'm sorry I was not there for lunch, Marta. I had another appointment and I forgot. I only just now remembered."

"I'm not very important," she said, indulging herself in a bag of caramels.

"Last night did not seem real," Ramon said, looking at her sadly. "Perhaps you should make your plans more real."

"Real, Ramon?"

"Yes," he said, "like the movies."

"Is that why, is that why you're here?"

"No, that's not why I'm here. I can't remember why I came to the matinee today. Pure boredom!"

"But your other appointment!"

"It slipped my mind too, Marta. You see, nothing nowadays seems real."

"Well," she said, "at least then it's not really just me."

During the middle of the film Marta leaned over and touched Ramon's shoulder. "Good-bye," she said, as softly as an insect being asphyxiated in a warm summery light. She pulled out an enormous white man's handkerchief and began to cry into it. "Is this good-bye, Marta?" Ramon said the words slowly, affectionately overcome with a sudden desire to embrace in his momentary displacement. "Good-bye?" he murmured. He was thinking of holding her in the corner of the theater with her hair all folded up under the kerchief and the abandoned springs of the theater seats deteriorating in the air. "It's so dark here, I can't see your face!" He pulled her face closer to him with his two hands and spoke into the center of it. "Good-bye," he said, releasing her, hoping that he had imparted an impression of hope, and then later on hoping that he had not.

When Ramon came out of the matinee the crowds around the theater were thin although he combed through them several times looking for Jalisco. After awhile he saw no one he knew and he began to walk home. Just after he was past the theater and the post office and onto the main lot between the theater and the road he had a sudden idea and turned back. "One package of cigarettes," he said, to the vendor. He held the cigarettes in his hand all the way home. He had a nervous apprehension that in some way the cigarettes would become damaged or destroyed.

There were several things Ramon held delicately, imagining how in some way all the strange possibilities of his future might rest on them. Once when he was a child he strangled a canary by holding it constantly in his hand.

In a few minutes, when he got home, he saw Jalisco de la Frontera hanging by his knees from a pepper tree near his house. It was the only tree of any distinction in the vicinity, all the others

were young and thin or dead. The pepper tree grew two or three feet from the tracks in a vertical line. Jalisco made chirruping sounds, and jiggled his arms as soon as he spotted Ramon.

"What an enormous joke I play on people!" he shouted. "So far, I've played this joke on three people. Imagine! Everyone has loved me all the more for it." While he was hanging upside down he started to strum an imaginary guitar on his chest. His eyelashes were black and heavy and made a luxurious line of his eyes. He sang, and when he reached the chorus of his song he looked up into the sky:

The little duck
won't go to the sea
because in saltwater
he can't swim.
O with love's love
love me,
don't use worn-out love
to love me.

"What are you doing in that tree?" Ramon asked, feeling his legs go stiff in his empty yard. Tiny rounded tin plates the size of goat's hooves blinked at him from the foliage of the pepper tree. They were decorations which remained from a party four years ago, which now burnt the light into the eyes of the passers-by.

It was a local holiday party which had somehow drifted into Ramon's yard. He had been very giddy and had danced with Marta until twilight in the yard. The tin plates seemed to complicate the tree in the day, but shone simply at night. It was a wild celebration, although they were the only couple that danced. When they danced he felt the buttons on the back of her dress were very cold, and when he looked at them over her shoulder, phosphorescent. Ramon's friends from the aluminum mine played the mandolin in the orchard and sang rodeo songs.

"What are you doing in that tree?" he whispered, not daring to look Jalisco in the face. He felt somehow that he was smelling Marta's perfume when he got close to Jalisco. "You are damaging the tree."

Jalisco de la Frontera reached up to the limb he was hanging from with his arms and somersaulted around in an arc to the ground. His face was very moist and red and stunned. A small collar of dust flew up around his feet, but then settled down. He put his arms out into the air propelling himself around Ramon like a helicopter. "Don't try to catch a butterfly," he said, turning

his eyes away from Ramon, "except with love. Come here," he said, letting his arms drop. He led Ramon over to the pepper tree and into the circle of shade under it. Ramon saw that Jalisco's hands were small and that the fingernails were black. "Like a child," Ramon said, "your hands are so fine." They knelt under the pepper tree and Jalisco de la Frontera waited for the sound of a cement truck to pass out into the distance. The sweetness from the sage blossomed out from under the pepper tree in small bushes. The desert was very still, but Jalisco put his finger to his lips to warn Ramon of making any noise. "What do you think happens when we get inside?" he said. He looked ahead of him where the bark of the pepper tree was moving with ants. "From now on I sleep in your room by your side. This tree isn't damaged," he said, standing up, "but in here—look in here!" He opened his mouth and pointed his finger down his throat. "My heart aches," he said.

Ramon followed Jalisco into his house and he saw that the furniture had been moved back into place. He saw that Jalisco's bed had been moved into his own room and was side by side with his bed. There was a small plastic figure of the Virgin Mary on each of the beds, resting on the pillows. "It isn't night yet," Jalisco said, blankly.

"This is very nice," Ramon said. There was no light in his room because it was on the north side of the house. He felt vague, and groped for some direction. When it was dinner time he put two plates of fish on the table with Marta's photograph in the middle. As they ate he turned the photograph from side to side.

"What do you think is a good life?" he asked Jalisco, eating the white meat of the fish. There was a bright pink shadeless lamp in the center of the table.

"What?" Jalisco said. "Why ask *me* that?"

"Well, what do you suppose a woman means to a man?" He separated a piece of the fish from the isolated bones.

"La vida y el placer." (Life and pleasure.)

"I feel something more," Ramon said. He blew his nose into his napkin. Outside, a strange bird pecked at the hollow of the pepper tree.

"By now I'm practically your son," Jalisco said, monotonously. "There are probably only certain things we should discuss. You see," he said, with the little flakes of the white fish sticking to his lips, "you see we must be so important to each other."

"That I know," Ramon said. "What should I do?"

"When you look at me, think, that is my son. And put all your

wishes on me. But not your troubles, thank you," he said, picking a piece of the spine out of his teeth. Impulsively he grabbed the photograph and rubbed the oil on his forefinger into Marta's abdomen.

"Dios mío!" Ramon said, "What kind of things you do!" He stood up, with his arms folded to his chest like a bird who had been chilled in the process of moving up a tree. It was dusk, and the light of the desert made the window white and lusterless as if it were painted with the dust. There were streaks of dust on the walls and on the chairs. Ramon moved away from the table. He isolated himself in the middle of the room and had the impulse to lie down and sleep.

Ramon went into his bedroom, which was grey and unlit, with years of powder accumulated in the cement units of the walls. He lifted the plastic Virgin from his bed and put it on the other bed, but then he placed both of the Virgins on the window sill near the Virgin which had become a permanent fixture. Jalisco de la Frontera followed him into his room, carrying in his arms a wooden chair. He pretended not to notice anything unusual and balanced the chair on the top of his head, and sat down on the floor.

"I'm staying in bed for the rest of my life," Ramon said, twitching the beads of his rosary. "Who is that chair for?"

"For Christ," Jalisco said. He stood up briefly and dusted off the seat of the chair with his hand. When he looked at Ramon his eyes narrowed, but his head sank downwards as if it wanted to be obscured. "God knows I've never done anything wrong." His lower lip made a distinct protrusion.

On the outside of Ramon Idalguez's house a vine had begun to grow that had not grown in the town Portales for fifty years. The vine was brought from a great distance, from a town that claimed to have the most delicate landscape in the world. The name of the town was Chimbote, and Ramon had once had the grand illusion of living there. Marta Torres brought the vine to Ramon over hundreds of miles on a warm, dry stinking bus. She held the vine in her hand in a piece of newspaper which she continuously wet with water from a vial. The vine grew around a small pond at a nunnery. After she gave the vine to Ramon she praised him for planting it and idolized him for how well it grew. The leaf was colorless but glossy as something that has just been licked. Inside the liquid was sweet and white and seemed artificial although it was used as a medicinal cure.

"Bring me some of that vine that grows around the house," Ramon said. Jalisco put the chair down and went out of the room, into the yard. Ramon stood up in the twilight and took off his gray coat and hat. Small moths with no instinctive direction beat on the windowpane. He went over to the window and pushed out the bottom glass up towards the sky. The air of the desert shocked him, because it was so still. The moths drifted into the room, illusory.

"Marta," he called out, and his arms groped out into the night as if to illuminate the world with an electric lamp. He knew intuitively that Marta Torres stood in the distance with her hands knotted together.

"Will I see you any more, Ramon," she said. A moth flew by, heavily, with the weight of a bird, past her eyes.

"You see me now, Marta. You see me now. You see how I am? I'm free," he said, rotating his hands on his wrists like a mechanical doll. "You're free too."

"And you have me now Ramon. I'm changed." It seemed to Ramon that she was talking to someone else.

"Is it true, Marta?"

In the dark light he saw more the pure whiteneess of the moths than the whiteness of her face. He rested his fingers on the thin image of the Virgin. They were weightless, and moved lifelessly.

Marta pulled out her handkerchief and began to weave it around her fingers. "It's true."

"Shall we take the bus then and go away?"

Her eyes were bright but tired like lights that shone in a town that was too far off.

"The bus!" Ramon's hands seemed to drift out and cup the black space around Marta.

"Take down your hair," he said, pleadingly.

Her hair fell down in red waves and she touched it. The line of her mouth had been painted uncertainly, in haste. Her lips were too red almost, and too bright. All her hair trembled around her face.

Marta came forward within reach of Ramon's hands by the window. A glaze lit across her eyes. It was twilight still, and her body moved clumsily, as if parts of it lingered behind. Ramon Idalguez could not penetrate Marta's eyes. He had never really been able to. The light there was old and extinguished yet alive. He looked instead at the line around her lips that was painted and made her mouth look crooked.

"We'll take the bus then," he said, but his throat ached and hurt.

"To another town?" Her voice was disappointed.

"Yes," he said, "meet me tomorrow in the morning. Bring what you like, but not too much. Meet me here, in my yard." He pushed the window down and listened to the glass shake between the strips of plywood. The light of dusk threw a strange light on his tin house which extended much farther out than the yard. He realized that Marta was three or four years older than he.

Ramon got into bed methodically and lay down and pulled the sheet up over his head. "Are you in the room?" he said to the walls.

"Yes, I'm in the room," Jalisco said. "I'm in the room, behind the door. Even when you pull down your sheet, you won't see me. You've been so kind to me, really, I just want to stay here. I'll just stay here all night behind the door to be near you. I can watch you all night so that nothing goes wrong."

"Nothing ever goes wrong," Ramon said. He heard the legs of the bird walking over the tin roof. "Good night," he said.

"You've been so kind to me! I love you so much, all of a sudden! I don't care, throw me aside, wound me! You've been so kind to me! Let me show you how I deserve you, behind this door."

"My vine," Ramon said; his face relaxed, soft and expressionless. He saw half of Jalisco de la Frontera's face twittering behind the door and the green vine coming out from his hand like a string. Jalisco had stepped on it until it was flat and the leaves elongated like the ears of a dog.

•

In the morning the first hyacinths of the year bloomed in the yard. There were five. Four years separated Ramon and Marta from the meaningful life of the track car system.

Ramon woke up that morning not by plan or restlessness or motivation even, but from the loud wailing screech of a guitar and the nasal sound of men's voices. There was clapping too, but no pretense was made to disguise the familiarity of the song. It was called the "dance of ill fortune" and it was a song a miner sang when his wife was found with another man. It was a common everyday occurrence since the men went to the mine in shifts and their wives were left behind, vulnerable to men whose shifts were not yet up. It was the song of two men and the tragedy of the graveyard shift.

"How repulsive!" Ramon said, turning his body over on his right side. He moved to get up but collapsed with his face falling into the pillow. He was afraid that as well as the song he smelled eels

being fried up in grease. He counted every eel, and every tomato that was possibly available and then he imagined each one being consumed. A thin shield of perspiration reached out from his body. The singers were reaching the last round of the song, in which the husband, the first man, is crippled by an accident on the conveyor belt in the mine. He loses both his legs during the graveyard shift while he thinks of his wife possessed by another man.

Ramon got up before the song was done because he knew exactly where the end fell and he wanted to see the faces of the singers before it was over. He walked out of his room and down the hall into the kitchen. He wore the same clothes he had worn for three days. When he got to the kitchen he saw Jalisco and Marta there, dancing in the middle of the room. Confetti was strewn all over the floor. There were twelve or thirteen other men, pressed up against the wall, holding plates of food. The atmosphere was dark and oily and nothing Ramon had ever experienced before, in the morning.

"Is it a reception?" Ramon asked. He hoped somewhere in the world someone would hear him.

"Please, of course!" Jalisco said. He swung Marta around so that Ramon would see exactly how closely they danced. There was, in fact, no space between them. Jalisco pushed out his face, beaming. He had a false jade stone glued to his forehead. "Let me just say this: I introduce Señora Jalisco de la Frontera!" Marta twisted her hips as if she were expressing confirmed pleasure. The jade stone came from the frame around Ramon Idalguez's platina mirror.

"Your wife!" Ramon exclaimed, clutching at the lining of his pockets. He stomped his foot on the ground but the confetti was too damp, and embraced everywhere the mud floor. "You say the most ridiculous things! It's always a joke with you. My son!"

"The father, the son, the wife," Jalisco said, putting his free arm around Ramon. "From now on, your life is in our hands. We will do everything for you. A chair," he said to one of the men along the wall, "get a chair for my father."

"By now you're an old man," he went on, "a lot of time has gone by."

"The things I believe in don't happen in a form like this," Ramon said. "I believe in goodness, warmth, charity, and I thank God for all that. Every night," he held up his hand and counted on his short, square shifting fingers, "Monday, Tuesday, Wednesday . . ."

"Old man," Jalisco said, depriving him of any further conversation, "our religious life was so beautiful. But still, everything goes on the same now, except that you're older. Sleep whenever you

want to! You gave me charity and I'm warmth. My wife is a good person too, that you know. 'Martita Lagartita,' " he whispered. (Little Martha-Lizard)

Marta held out her hand to Ramon and pressed it on his palm. "How do you do," she said. The farther he looked into her eyes the less he saw. They were fallow things, two voids in a state of recovery, and although they blinked at him they took their involvement somewhere else. She drained him, by this sudden inversion in her role.

"Congratulations," Ramon said. The men howled out again the chorus of the dance of ill fortune. Two of the men who had guitars Ramon recognized as caramel vendors from the theater. "Well, what happens now? I'd like to know how I fit in a world that no longer even allows me the property of my own house. Maybe I should just say 'get out of here.' " Ramon stood up from his chair. "Get out of here!" he shouted hoarsely. He felt prepared to perceive a collapse as if all of this had been mere pretense and would gladly disassemble itself. Suddenly he could see the men put down their plates and move out the door of the kitchen. They went out effortlessly, as if they had only been there to wish him well. It suddenly occurred to Ramon that perhaps they had been there for those good purposes, and that he was unable, any longer, to perceive good fortune.

Ramon asked Marta Torres if she would wash the dishes and sweep his floor before she left. He felt weak and strong, and wished that the invisible string which he had always imagined connected him to God would nurture him more and give him more strength. He saw Marta and Jalisco standing together in the room as two objects whose immorality he wanted to be simultaneously separate from and close to. "I'm glad this party is over," he said. "It's been such a long one. Clean my house please before you leave. Do me that one favor." He went to the side of the room to get a broom and a pail for water. "It's been too long."

"This is a fine way to treat a son and a daughter-in-law," Jalisco said. He stuck out his chest and held fiercely to Marta's waist with his left arm.

"Take that jade off your face," Ramon said to him, "I don't like it there."

"Well, if that's the way you want it," Jalisco said. He started inching around with his feet until he pushed a cockroach out from under him with his shoe.

"What is that doing here?" Ramon shouted. He squatted down and pushed his face near the cockroach. "Did you find it necessary to include this also?"

Jalisco bent over and picked the insect up with his fingers. After he pulled off all its legs he tucked it under his yellow bandana. It wiggled some but then it was still. "A sign of the times," Jalisco said. "Don't you know what this means? It means you'll have evil here, and dirt to live with, without me."

"It hardly seems that way to me."

"Why doesn't any fruit come off your trees?"

"They're too young, too thin, too—"

"Too lonely!" Jalisco screeched.

Ramon felt both hot and cold as if a long way off in the future he saw that he would be taking a journey and then he realized it was a journey he was already on and he was terrified that he could not see clearly what point he had reached, and that he had come into the journey so unprepared.

"What kind of loneliness isn't worse with a married couple living in the lonely man's house?"

"I see you don't understand a fine thing when you have one," Jalisco said.

"Possibly I don't," Ramon said, "possibly I thought that you and what you have were mine. But in a different way, understand that. And not that it would be all for myself either. One shares or there's nothing."

"Martita Lagartita," Jalisco whispered. He poked her from behind where Ramon could not see, so that she stepped a foot closer to Ramon. "I married her for you," he said, puckering his lips into the soft, familiar roundness of a cherry. Into the cool, dark, confused room he blew a kiss towards Ramon. "You were asleep. Señor! On such an important day! Really, it was meant another way. So I told the priest my name was Ramon Idalguez. He never suspected. You see? No one in this town knows who you are. It's so easy! And so sweet! When you think of it!"

"In that case, it is all very different. I might have expected that from you. I might have known that under all your teasing you were only reaching out to me, giving me a gift. Still, you might have told me right away. You might have saved me so much pain. This morning, for instance, when I woke up, I felt that music eating away at my liver. Please! But never mind. Just explain to me this new arrangement again." He sat down for the second time in his

chair. All this time Jalisco was sitting on the floor in front of him picking out of the dirt a corona of confetti. Sharp little black lines filled up under his fingernails.

Jalisco pulled the cockroach out from his bandana. It made a hard, amputated shield the size of a fifty-peso coin. He laid it softly on the ground in the clearing. All around the house the wind was blowing, dislocating loose fragments of tin. A fine plate of sunlight came through the room from the two windows over the sink. It was by the precision of the light that Ramon knew it was near twelve o'clock. "Don't you care to explain it to me again?"

Jalisco flipped the cockroach over on its back, exposing the segmented underside. "An insect made of so many parts," he said, "just look at that."

"I think, Ramon," Marta began, "that you can kiss me now." She came close and leaned towards him stretching her arms into a circle around his neck. She smelled of the sweet inexpensive almond candies at a large wedding. Ramon seized her and kissed her fiercely on the cheek. She kissed him back, several times, but at such contrived points of his face that it terrified him, because of the implied professionalism.

It was a day however that ended victoriously in Ramon's affairs. It was not a flirtation or an illusory love. The beauty of it was that he felt he had at long last grasped the euphoric consequences of good fortune, and the beauty of the day was that it would radiate a brilliance far forward into his future, and, simultaneously, create some significance out of his dull past. He had reached the point that he knew the Blessed Mary had lifted him towards all his life. Everything had been mere preparation for this.

The arrangement that was made was as satisfactory as possible for all three involved, without the usual delineation of specifics which accompanies an arrangement or the obligatory sense of awe that might ensue. Jalisco was, of course, not impressed by whatever power Ramon represented, and Ramon was grateful that it was all so vague. The arrangement was a kind of open-ended waltz in which three people repeated the same emotional and physical invitations over and over in either direction and tapped out, almost blindly, the same identical responses with their feet. In the arrangement Ramon was married to Marta and Jalisco was their child, although not by birth. Jalisco was, he himself implied, a prodigy, but this was not to say he would not work. Marta would also work, but in some modest domestic sense, since the arrangement made no mention of the word burlesque or of the idea of the Portales Bar.

Ramon would sleep with Marta in one room, and Jalisco's room would fluctuate down the hall. Ramon felt there was no extravagance allowed for in this arrangement that could not be explained fully before God. Jalisco and Ramon and Marta would go to church twice a week and every Sunday and drink tea afterwards somewhere along the road.

The arrangement went on for several weeks like a party that is sustained by the mere detailing of a place setting, or the formality of men who refuse to acknowledge the perspiration along a woman's dress. It was a glossy surface that worked best when there was nothing underneath. Ramon Idalguez was so occupied with the fact that he now had a wife and a son that he spent very little time wondering if it was real. He fixed his eyes on the hyacinths that had flowered in his yard whenever he was uncertain of what to do. He enjoyed the predicament of being a good father and a good husband, although there was something in the relationship between his son and his wife he did not want to understand. Whenever Ramon felt uncertain about the way things were he reminded himself that there were always two other chairs at the table each night and that the food was always served in multiples of three. When he woke up in the morning he could hear Marta breathing just as regularly as he could hear the small handfuls of birds strung out on the electrical wires outside the house. All of this pleasure was, to him, symbolized by the bright yellow of Jalisco de la Frontera's bandana, which he saw as an omen every day.

•

Jalisco de la Frontera went out in search of work for four days and each day he came back his face was whitened by a cosmetic powder he had stolen at the pharmacy in Portal and his mouth turned downwards as if it were being pulled by a hook.

On the fifth day he did not get out of bed at all except to stand in the hallway and exclaim how hilarious life was, and how ridiculous the three of them were in it. He shouted this out at two different times and at the end of the day he called Marta in to cure him of a terrible headache. Marta had been in the room with Jalisco for a long time when Ramon came in. He saw her sitting on Jalisco's bed, squeezing his hand. She dropped it as quickly as she saw Ramon walk in. Marta blushed instantly, as though a fast light were seeking her out.

"Well, do we need a doctor?" Ramon asked. Jalisco began to cough a dry empty cough that had only a strained force to it. Ramon went over to the black wooden dresser with the chipped gold circular knobs in the corner. "We may as well use this," he said. He took a crucifix of palm fronds out of the drawer, "Even though there are already so many under the bed." When he turned around he saw Marta squeezing Jalisco's hand again. Then Jalisco started coughing, the same empty way, wailing his arms over his head.

"Ramon, we might ask you to leave the room," Marta said. All the color had drained from far down in her face. She was wearing a three-piece lavender suit she had been given by a bartender.

"And why that? Do you find something wrong with our life here? Am I so unpleasant, all of a sudden?"

Marta squeezed Jalisco de la Frontera's hand so that he coughed again.

"The boy is sick," she said, simply, "don't you have eyes?"

Ramon circled around the bed and pressed down at Jalisco. He tried to stare closely at his face, to sort out the sickness from the artificial powder. He got very close and was about to say something when Marta pushed him away. "You should be running all the way to the doctor's by now," she said, "you have the responsibility of a family man."

Ramon felt the small burst of flattery that she should phrase it this way. Although Marta almost pushed him out of the room he hardly noticed, thinking only of the final turn in the run to town and the heat and of wearing his weightless straw hat.

After Ramon left the room was all empty with the peace and quiet of two people who are relieved of a tedium. Marta lay down in her suit next to Jalisco and pressed herself into his side. The lavender color of her suit was very subtle, with persimmon leaves embroidered on the hemline.

"That was very good," Jalisco said, "but hardly enough."

"For a young boy?"

"Young boys are not all like this," he said. He held his arm up in the air and flexed it until the thin string of muscles broke out into a small bulge. His face was bright and oily from the exertion. "We've done well so far, but we aren't finished yet; eating a man up is a long job!"

"May God pardon me for the words you use. I loved Ramon once. Ay!" Marta gave a short cry and contracted her legs so that the points of her high-heeled shoes projected over the bed in darts.

"May God forgive me this! For two weeks I've slept in one bed and then another. For a sixteen-year-old boy! I didn't know sixteen-year-old boys like you once." She began to giggle, and wrapped her arms around Jalisco. She got an excruciating pleasure out of holding him, to the point that she had, several times during the past two weeks, stood up from the table just to embrace him. Ramon would blink sadly when this happened and look at his plate. He quickly forgot, however, the things he could not define.

When Ramon came back from the town it was several hours later. He found Marta ironing his shirts with an old iron he had never seen before and a sheet draped over a dresser for a board. She had removed the jacket from her suit so that her breasts were exposed, and, from the side, overwhelmingly large. Jalisco was working behind the house, in a thin, undeveloped strand of orchard. Ramon pulled the doctor into his house by the fabric of his coat. As soon as Jalisco spotted them he ran down from the orchard and into the front door of the house. His whole body was thrown into the shadow of dirt.

"Holy mother of God," he cried, grabbing the two diminutive hands on the doctor. "Is my father sick?" He did not wait for an answer, but began to wipe Ramon's forehead with a cloth. Marta came over from the ironing board and stood in front of the doctor. After she felt she was showing an angle he could appreciate she said:

"My husband is terribly ill." Then she leaned over and whispered into his ear, "I try to keep it from his son."

Jalisco and Marta pressed Ramon down into a chair and Jalisco undid his shoes and began to massage his feet. "Cu-cu-ru-cu-cu," Jalisco said, while he rubbed Ramon's feet, simulating the voice of a dove.

All this time the doctor stood staring at Ramon who did not, in his confusion, respond to anyone.

"Is there a sick boy in this house?" the doctor said. "Because I don't see one." He was irritated and impatient and felt the un-pleasantness of the afternoon heat. He had probably walked half an hour to get to Ramon's house. He looked down at Ramon in the chair and saw that his legs rested in Jalisco's lap and his forehead was being wiped at intervals by Marta. "Someone will pay me for my time, no matter who is really ill. This all seems ridiculous to me."

"Have a little pity at least," Marta said, "my husband is so ill. Here," she said, pressing two bills into his hand. "Now let me show

you out the door. But perhaps there's something you can suggest that I do for him." They went out of the house and stood for a while talking behind the door. When Marta came back inside her face looked ecstatic and enlarged like a flower whose petals have been unnaturally stretched out.

"Well now we know what to do with you." She kissed Ramon softly on the neck and pulled at him by the hands. "The doctor told me what to do with you. A sick man who doesn't know he's sick! Ha! You didn't look in the mirror today, Ramon, did you?"

"No, I didn't. I haven't looked in the mirror lately. I've been too, too happy." He squeezed one of her hands.

"You look yellow," she said. She pulled him out of the chair. "Jalisco, prepare the bed. I ironed the sheets today," she said into Ramon's ear as she led him down the hall.

They put Ramon in bed and told him he was suffering from a mild hereditary disease that was felt in the heart. They gave him several glasses of wine. When he said that he felt no pain Marta said that that was exactly the symptom of the disease. They gave him more wine and told him it would probably pass, in a few days. After a while he fell asleep.

•

When Ramon woke up the next morning he was strapped to his bed with long strips of canvas that he recognized as material he used to mark the trees in his orchard. He called out for Marta and Jalisco and was astonished at how empty the house seemed. After he managed to get out of bed he walked down the hall and through the rooms and into the kitchen but it was completely empty. There was not a single possession of his left anywhere. Only the platina mirror was left on the wall because it had been cemented to the brick. There was a piece of paper stuck to it that said "Good-bye, Ramon" and showed an amateur diagram of three stick figures embracing. A long way off he heard the birds singing, as he had every morning of his life.

OH MANDRAKE!

MAUDE HUTCHINS

Aspice Judas pendu

I
I heard a mandrake
                    scream
I live
I shut my ears and wait
        It is written that
such a one as I who
        hears the mandrake
                    wail
goes mad
I do not care to
I wait
It was not I I reasoned
who did this thing
It is I
who sent away my brown dog
trained as he is to sacrifice
                    himself
for me.
Go home I said brown dog.
Oh Jew, Josephus
It was you who said
                    the dog dies

Carefully I remove my fingers
                    from my ears
And the labyrinthine shriek
                    stays on
an awful memory repeat, repeat,
"And shrieks like a mandrake's
torn out of earth
that living mortals hearing them
                    run mad."*
I do not run
I am not mad
I wait
Silence
A black man stands tall
                    beside me
Is he my shadow?
He speaks
I am he you have wounded
                    he said
Not I, I swear it, I
                    replied
You do what you read
                    he said
being poet.
And you? I said, a
                    shade?
Not at all. Look!
I see a kind of umbilical
as yet attached to his navel
and buried in the ground
                    nearby
How old are you I said
                    astounded
I am Yadúa he said
twelfth century
You have read the Talmud?
Not lately, I said
And Albertus Magnus?

*Shakespeare, *Romeo and Juliet*

Yes.
Pliny?
Of course.
Then take this sword and
   trace three circles on the
      ground
Look to the West! he
     commanded
Oh no you don't I cried
I've read that too
And the powerful smell of your
  leaves will deprive me
     of speech
If you be Yadúa
give me an arrow,
Nameless Jewish commentator
     I said
He did.
I cut the cord
    he died.
I really must go . . .
A beautiful woman stands
     beside me
Even as Yadúa had
Her skin is like milk
I am Moly
Yes I know
And I patted the copy
    of the Odyssey
I carry always in my jacket
I am only a flower
    spare me,
I am tempted. I would pluck you
   but you are for the Gods
     it says here
I am only mortal man
And I whistled for
    my brown dog.

II
Well we're home brown dog
But brown dog speechless
            lifts his nose
            and sniffs the air
            his hackles high
Flavius Josephus
            is at my window
Speak Jew I say, of your
                  Jewish wars
                  and go away
Your dog, he begins
Is alive, I cry, no thanks
                  to you!
Come, he said and I did
Stay! Brown dog, sit!
You will most likely find it
            if you are still interested
At the foot of a gallows
Josephus said in Hebrew
Find what? I said, and I
            am not longer interested
            I long only for sleep
You are asleep he replied
It is a powerful narcotic
What! I yelled
The mandrake! Look you up
but first look you down
I saw the mandrake at
            the foot of the gallows
I should like to present Thomas
            Brown author of
            Pseudodoxia
            Epidemica 1646
said the Jew Flavius.
How do you do I have you in
            paperback I said
It likes the "grease" of
            hanged men

Say semen
Right he said dare
        you look up?
And I saw the powerful
        erection on the hanged man
And at the foot of the gallows
Mola white as milk
Horrified I put the
        book away
        for it is the end.

III
However sleepless
There is more . . . yes . . .
Here's Genesis
Go away I murmur
And take your metaphors
        with you
Is it a small matter said
        Leah
. . . And wouldst thou take
    away my son's mandrakes
        also?
. . . and Rachel said
Therefore he shall lie with
    thee tonight for thy
        son's mandrakes
I am not Jacob!
You do what you read
        said Yadúa
. . . for surely I have hired
    thee with my son's mandrake
. . . thou must come in
        unto me
    thou must come in unto
        me
    thou must come in unto
        me
Mola I sigh
white as milk

And God harkened unto her
said Genesis and
                she conceived.
A kind of cord comes out
of a root in the ground says
a German Jewish commentator
back in my window again.
The cord should be cut
            by an arrow
            I yell
In all respects like a man:
face, body, hands, and feet. Yadúa!
Jacob the fifth son
            said Genesis.
Brown dog where are you?
No longer speechless brown
            dog replies
I am here, master, go to sleep.

SIX POEMS

RICHARD PEVEAR

TWO RUSSIAN GOAT SONGS

1   Intoxication

for Andrei Amalrik

A dark drink of mud and crushed leaves
In water-holes after the squall, the year's end
Comes suddenly, small rain from the sky,
Immense rain from the trees.

Open on all sides to the light now,
There are no more secrets.
Nothing is happening now but
What you see.

No divination in these pools.
Yeasted with earth, black decay
Works at the parings of a rich season.
This is the god's sign: lightness of view

And the heavy breath of the earth. Imagine
What futures the Romans argued for themselves
In the fifth century. In the sixth
Century goats are grazing in the Forum.

2   The Monument at Kuibyshev Transit Prison

So Eden appears,
The same scene taken into
The notched eyes of goats,
The round eyes of children.
But the woman, shading
Her eyes, one hour
And then two hours,
Scarcely moving, saw
Prison and death
Below the green hill.

Three kinds of innocence:
The innocence of sleep,
The innocence of waking,
The innocence of knowing,
Looked into the dark
Of meaningless affliction.

The woman stood
In a hard wind,
A cloudy summer day,
An hour, two hours,
A hand raised, an arm,
A great strain of wings
Broken, broken
And so completed.

This is the monument
Set up for his comrades
By one prisoner
Who looked back, there
Where there is no monument
But the long hill,
The perdurable goats.

BUILDING AS FARMING

The purposeless branches
Of my attention,
A bird somewhere in them
And in the bird's beak

A seed of the music
To re-tune the stones.
Anonymity hides
What labor reveals:

The hierarchical
Moment goes quickly
But leaves the ground turned up
And staggered with light.

AUBERGE DE PEYREBEILHE

Station to station, swallowing
Humble dust, clear water:
We are all on the same way
Though not by some law together.
But you, my scattered companions,
How faint your letters are,
What poor warmth they offer
In a cold month, on a hard bed,
In a strange house. What should have been
Would have been stronger, drawn
To a final meeting and the tongues of flame.
Rain above the tree-line, I remember
A skull of stone, and the last road ends
In air, and happening onto
The Auberge de Peyrebeilhe where travellers
Were murdered in their sleep.

LES ILLUMINÉS

Ice-fields polished by wind
From the mountains behind us,
The frozen ocean ahead, the glare
Of a thin heatless light
Not sun enough
To resurrect the finally dead.
Between here and Kolyma
There is no measurable distance,
From '38 to now
No accountable time. If change is
Motion or mutation, the wind
Is changeless, disembodied, an unmoving
Force exerted equally over
The totality of matter.
On the map the baby face puffs
Its cheeks, the official
Deploys his troops,
New lines of power along old borders.
Not on the map, the small
Fire, the circle of faces touched
By its troubled light.

THE CITY

The city, which labor has raised up, stone
In fountaining arcades, shelters more
Than the builders imagined: moments or sudden
Glimpses of past life,

Their own acts caught in the high traceries,
The architect's blind geometry; birds come
To nest there, martin and swift, their songs
Drift down the roofed air

But fly back again at night as stars seen
To move by a great law—dance, the first sketch
Of the dance floor; place, word, image: history
Roars through the streets,

Up above, balconies and oriels
Guard a strict silence, like the nameless dead,
Like the soldiers who obeyed and were buried under
The stone at Thermopylae

Whose silence says, "We have no interest
In these momentary survivors and their obscure fate.
We rest in the gathering place like
Water in a well."

In the same way, even to ruins, the birds
Return, the flowering vines cling, the bees
Thrive in rough hollows, in perfect chambers
Deposit their honey.

TRUE

JAMES PURDY

Dedicated to John Uker

CHESTER. I've never lied to you, Ewen, never.

EWEN. Oh, you've lied to me from time to time ever since you could talk. Not real lies, little made-up things. But today you see you lied. You lied big to me today. (*He mumbles and shakes his head.*) So as a result I may have to give you away.

CHESTER. Give me away? Why, isn't that what you'd call a threat?

EWEN. I don't need to threaten you . . . You threaten yourself when you talk the way you've been talking. (*Drowsily*) You see you scare yourself.

CHESTER. All of a sudden you are mean to me, after all the years you were good to me. Suddenly you give me the shitty end of the stick.

EWEN (*slapping him*). Don't ever let me hear you use such words. I brought you up better than that.

CHESTER (*whimpering*). You see, you have changed. Threats, slaps.

EWEN. Calm down now . . . There, there. (*He holds him gently on his lap.*) You musn't make yourself sick now . . . Now now.

CHESTER. Tell me how I lied to you.

EWEN. It don't matter. You're my only brother and it don't matter.

CHESTER. I want to be true.

EWEN. Just rest in my arms, why don't you? See, get quiet . . . That's right. When you get riled you don't feel so good . . . It don't matter anyhow about your thinking you lied or if I said you lied . . . It don't matter. You can lie to me or you can tell me the truth. I am your brother.

CHESTER. But I didn't lie, Ewen. Or imagine. I saw him kill the boy.

EWEN. Oh, here we go again. Oh, oh.

CHESTER. I swear to you, Ewen. I swear by . . . by (*looking out*) the church spire.

EWEN. And you just watched him kill him, you didn't try to stop it . . .

CHESTER. Him? Oh . . . what could I do, Ewen . . . He raised the knife before I could get ready to scream . . . The man who saw the knife raised over him started to cry out, at last he opened his mouth wide, but the knife plunged downwards, down, down. (*He cries and hides his head in his brother's shirt.*) Oh, oh, oh.

EWEN. Chester, Chester . . . See here, you imagined it . . . See here. (*He slaps him.*) Wake up!

CHESTER. Don't hit me for telling the truth now . . . Don't.

EWEN. All right . . . He stabbed him then. You saw it . . . Why did you wait so long then to tell me . . . Why?

CHESTER. A day—is that long?

EWEN. Yes, it's long . . . (*Quickly*) Chester, you lied.

CHESTER. No, no, I told the truth . . . Ewen, my hand—you hold it too tight.

EWEN. You lie. There was no murder.

CHESTER. Did I call it a murder?

EWEN. You said he raised a knife and killed him.

CHESTER. Is that murder?

EWEN. Well, it ain't givin birth to a baby is it.

CHESTER (*dreamy*). I wish I had not seen it . . . Ewen, what are you thinking about.

EWEN. I'm tired of you burdening me with your lies.

CHESTER. You shouldn't ever be tired of me . . . I'll quit lying then.

EWEN. Then you admit it was a lie, do you. Damn it all.

CHESTER. Oh, no, no. It was true, but if it makes you feel better I'll say it was a lie. For you, you see, I'll say any—

EWEN. Oh, God Almighty. Stand up . . . Go on, stand up, Chester. (*Chester stands up. He is very small and stunted in growth for a boy of thirteen.*) Now, answer me truthful, tell me the very rock-bottom truth . . . Did you see another man stab a man.

CHESTER. No.

EWEN. You lied to me then.

CHESTER. I'm telling you I didn't see him do it to make you feel better, Ewen. No, I saw nothing. No stabbing.

EWEN. Oh, God. My God. I think I'm going crazy . . . Now see here . . . Did you see it, and if so, where . . . Where did it take place . . . ?

CHESTER (*whispering into his brother's ear*). In the back room of Hattie's saloon.

EWEN. What in hell were you doing in there, you're no more than a child, huh.

CHESTER. I went to . . . (*Lowering his voice*) . . . take a leak.

EWEN. At Hattie's? (*Frantically*) Why there?

CHESTER. Well, I dunno . . . Let me see. It was raining . . . I couldn't wait.

EWEN. And so you went right to the back of the saloon and see him stabbing this other fellow.

CHESTER. I swear I did. Yes.

EWEN. Didn't other people notice it too . . . It's not in this paper, for instance. I've gone through it with a fine-tooth comb. (*He almost tears the newspaper to pieces.*) There are no murders mentioned in the paper . . . Just a few suicides . . . Oh, Chester, Chester, what is to become of you? (*Swiftly*) Did you take a leak when you got there, or just go spying?

CHESTER. Oh yes, I did that . . . (*Shamed*) You see (*whispering again*) I saw the murder when I was . . . peeing. Through a hole in the wall . . .

EWEN (*dazed*). I see . . . Go on.

CHESTER. But I dried my hands and come out into the room afterwards and he . . . was standing over the body.

EWEN. Well, didn't he see you.

CHESTER. I don't think so . . . I came like a shadow. He didn't look in my direction.

EWEN. Then what?

CHESTER. I hid behind a curtain that leads to the toilet.

EWEN (*wildly*). And, Chester . . . And?

CHESTER. The man went in the toilet . . . He looked down in the bowl . . . (*Bemused*)

EWEN. Yes, yes!

CHESTER. He said, *Who pissed here? On account of I flushed it just a minute ago. Who has pissed here . . .*

EWEN. (*He suddenly puts his hand over Chester's mouth as if to protect him.*) Oh, my God in heaven . . .

CHESTER (*breaking away from the protecting hand*). I almost answered him back where I was hid behind the curtain . . . I was so mixed up, Ewen.

EWEN. But instead you said nothing.

CHESTER. I hid for an hour till all was quiet. (*Ewen holds him protectively.*) Then I went back in the room where he had done it, on account of the . . . stabber had flushed the toilet with the two . . . urines . . . (*Ewen puts his hand over Chester's mouth.*) . . . I . . . I . . .

EWEN (*explosively*). But where were the other people all this while? Hattie, for example, where was she? You mean to say you were alone in that whole God-damned tavern?

CHESTER. Yes, because, they was having a drawing upstairs and everybody went up there for a few minutes to see who won . . . That was when the murderer struck . . .

EWEN. Look, we will go to Hattie's now, and we will ask around and find out . . . If you aren't telling me the truth, though, watch out . . .

CHESTER. Watch out for what? (*Terrified*) Watch out for what, Ewen.

EWEN. Nothing.

CHESTER. I know now I am not lying. (*Stares at his brother's hands.*) I know the murderer.

EWEN. Well, that is big news.

CHESTER (*moony*). But I imagined it, you see . . . Ewen (*terrified*), there is a difference . . . I did take a . . . leak, but the rest of it, I must have imagined it. Tell me I did.

EWEN. Haven't I always been good to you, Chester, save a few times when I lost my temper . . . After all I have been both mother and father to you . . . Haven't I been good to you for as long back

as you can remember. I was already in the second grade when you were born . . .

CHESTER. I imagined it all, Ewen . . . After I went in the toilet . . . I just thought I saw a stabbing.

EWEN (*strangely*). You're not afraid of me, are you, Chester.

CHESTER. I can't think . . .

EWEN (*screaming*). See here! You must have known it was me all the time . . . Didn't you. See, I'm making a clean breast of it all . . . Look at me! You must have known I did it . . .

CHESTER. No, I didn't . . . No . . . Not till . . .

EWEN. Not till just . . .

CHESTER. A minute ago. When I saw your cut fingers . . .

EWEN. (*He looks at his own hands.*) Only a minute ago I was just your brother . . .

CHESTER. Are you going to do it to me too now, Ewen . . . Stab me too?

EWEN. Why ever would I do that to you?

CHESTER. I thought I would be next.

EWEN. You mean, Chester, you really didn't know it was me who stabbed him until just now . . .

CHESTER. I have never lied to you, Ewen . . . Sometimes I imagine, but never lie—because you are so close to me . . .

EWEN. Well, you used to make up things when you were little . . . Stories . . . You amused yourself telling stories.

CHESTER. Ewen, I will never tell on you. I am true. Maybe I make up stories from time to time because of my condition, but I am true.

EWEN. But why would you think I would kill you, Chester . . . That is a blow to me you think that . . . Anyhow, even if you told the police what you saw, nobody would believe you . . .

CHESTER (*aroused*). Why ever not?

EWEN (*bitterly*). *Why ever not,* he asks.

CHESTER (*passionately*). Yes, why ever not, Ewen!

EWEN. (*He kisses him.*) You're not like other boys.

CHESTER. I'm like you, ain't I? Ain't I your own flesh and blood, like you used to always tell me.

EWEN. Yes, but you're different too. That's precious.

CHESTER. No, no. I'm not different. I'm like you . . . You told me once . . . when I was . . . little that I would grow up to be like you too if I waited long enough.

EWEN (*abstractedly, to himself really*). That was why I killed the man at Hattie's tavern. He mocked you. He mocked the way I kept such good care of you . . . (*Insanely*) He dared to question why I cared for you!

CHESTER. But you didn't believe what he said . . . about me . . .

EWEN. Of course not!

CHESTER. (*acting strange*). But see here . . . What exactly did he say about me . . .

EWEN. You be quiet now . . . We are going to pack and leave, hear? We're leaving New York City for good.

CHESTER. What did that man say about me, Ewen . . . You tell me.

EWEN. He didn't say a thing. (*He begins to put some clothes in a valise.*)

CHESTER. You tell me what he said . . .

EWEN (*deliriously, forgetful anybody else is hearing*). He stung me! He stung me by his words . . .

CHESTER. So he did say it to you then? (*In violent collapse*)

EWEN (*fearful*). No!

CHESTER. Who is the liar now? You tell me what he said because I am true, or—(*He shows the murder weapon to a terrified Ewen.*) You must tell me because I am true . . . (*He waits.*) He spoke the truth against me, didn't he, Ewen?

EWEN. Put that knife away! That is a dangerous . . .

CHESTER (*maniacally*). I am true, true. You should not have told me different . . . Admit it now, Ewen, that you have lied to me, that I will not grow up to be like you, though of the same flesh and blood . . . You have lied, and the man you murdered spoke true . . . See, see . . . (*He stabs Ewen in the throat again and again, and then pulling the blade out with difficulty he stabs himself.*)

EWEN. Here, here, Chester (*taking the knife*). You have not done it quite, have you? (*He stabs Chester vehemently, then takes him in his arms.*) You stabbed me so good, but you failed on yourself . . . Such bright blood . . . Well, so what . . . It's better this way . . . You would have died anyhow with me in jail . . . (*He hugs him.*) Chester, Chester say I done good for you even if I did lie . . . Say I done good . . . Are you gone already? (*He rolls back the dead boy's eyes.*) Well, well . . . Dying is not all they write home about, is it? It's not any worse than life, that's sure . . . Chester, Chester . . . Well, well . . . (*He dies.*)

FOUR POEMS

PARAKRAMA KODITUWAKKU

Translated from the Sinhalese by Ranjini Obeyeskere and Reggie Siriwardene

TRANSLATORS' NOTE: *Parakrama Kodituwakku was born on September 13, 1943, in rural Sri Lanka. The son of a Catholic mother and Buddhist father, he was raised in the Church. As a young man, however, he increasingly rejected his early religious training and finally abandoned Catholicism. Today Kodituwakku sees himself as a Marxist—but one who does not entirely disregard traditional Buddhist values, which he considers an inextricable part of the culture and worldview of the Sinhala people.*

Kodituwakku is, in a fundamental sense, a revolutionary poet, and his antiestablishment attitudes pervade both his life and his work. Graduated from high school, he decided not to seek the generally accepted road to upward social mobility and economic advancement—a university education and a job in the central administrative bureaucracy. He states he was "not prepared to waste three to four years of his life in an institution patterned on outdated imperialist values, providing a system of education totally unrelated to the real needs of the country." Instead, he spent those years traveling in remote parts of the country. His poetry, he claims, deals with the incidents and realities of his actual experience—not a fictional world of the imagination.

He is presently employed as a trained teacher in a secondary

school in the provincial town of Ratnapura. While his reputation as a poet has been growing (he is now acclaimed the foremost of the younger writers), he has chosen to remain a schoolteacher in the provinces.

An educational system geared to white-collar employment within the country's administrative system is a familiar feature of the developing nations of Asia and Africa (formerly colonies). Similarly, a self-conscious rejection of that system by today's youth is also becoming a pervasive syndrome among these nations. Poets like Kodituwakku, whose writings reflect their intense sense of social and political commitment, have their counterparts in Indonesia, Malaysia, Bangladesh, India, and many African countries. However, the authenticity of Kodituwakku's poetic voice, his sureness of touch, and his control of language, ensure that his work does not degenerate into mere propaganda or political dialectic.

The following poems are from The World of a Disobedient Son *(1974). An earlier collection,* Little Brother, *was published in 1973.*

COURT INQUIRY OF A REVOLUTIONARY

I (School Report)

Doubts all teachings.
Questions continuously.
Thinks individualistically.
Disregards discipline.
Works as he chooses.
Conduct unsatisfactory.

II (Sunday School Report)

Disbelief verily signifiieth a sinful mind.
The horoscope too indicateth a lack of merit.
Choleric humours have become excited and turbulent.
Hath no knowledge of the doctrine of the gods.
I take refuge in the Buddha. He should do likewise.

III (Court Report)

(a) Attempted to break the law.
(b) Destroyed the peace.
(c) Should be ordered a whipping.
(d) Be made into a good citizen.

IV (Doctor's Report)

Sick.
Psychiatric treatment advised.
Phobia, mania, paranoia, hysteria,
Neurotic, psychotic,
Abnormal—criminal
Behaviour unnatural.

Brain surgery recommended
Demonic fantasies to be controlled
Before going to bed
Several tablets of phenobarbitone.

V (Statement of the Accused)

Turn me not into a snail
my feelers chopped off.
Turn me not into a coward
by preaching of gods.
Turn me not into a buffalo
burdened with false views.
Make me not a "good boy"
with hands and mouth gagged.

Allow me to question like Socrates
Doubt like Descartes
Crash through like a gushing river
Cut clean as a knife.
Let me rise, erect
Like a penis.

AN UNFINISHED LESSON . . .*

One by one each burnt-out leaf
falls and fills the yard.
A blackbird cries a sharp tu . . . week
perched upon the ground.

O blackbird is that a question
that you too ask of me
because you know me for a schoolteacher?

A full half of my life I've spent
answering questions.
And now my white-haired head
has no more strength.

Those who asked me questions then
where are they now?
To questions that are posed to them
what answers do they give?

Children, you who tramped to school by flowering forest trails,
You who carried clouds with you, down the mountain slopes,
you who splashed through cool stream beds to wash your feet,
tell o tell where are you now, in what far place?

There was no playground for the school
you trained on the bus route,
the hundred-metre race was run
on the scorching road, barefoot.
While I stood at the bend, alert
for passing cars.

Where are you now, the lot of you?
whether far or near
Raise your hand for me to see
and answer clearly "here."

*This poem was used as a dedication to the young men and women
killed in the 1971 insurrection.

...Do you still, now, as you did then,
get drenched in the pouring rain
trapped in the threatening storms,
wade across rushing streams,
see laughter in the sun,
run races on the road
see a winning post ahead?

A full half of my life I've spent,
answering questions.
And now my white-haired head
has no more strength.

KISA'S SON

"Find a house where no child has died
and bring me from there some mustard seed"

—You told me, Lord, I remember
when my son was dead

Oh I knew well
the mustard seed you spoke of
was impossible to find

—Yet I went hastening
from street to street
from house to house
Lord, not to find
your mustard seed

but in each village home
to see and embrace
my son, reborn and dancing
at the breasts of the mothers!

ON MOVING INTO YET ANOTHER RENTED HOUSE

Gnanawathi, Gnanasena,
buried down beneath the baggage
loaded into the half-truck;
ears uplifted,
eyes wide open,
why do you keep looking out?

Cats, can you not keep count?
This will be the 17th rented residence
that we now head for.

The 16th rented house we have just left
to the 17th rented home we now proceed.

It struck me during the history lesson
that our life was like
that ambling steam engine
that Watson once built.

In the giant tree of life
let us live like birds,
flit from limb to limb
in search of ripening fruit.

But gentle sirs forgive us, and listen to our tale.
We move from one house to the next
not because we want to change.
We pay our rent
and would so like
to close our eyes in peace,
safe, in a single place.

But the government by telegram
from Her Majesty the Queen*
transfers our father from school to school.

*Until Sri Lanka was declared a republic in 1972, the Queen of England was legally the head of the state.

We've already moved from seven.
Because he does not care to creep
beneath the Parliamentarians' feet,*
from house to house we slide,
our goods and chattel tied,
our bag and baggage clutched,
sliding, slipping, shuffling, shoving
a vagrant life.

Why we moved out of one house
was when we couldn't take much more.
The moment we put out the light
countless roaches rained on us.
In the rafters lived a snake
his underbelly white and slithering
moving up there overhead;
little sister screaming, shrieking,
as if nearly dead.

Then in a twin house once we lived
in perfect amity.
Passing dishes back and forth
in friendly harmony.
One from this house
one to that house
One from that to this
feeling there was no distinction
between that and this.
Until one day,
Buddhadas, the boy next door,
kissed my young sister's breast.
To preserve her (golden) future
we hurriedly packed and left.

*The official government policy of "politicisation of the bureaucracy"
presently in operation has meant that all government appointments and
transfers depend on the whims or wishes of the Parliamentary represen-
tative of the area.

I swear it's true.
There was one house
on the banks of the broad Black River,*
so beautiful! it looked almost
like a movie picture.

Then without any warning
not a letter or a note,
the Black River maiden
ripped her cloth apart
crept into our house.
The three watches of that night we spent
awake
upon a beam.

..."This world is an illusion
this life a drop of dew
all carrion and waste,
a mere ball of spit."
So said our next landlord
a saintly gentleman
who...
because mother picked up a coconut
that fell from his tree
gave her notice, at once,
with great equanimity,
to quit the house
in twenty-four hours!

Gnanasena, Gnanawathi,
Cats I have some questions
which I will put to you:

*Kalu-ganga (Black River) is the name of a major river in south
Sri Lanka.

Our 17th rented house
has just one room.
They say there is not space enough
for baby sister to crawl.
Do you think then when she grows up
she won't be able to walk?

Because I will not have a room
in which to read and write,
Will I not have a chance one day
to become a famous poet?

Living in a single room
will my young sister ever
find herself a lover?

Flitting thus from tree to tree
will my mother and my father
turn to birds?

SIX GRAPHICS

CHARLES TOMLINSON

Introduced by Octavio Paz

BLACK AND WHITE: THE GRAPHICS OF CHARLES TOMLINSON[*]

Octavio Paz

When I first read one of Charles Tomlinson's poems, over ten years ago, I was struck by the powerful presence of an element which, later, I found in almost all his creative work, even in the most reflective and self-contemplating: the outer world, a presence at once constant and invisible. It is everywhere but we do not see it. If Tomlinson is a poet for whom "the outer world exists," it must be added that it does not exist for him as an independent reality, apart from us. In his poems the distinction between subject and object is attenuated until it becomes, rather than a frontier, a zone of interpenetration, giving precedence not to the subject but rather to the object: the world is not a representation of the subject— rather, the subject is the projection of the world. In his poems, outer reality—more than merely the space in which our actions, thoughts and emotions unfold—is a climate which involves us, an impalpable substance, at once physical and mental, which we penetrate and which penetrates us. The world turns to air, temperature,

[*]Translated from the Spanish by Michael Schmidt.

sensation, thought; and we become stone, window, orange peel, turf, oil stain, helix.

Against the idea of the world-as-spectacle, Tomlinson opposes the concept—a very English one—of the world as event. His poems are neither a painting nor a description of the object or its more or less constant properties; what interests him is the process which leads it to be the object that it is. He is fascinated—with his eyes open: a lucid fascination—at the universal busyness, the continuous generation and degeneration of things. His is a poetry of the minimal catastrophes and resurrections of which the great catastrophe and resurrection of the worlds is composed. Objects are unstable congregations ruled alternately by the forces of attraction and repulsion. Process and not transition: not the place of departure and the place of arrival but what we are when we depart and what we have become when we arrive . . . The waterdrops on a bench wet with rain, crowded on the edge of a slat, after an instant of ripening—analogous in the affairs of men to the moment of doubt which precedes major decisions—fall on to the concrete; "dropped seeds of now becoming then." A moral and physical evocation of the water drops. . .

Thanks to a double process, at once visual and intellectual, the product of many patient hours of concentrated passivity and of a moment of decision, Tomlinson can isolate the object, observe it, leap suddenly inside it and, before it dissolves, take the snapshot. The poem is the perception of the change, a perception which includes the poet: he changes with the changes of the object and perceives himself in the perception of those changes. The leap into the object is a leap into himself. The mind is a photographic darkroom: there the images—"the gypsum's snow/the limestone stair/and boneyard landscape grow/into the identity of flesh" ("The Cavern"). It is not, of course, a pantheistic claim of being everywhere and being everything. Tomlinson does not wish to be the heart and soul of the universe. He does not seek the "thing in itself" or the "thing in myself" but rather things in that moment of indecision when they are on the point of generation or degeneration. The moment they appear or disappear before us, before they form as objects in our minds or resolve in our forgetfulness . . . Tomlinson quotes a passage from Kafka which defines his purpose admirably: "to catch a glimpse of things as they may have been before they show themselves to me."

His procedure approaches, at one extreme, science: maximum objectivity and purification, though not suppression, of the subject. On the other hand, nothing is further from modern scientism. This is not because of the aestheticism with which he is at times reproached, but because his poems are experiences and not experiments. Aestheticism is an affectation, contortion, preciosity, and in Tomlinson we find rigour, precision, economy, subtlety. The experiments of modern science are carried out on segments of reality, while experiences implicitly postulate that the grain of sand is a world and each fragment figures the whole; the archetype of experiments is the quantitative model of mathematics, while in experience a qualitative element appears which up to now has not been limited to measurement. A contemporary mathematician, René Thom, describes the situation with grace and exactness: "*A la fin du XVIIième siècle, la controverse faisait rage entre tenants de physique de Descartes et de Newton. Descartes, avec ses tourbillons, ses atomes crochus, etc., expliquait tout et ne calculait rien; Newton, avec la loi de gravitation en l/r², calculait tout et n'expliquait rien.*" And he adds, "*Le point de vue newtonien se justifie pleinement par son efficacité . . . mais les esprits soucieux de compréhension n'auront jamais, au regard des théories qualitatives et descriptives, l'attitude méprisant du scientisme quantitatif.*" It is even less justifiable to undervalue the poets, who offer us not theories but experiences.

In many of his poems Tomlinson presents us with the changes in the particle of dust, the outlines of the stain spreading on the rag, the way the pollen's flying mechanism works, the structure of the whirlwind. The experience fulfills a need of the human spirit: to imagine what we cannot see, give ideas a form the senses can respond to, *see* ideas. In this sense the poet's experiences are not less truthful than the experiments carried out in our laboratories, though their truth is on another level from scientific truth. Geometry translates the abstract relationships between bodies into forms which are visible archetypes: thus, it is the frontier between the qualitative and the quantitative. But there is another frontier: that of art and poetry, which translates into sensible forms, that are at the same time archetypes, the qualitative relationships between things and men. Poetry—imagination and sensibility made language—is a crystallizing agent of phenomena. Tomlinson's poems are crystals, produced by the combined action of his sensibility

and his imaginative and verbal powers—crystals sometimes transparent, sometimes rainbow-colored, not all perfect, but all poems that we can look through. The act of looking becomes a destiny and a profession of faith: seeing is believing.

It is hardly surprising that a poet with these concerns should be attracted to painting. In general, the poet who turns to plastic work tries to express with shapes and colors those things he cannot say with words. The same is true of the painter who writes. Arp's poetry is a counterpointing of wit and fantasy set against the abstract elegance of his painting. In the case of Michaux, painting and drawing are essentially rhythmic incantations, signs beyond articulate language, visual magic. The expressionism of some of Tagore's ink drawings, with their violence, compensates us for the sticky sweetness of many of his melodies. To find one of Valéry's water colors among the arguments and paradoxes of the *Cahiers* is like opening the window and finding that, outside, the sea, the sun, and the trees still exist. When I was considering Tomlinson, I called to mind these other artists, and I asked myself how this desire to paint came to manifest itself in a meditative temperament such as his—a poet whose main faculty of sense is his eyes, but eyes which think. Before I had a chance to ask him about this, I received, around 1970, a letter from him in which he told me he had sent me one of the New Directions anthologies (*ND22*), which included reproductions of some of his drawings done in 1968. Later in 1970, during my stay in England, I was able to see other drawings from that same period—all of them in black and white, except for a few in sepia; studies of cow skulls, skeletons of birds, rats, and other creatures which he and his daughters had found in the countryside and on the Cornish beaches.

In Tomlinson's poetry, the perception of movement is exquisite and precise. Whether the poem is about rocks, plants, sand, insects, leaves, birds, or human beings, the true protagonist, the hero of each poem, is change. Tomlinson hears foliage grow. Such an acute perception of variations, at times almost imperceptible, in beings and things, necessarily implies a vision of reality as a system of calls and replies. Beings and things, in changing, come in contact: change means relationship. In those Tomlinson drawings, the skulls of the birds, rats and cows were isolated structures, placed in an abstract space, far from other objects, and even at a remove from themselves, fixed and immovable. Rather than a counter-

pointing of his poetic work, they seemed to me a contradiction. He missed out some of the features which attract me to his poetry: delicacy, wit, refinement of tones, energy, depth. How could he recover all these qualities without turning Tomlinson the painter into a servile disciple of Tomlinson the poet? The answer to this question is found in the work—drawings, collages, and *decalcomania**—of recent years.

Tomlinson's painting vocation began, significantly, in a fascination with films. When he came down from Cambridge in 1948, he had not only seen "all the films"; he was also writing scripts which he sent to producers and which they, invariably, returned to him. This passion died out in time but left two enduring interests: in the image in motion, and in the idea of a literary text as support for the image. Both elements reappear in the poems and the collages. When the unions closed the doors of the film industry against him, Tomlinson dedicated himself energetically to painting. His first experiments, combining *frottage*, oil, and ink, date from that period. Between 1948 and 1950 he exhibited his work in London and Manchester. In 1951 he had the opportunity to live for a time in Italy. During that trip the urge to paint began to recede before the urge to write poetry. When he returned to England, he devoted himself more and more to writing, less and less to painting. In the first phase of his painting, the results were indecisive: *frottages* in the shadow of Max Ernst, studies of water and rocks more or less inspired by Cézanne, trees and foliage seen in Samuel Palmer rather than in the real world. Like other artists of his generation, he made the circuit round the various stations of modern art and paused, long enough to genuflect, before the geometric chapel of the Braques, the Legers, and the Gris's. During those same years— getting on towards 1954—Tomlinson was writing the splendid *Seeing Is Believing* poems. He ceased painting.

The interruption was not long. Settled near Bristol, he returned to his brushes and crayons. The temptation to use black (why? he still asks himself) had an unfortunate effect: by exaggerating the

---

*"*Decalcomania* without preconceived object or *decalcomania* of desire: by means of a thick brush, spread out black gouache, more or less diluted in places, upon a sheet of glossy white paper and cover at once with a second sheet, upon which exert an even pressure. Lift off the second sheet without haste." Oscar Dominguez, quoted in *Surrealism* by Roger Cardinal and Robert Stuart Short.

contours, it made his compositions stiff. "I wanted to reveal the pressure of objects," he wrote to me, "but all I managed to do was thicken the outlines." In 1968 Tomlinson seriously confronted his vocation and the obstacles to it. I refer to his inner inhibitions and, most of all, to that mysterious predilection for black. As always happens, an intercessor appeared: Seghers. Tomlinson was wise to have chosen Hercules Seghers—each of us has the intercessors he deserves. It is worth noting that the work of this great artist— I am thinking of his impressive stony landscapes done in white, black, and sepia—also inspired Nicolas de Stael. Segher's lesson is: do not abandon black, do not resist it, but embrace it, walk round it as you walk round a mountain. Black was not an enemy but an accomplice. If it was not a bridge, then it was a tunnel: if he followed it to the end it would bring him through to the other side, to the light. Tomlinson had found the key which had seemed lost. With that key he unlocked the door so long bolted against him and entered a world which, despite its initial strangeness, he soon recognized as his own. In that world black ruled. It was not an obstacle but an ally. The ascetic black and white proved to be rich, and the limitation on the use of materials provoked the explosion of forms and fantasy.

In the earliest drawings of this period, Tomlinson began with the method which shortly afterwards he was to use in his collages: he set the image in a literary context and thus built up a system of visual echoes and verbal correspondences. It was only natural that he should have selected one of Mallarmé's sonnets in which the sea snail is a spiral of resonances and reflections. The encounter with surrealism was inevitable—not to repeat the experiences of Ernst or Tanguy but to find the route back to himself. Perhaps it would be best to quote a paragraph of the letter I mentioned before: "Why couldn't I make their world my world? But in my own terms. In poetry I had always been drawn to impersonality— how could I go beyond the self in painting?" Or put another way: how to use the surrealists' psychic automatism without lapsing into subjectivism? In poetry we accept the accident and use it even in the most conscious and premeditated works. Rhyme, for example, is an accident; it appears unsummoned but, as soon as we accept it, it turns into a choice and a rule. Tomlinson asked himself: what in painting is the equivalent of rhyme in poetry? What is *given* in the visual arts? Oscar Domínguez answered that

question with his *decalcomania*. In fact, Domínguez was a bridge to an artist closer to Tomlinson's own sensibility. In those days he was obsessed by Gaudí and by the memory of the dining room windows in Casa Batlló. He drew them many times: what would happen if we could look out from these windows on the lunar landscape?

Those two impulses, Domínguez's *decalcomania* and Gaudí's architectural arabesques, fused: "Then, I conceived of the idea of cutting and contrasting sections of a sheet of *decalcomania* and fitting them into the irregular windowpanes . . . Scissors! Here was the instrument for choice. I found I could *draw* with scissors, reacting *with* and *against* the *decalcomania* . . . Finally I took a piece of paper, cut out the shape of Gaudí's window and moved the mask across my *decalcomania* until I found my moonscape . . . The 18th of June 1970 was a day of discovery for me: I made my best arabesque of a mask, fitted it round a paint blot and then extended the idea of reflection implicit in the blot with geometric lines . . ." Tomlinson had found, with different means from those he used in his poetry but with analogous results, a visual counterpoint for his verbal world: a counterpointing and a complement.

The quotes from Tomlinson's letter reveal with involuntary but overwhelming clarity the double function of the images, be they verbal or visual. Gaudí's windows, converted by Tomlinson into masks, that is, into objects which *conceal*, serve him to *reveal*. And what does he discover through those window-masks? Not the real world: an imaginary landscape. What began on the 18th of June 1970 was a fantastic morphology. A morphology and not a mythology: the places and beings which Tomlinson's collages evoke for us reveal no paradise or hell. Those skies and those caverns are not inhabited by gods or devils; they are places of the mind. To be more exact, they are places, beings and things revealed in the darkroom of the mind. They are the product of the confabulation—in the etymological sense of that word—of accident and imagination.

Has it all been the product of chance? But what is meant by that word? Chance is never produced by chance. Chance possesses a logic—is a logic. Because we have yet to discover the rules of something, we have no reason to doubt that there are rules. If we could outline a plan, however roughly, of its involved corridors of mirrors which ceaselessly knot and unknot themselves, we would know a little more of what really matters. We would know something, for

instance, about the intervention of "chance" both in scientific discoveries and artistic creation and in history and our daily life. Of course, like all artists, Tomlinson knows something: we ought to accept chance as we accept the appearance of an unsummoned rhyme.

In general, we should stress the moral and philosophical aspect of the operation: in accepting chance, the artist transforms a thing of fate into a free choice. Or it can be seen from another angle: rhyme guides the text but the text produces the rhyme. A modern superstition is that of art as transgression. The opposite seems to me truer: art transforms disturbance into a new regularity. Topology can show us something: the appearance of the accident provokes, rather than the destruction of the system, a recombination of the structure which was destined to absorb it. The structure validates the disturbance, art canonizes the exception. Rhyme is not a rupture but a binding agent, a link in the chain, without which the continuity of the text would be broken. Rhymes convert the text into a succession of auditory equivalences, just as metaphors make the poem into a texture of semantic equivalences. Tomlinson's fantastic morphology is a world ruled by verbal and visual analogies.

What we call chance is nothing but the sudden revelation of relationships between things. Chance is an aspect of analogy. Its unexpected advent provokes the immediate response of analogy, which tends to integrate the exception in a system of correspondences. Thanks to chance we discover that silence is milk, that the stone is composed of water and wind, that ink has wings and a beak. Between the grain of corn and the lion we sense no relationship at all, until we reflect that both serve the same lord: the sun. The spectrum of relationships and affinities between things is extensive, from the interpenetration of one object with another—"the sea's edge is neither sand nor water," the poem says—to the literary comparisons linked by the word "like." Contrary to surrealist practice, Tomlinson does not juxtapose contradictory realities in order to produce a mental explosion. His method is more subtle. And his intention is distinct from theirs: he does not wish to alter reality but to achieve a *modus vivendi* with it. He is not certain that the function of imagination is to transform reality; he is certain, on the other hand, that it can make it more real. Imagination imparts a little more reality to our lives.

Spurred on by fantasy and reined in by reflection, Tomlinson's work submits to the double requirements of imagination and perception: one demands freedom and the other precision. His attempt seems to propose for itself two contradictory objectives: the saving of appearances, and their destruction. The purpose is not contradictory because what it is really about is the rediscovery—more precisely, the reliving—of the original act of making. The experience of art is one of the experiences of Beginning: that archetypal moment in which, combining one set of things with another to produce a new, we reproduce the very moment of the making of the worlds. Intercommunication between the letter and the image, the *decalcomania* and the scissors, the window and the mask, those things which are hardlooking and those which are softlooking, the photograph and the drawing, the hand and the compass, the reality which we see with our eyes and the reality which closes our eyes so that we see it: the search for a lost identity. Or as Tomlinson puts it best: "to reconcile the I that is with the I that I am." In the nameless, impersonal I that is, are fused the I that measures and the I that dreams, the I that thinks and the I that breathes, the I which creates and the I which destroys.

Seal It in Sea-Caves. August 1972

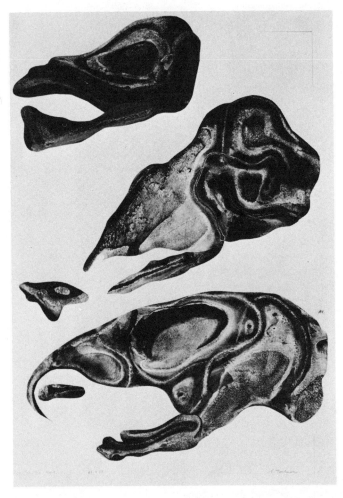

Three Prehistoric Masks. May 28, 1973

The Milk of Silence. 1972

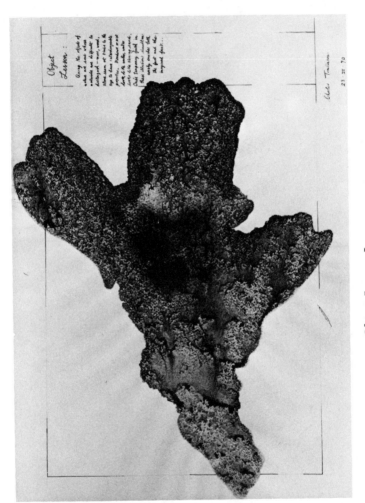

Object Lesson. June 23, 1970

The Four Elements. October 24, 1970

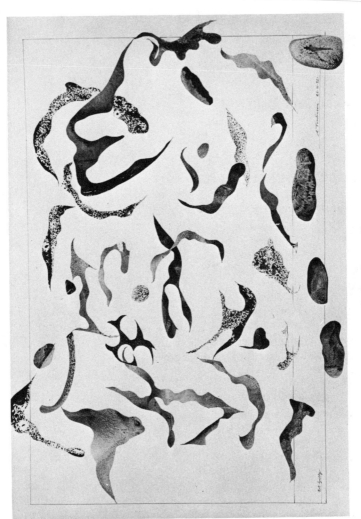

Not Guilty. June 26, 1972

SEVEN POEMS

JONATHAN GREENE

REMEMBERING

The details are devils,
they disturb with
their little intrigues
asking for dream articles.

For often if we reach
the heights, these devils
renew their interest,
bring up lost childhood desires,
give us a table to overeat from,
some flesh eyeing you from the corner,
the easy outs.

Or, beginner's luck, you are desposited there
where others desire and cannot reach.
You feel then a clarity beyond speech,
a knowing-before-it-happens, a levity,
a strength to the body.

But you fear this for its strangeness,
need weights for the ankles
to slow the dance,
to catch breath:

As it was said: *Whenever Shems-ed-din, in his exile,*
was overwhelmed by the frequency and duration
of divine presence, and becoming lost
in perfect ecstasy, felt that human strength
could no longer bear this beauty, he would
undertake menial tasks to ease his situation.
Hiring himself out as a labourer, he would
work far into the night.

But your weights are not as pure,
you lose the vision. Another dozen years
of forgetfulness, perhaps, until
you remember that gift, start
to work for what had been too easy.

VISIT TO COOLE

Yes, all in ruin now
as Yeats foresaw,
a few stones from the garden wall
is all that stands
of things man by man.

The 'Autograph tree, a copper beeach'
with the names of the famous
(AE, Yeats, O'Casey, Shaw, & Synge)
is still there to be deciphered
with book in hand—now surrounded
by a gate for time, not vandals,
to erase.

And at the lake no wild swans,
but the huge irregular rocks
& a Jaguar beside which
an Englishman & his son fish.

Yet the solitude remains
in the wildness of the place:
the overgrown orchard, the thorns
we made our way through to the lake,
the clouds fast-travelling there,
a slight rain that closed off
this ground from all else.

I stood there & the power
of the place stood inside me.
It was as hard leaving
as all these small deaths are.

THE COMPARISON

The car, a room
we want more privacy in,
freedom of the road
not road to ourselves,
an insularity, private yacht
rolling down the highway,
another self-image symbol
to the world of how to know us.

The feet, a more individual
instrument of attainment.
Compare toes, compare chrome.
The walk, a way the body thinks.
Keeps tune with the earth.
The walk eases the mind
into a vantage, a roadside
overlook into all the busy
doing of the town below.

Live the day.

Both more real/more dream-
like. A knowing we touch
& know nothing of how
it comes.

BEYOND ANYTHING SOLID

All this before us: projections
of ourselves, of those before. Ideas
made solid: this house, what
resides here. At times
the wind thru the trees
forgotten.

       But then travelling
the short distance between rooms,
there is a storm, the heart
stops, endless space
comes to us.

       We fall down,
cleave creature comfort,
the cold, the warmth,
the known.

       But forever now
we know the Other. But forever
now 'forgets' it's there
on the outskirts, waiting
on the cliff till we come into sight,
a small dot of shadow, our momentary
forgetting of all the world hands us
of who we are.

BEYOND THE PARADIGMS

We let the world in slowly,
bit-by-bit; take a bite,
chew in slowly, then digest.
As a child—one room would do.
And for the longest time
we hold back the larger vision
of things, though obvious
to ourselves we are wrong.

Does the tree outside
hold its breath
before deciding to produce
another ring? The *no* affirms
our stilted behavior.

But finally we accept, grow
into another era of ourselves.
Walking the streets of the everyday,
at times it's like waking
in a foreign country,
only every third word
understandable.

And we open
to how much is beyond us.
Building model-after-model,
reality-after-reality,
photographs at different
distances, poems.
And still it is
beyond us.

And when we compare the pictures:
how much the microscopic
& the telescopic look alike,
how much airyness there is
in the solids, how
each of us is a mystery
in all this mystery

large as space,
small as grain,
just breathing.

THE UNDERPINNING

We all avoid it.
Turn the car to miss
the cat with its entrails
splayed on the road.
The toothless farmer grins
when we fail to meet his eyes.
The hungry wino moaning
asleep on the sidewalk
as we walk home from
the movies.

There is this nightmare
underpinning this other dream.
Nightmare of dirt, sweat, & blood,
obscene gestures, rape, violence,
men locked in the furnace room
of a luxury liner without rudder.

An underpinning we feel at
the edges of our knowing.
For we refuse the knowing—
land & men are wasted
so that the rest of us
can live unmindful & heedless.

We've never talked to them,
never knew them. Fear a violence
there. I cannot speak what
they think of us, only imagine
a slow built-up curse. And perhaps
an ignorance like ours
mystifies us in their eyes.

DESIRE

for Carol

I desired so much;
years & years
to tame it.

Tamed,
the wished-for
was given.

Then taken away.
Then given.
Then gone.

So that beginning
& end are known
beforehand

the first sight,
eye-blink,
your intangible smile

brought all the way
from childhood
when you wave

good-bye.
The unreality
haunts . . .

as if this
were being filmed
with only

one take allowed
& thus it's
perfect.

SEVEN STORIES ALIAS SUBSIDIARIES

GANGA PRASAD VIMAL

Translated from the Hindi by K. P. Saradhi and Millen Brand

TRANSLATORS' NOTE. *Although relatively unknown in the United States, Ganga Prasad Vimal at the age of thirty-eight is considered one of the most important young writers in India. He was born in Utrakashi, studied at Allahabad and Punjab universities, and now teaches at Delhi University College. His Ph.D. thesis was on "Symbols and Images in Modern Hindi Poetry." He has to date published eight books of his own work: three novels, two collections of short fiction, two volumes of criticism, and one of poetry. In addition, he has edited two collections of essays on major Hindi writers and* An Anthology of Modern Hindi Poetry, *and has translated many short stories, poems, and articles from both English and Japanese.*

1.
I'd like to disown all the stories I've been getting printed so far. I don't claim they're even a prelude to what I'll write. Not that I'm sure what may follow will be my real stories.

In fact, all these stories I've done have been written under extreme pressure. I don't know how long that's going to go on. The truth does seem to be that I'll have to learn to accommodate myself to this pressure, though in a weak and submissive way. This at least is more obvious to me than ever before. I'm surrounded by people who avoid the paths of life that are manifestly clear to

177

them and take to devious detours because in facing life squarely they'd only be ringing their own death knell. It's no great thing after all to face the truth and be a victim of valor. It's equally futile to try to hide the truth. In both cases man only becomes a scapegoat for valor.

What I'd like to say is simply what I've been saying, using, perhaps, feeble and roundabout means of expressing myself. I fully realize that it's difficult to express myself completely through ineffective and faulty means, still I use them, even if it's just to prove their falsity and uselessness. Persisting in these faulty means, I'd like to relate the tale of my own likes and dislikes.

You may exclaim, what is this, hypocrisy? The word shudders and says nothing: I could say hypocrisy is a figure of speech written on each and everyone's face. Everyone puts it on as a mask—lawyers, various authorities, teachers, and intellectuals. I don't like making them the subject of my stories, committing the fault of covering up sin with false language. Speaking of sin, I think, Only Valmiki, Vyas, or Tulsidas can claim to be the greatest sinners. Or, at best, the people who, on the pretext of celebrating his (Tulsidas's) centenary, fill their own pockets with money. You say, "How am I bothered?" Yes. How does it matter to some ryot who, alone on his small stretch of land on the banks of the Narmada, sheds tears on the bellflowers that interlace his corn crop? How is he affected if some committee president or some politician makes a crore of rupees for his personal ends?

I want to particularly reassert this point. How does it matter after all to the ryot? The problem, where this world is heading and why, is not my concern. What am I, after all, to bother about the course of the universe? I'm only a maniac struggling hard to suppress my instinct of self-immolation.

May God pardon me. I want this kind of language to go. It's an insult to man. It's a social hangover of those who are hungry and naked. McNamara, you are indeed blessed. You've ruined all the languages of the world so badly that one should think twice before using any one of them.

Down with society's elite. The portals of the prostitutes are wide open for them.

I want you to give me a new language to speak—the least inhibited one. I want to abuse Mao Tse-tung. Not that I don't respect him. He's the only people's poet. He's turned all culture

inside out, laying bare its poverty and hunger. But I want to abuse him brutally.

Indeed, it's all I want to say. To check my bona fides, open up the four hundred and eighth page of *Atharva Ved* or the *Thought* of Mao. You'll find the same thing in both places.

2. DECEIT
(Two tramps)
My dear fellow, nothing is turning up
What?
no meager luck even
then came along . . .
Where?
on to the dais
What will we do?
Throw up two chairs and shout out slogans
On what issue?
Forget it. Life itself is an issue
but deceitful
Deceit is its justification.

(Both of them slide into the pages of history to find out the weakest of the tribal races that still exist.)

Then they sent out a slogan. And the entire town reverberated with the noise. (Excuse me for this old revolutionary zeal. Nowadays there is no use working, one must meditate.)

THE THIRD STORY
Brothers and sisters, I have just set my mind thinking. I'll write out my ideas next year . . .

THE FOURTH STORY
For my part, I didn't stray into the pages of history. One fine morning I saw him outside the church gate, reading the posters on the walls. (Excuse me. I'm not sure whether he was reading or just looking. It's hard to differentiate between reading and looking. The difference exists only psychologically with any degree of precision. But, could the same thing be said of the effort to translate others' thoughts into language? We had better ignore what causes the confusion regarding the difference between reading and looking.)

He broke into a long laugh, startling an old passer-by who was

on his morning walk. He stopped and straightened up and said, "What are you doing here?"

The old man's nose was running, and as he spoke the words, he sounded as if he was sobbing. Through his sobs he said, "This damn nose is still running."

Meanwhile another old man came by. Pointing his walking stick at the laughing man, he muttered, "This young man has gone mad. Why is he laughing at the posters like this?"

Lately I've been strolling out in the mornings on a doctor's advice. After a thorough checkup, he gave me this foolish prescription of taking long walks. So what does it bring me? The nauseating sight of old men with running noses so early in the morning. Some of these customers brush their teeth with a tooth stick as they walk along. I'd rather be sick than see all this.

"Only water flows from both the eyes and the nose," the first old man said as if explaining himself. He continued, "There must be something really interesting in the poster. How unlucky, I've left my glasses at home. I can't read."

A middle-aged man who had by now got into the crowd made his way to the one who was laughing and said, "What's the matter?"

The man began laughing again, keeping on repeating the question, "What's the matter?" in diverse derisive tones. "Nothing's the matter," he reassured himself in a mood of self-mockery, and went on laughing.

"Drunkard," shouted the middle-aged man. Then, turning to the crowd, he said with the air of a sidewalk advertiser, "Sirs, this is the current fashion. I can vouch cent per cent this is what the drug has done to him. Let's praise this demigod."

"You fool," whined the one who was laughing. He said the word "fool" with the growl of a dog. "You fool," he continued with some animation, "you auspicious fool living in the world of wealth, have you ever been to the prostitute of knowledge, I mean, the university? The citadel of knowledge?"

On seeing the laughing man get into a rage like this, the first old man slipped silently into a nearby lane. I noticed he was trying hard to hide his running nose.

I still had to walk a long way to complete the day's quota. I began to pace ahead absent-mindedly. Suddenly the laughing man caught hold of me from behind. He said, "Have you any idea about linguistics? Look, language leads you through knowledge to wisdom."

"No . . . no . . . no . . ." I said, "I'm only. . . ."

He turned to the posters again, and began to laugh. The middle-aged man was still there. He said, "He has gone mad. There's no doubt about this."

"Shut up," said the laughing man. "Come on here and I'll tell you what the poster means."

"Great," I cried out, and took to my heels.

Even today you'll find the laughing man standing in the same spot, perhaps reading or looking at the posters, but laughing endlessly.

"Great," I tell myself. I've found out what he should get instead.

THE FIFTH STORY

The tonga in the movie film was skidding into loose earth. It was crammed to capacity. There was a girl among the occupants. You'd never have an idea of her beauty unless you saw the African film. *Gamba-Kotira:*

For a minor fraction of a second my eyes flickered, from fatigue. And, all of a sudden, the scene changes. Something flashes into my mind.

I remembered a quick-witted fish and a newborn child reincarnated Jatarka and then the empty bus parked at the Indraprastha depot. There should be a girl at places like this. They look so drab without these blooming stars. The lone girl in the tonga could appear in a dream or in the form of the resourceful fish, or in the empty bus as the Indraprastha depot.

"Ticca . . ." the wheel rolled out. In the blaze of light one could perceive the fleeting shade of darkness.

Side by side with *Gamba-Kotira* there had been rolling out in my mind another story.

I have an appointment with Biatthis at nine. If the film ends at quarter to nine, I'll still have five minutes to call up a conveyance, and the meeting can take place on time in the house near the twenty-third pole.

The tonga skidded and overturned. And it rolled away to become one with the trees of the forest nearby.

The routine of the day stares into my eyes, hands in pockets. I blink. Where do I stand? Do I wait for a conveyance or for some one?

THE SIXTH STORY

As the garbage truck moves along, a dead dog is thrown on it. Its rotten skin stinks menacingly. "Oh, it's alive," a woman shrieks in burkah.

A big crowd collects around the truck. A number of hands go up to pull the dog down.

The dog seemed alive when it was being pulled out.

"He can't bark," someone offered as an explanation.

A dog or a man, whether alive or dead—being what they are but whenever seeming to be belonging to others—become the center of attraction or repulsion, dispute or sympathy—as Independence in Democracy or Poverty in Capitalism.

THE SEVENTH STORY

This is not my story. Nor is it his. Nor someone else's. Nor anybody's. Nor this man's. Nor that man's. Nor someone else's someone's. Nor a third somebody's. Nor that somebody's someone's. Nor his someone's somebody's. Neither mine nor yours. Nor yours nor mine. Neither mine-yours nor yours-mine. Nor someone's anyone's. Nor anyone's someone's.

(I'm now at the tether end of my knowledge of pronouns. For the pronouns that refer to persons who don't exist, I have to look in a grammar. But you can look in a grammar, can't you, dear reader, to complete my story? You can get grammars anywhere. They're available in series ranging in cost from a meager six annas to six rupees. I can give you the address of my publisher. But he's slow doing things and also stingy in money matters. He won't let you have a pie's discount. That's why his signature is so bad. If only his sight was bad. I'd then have taken you on a pleasure tour of the world to relate my story.

The fall of youth—the fall of the Yavanas—the fall of sex—and the fall of the curtain.

NOTES ON CONTRIBUTORS

PETER ARONIAWENRATE BLUE CLOUD, former poetry editor of *Akwesasne Notes,* presently resides in Bombay, New York. His first book of poems was published by Akwesasne Notes in September 1976. At one time Blue Cloud worked as a structural ironworker. A native American, he traces his lineage to the Mohawk Nation at Caughnawaga, Quebec, Canada.

A frequent contributor to the New Directions anthologies, CID CORMAN lives in Kyoto, Japan, where he has edited for many years the influential literary periodical *Origin.* In the recently published *The Gist of Origin* (Grossman, 1975), he collected highlights from various numbers of the magazine, providing a valuable sampling of the major poetic trends of our times. New Directions has published two volumes of his poetry, *Livingdying* (1970) and *Sun Rock Man* (1970). His work has also appeared under The Elizabeth Press imprint.

Since the publication of *Bending the Bow* (New Directions, 1968), ROBERT DUNCAN has been at work on a fifteen-year project, which he conceives of as *Ground Work,* to appear in 1983. This San Francisco poet, the recipient of numerous literary awards and prizes, including a Guggenheim Fellowship (1963), was one of the key figures in the Black Mountain school of poetry and the San Francisco renaissance of the 1950s.

For biographical information on HENRY ELINSON, see the introductory essay by ALEKSIS RANNIT preceding "Eight Drawings." Rannit's own poetry has appeared in translation from the Estonian in earlier New Directions anthologies. Curator of Russian and East European Studies at Yale, he has published five monographs on modern artists through UNESCO, and in 1976 the Elizabeth Press brought out a bilingual selection of his verse.

Raised in a mining town in the Andes, IPPY GIZZI now lives in Rehoboth, Massachusetts. She is employed as a free-lance illustrator for *House Plants and Porch Gardens*. After attending the Rhode Island School of Design, she graduated from Brown University, where she studied with the novelist John Hawkes. Burning Deck Press published her *Letters to Pauline* in 1975.

Information about YVAN GOLL will be found in the Translator's Note introducing his "Paris Georgics." FRANK JONES, who teaches English and Comparative Literature at the University of Washington, has translated Euripides, Gide, Horace, Lucian, and—in collaboration with Simon Mpondo—David Mandessi Diop. His translation of Brecht's *Saint Joan of the Stockyards* (Indiana University Press, 1970) won a National Book Award in 1971.

Born in Carnac in 1907 of peasant stock, GUILLEVIC is one of the most highly regarded of living French poets. His work reflects the elemental austerity of his native Breton landscape. A bilingual edition of his *Selected Poems*, translated by Denise Levertov, was published by New Directions in 1969. MARY FEENEY, a native of New York state, currently lives in Paris, where she and Guillevic have together taught a translation workshop. They have read at colleges in the United States and in Kilkenny, Ireland. She has recently collaborated with William Matthews, translating Jean Follain's prose poetry, soon to appear in book form.

JONATHAN GREENE lives in Kentucky, and in 1976 edited an anthology of Kentucky writing for his Gnomon Press. He has been teaching in the Poetry-in-the-Schools program, while designing books and helping to build a house on his recently purchased farm. His three latest collections of poetry are *Scaling the Walls* (Gnomon Press), *Once a Kingdom Again* (Sand Dollar) and *Quiet Goods* (Larkspur Press).

Sculptor, painter, novelist, and poet, MAUDE HUTCHINS resides in a seaside town in Connecticut. Her published fiction includes *Georgiana* (1948), *A Diary of Love* (1950), *Love Is a Pie* (1952), and *My Hero* (1953). Her work has appeared in numerous literary magazines, such as *The Kenyon Review* and *Mademoiselle*, as well as in earlier New Directions anthologies.

For information about PARAKRAMA KODITUWAKKU, see the Translators' Note preceding his "Four Poems." REGGIE SIRIWARDENE, a critic and filmscript writer, teaches English at the University of Sri Lanka. He is presently editing an anthology of American and European poetry in Sinhalese translation. RANJINI OBEYESEKERE, a professor at the University of California, San Diego, has published *Sinhala Writing and the New Critics* (Colombo, 1974) and several translations of poetry from the Sinhalese.

Belgian-born ANDRÉ LEFEVERE teaches English literature at the University of Antwerp. One of the growing number of Euro-English writers—Continental Europeans who write in English—he has translated widely into English from Greek, French, Dutch, and German. New Directions is bringing out this spring his translation, with Michael Hamburger, of Philippe Jaccottet's *Seedtme ("Le Semaison")*.

RICHARD PEVEAR, who now lives in New York City, is the translator of *The Gods*, by the French philosopher Alain, published by New Directions in 1974.

A prolific writer, JAMES PURDY is a frequent contributor to these pages. *Children Is All*, a collection of two plays and ten stories, is available as a New Directions Paperbook. His most recent gathering of short fiction and drama, *A Day after the Fair*, is to be published this spring by The Five Trees Press, while his latest novel, *Narrow Rooms*, is soon to be brought out by Arbor House.

ANTONIS SAMARAKIS holds a degree in law from Athens University and was an official in the Greek Ministry of Labor from 1935 to 1963. As a fighter in the Underground during the German Occupation, he was arrested and condemned to death. Though he began publishing as early as 1932, his first book, a collection of short stories called *Wanted: Hope*, was not brought out until 1954. This was followed by the short novel *Danger Signal* (1959) and a second collection, *I Refuse* (1961), which received the Greek National Book Award. His fourth book, the novel *The Flaw* (1966), was awarded the highly prestigious Kostas Ouranis Prize of the Twelve as well as the French Grand Prix de Littérature Policière. A further volume of short fiction, *The Jungle*, also appeared in

1966. ANDREW HORTON, who translated "Anatomy Lesson, etc.," lives in Virginia.

ROBERT STEINER's "A Parable of Guerrillas" is excerpted from his second novel, *Mesmer Facing Algiers*. His first novel, *Quill*, was published by Harper & Row. At present, he teaches comparative literature at the University of Massachusetts.

"Narrative of the Great Animal," by NATHANIEL TARN and JANET RODNEY, is a section from their *Alashka* sequence, inspired by recent visits to Alaska. Among Nathaniel Tarn's many earlier volumes of poetry are *A Nowhere for Vallejo* (1971) and *The Persephones* (1974). In 1975, New Directions published his *Lyrics for the Bride of God*. Janet Rodney returned to the United States in 1973 after living in Madrid and Barcelona for fifteen years and is currently working on a book of poems called *Crystals*.

An earlier selection of the British poet and critic CHARLES TOMLINSON's graphics, "Skullshapes," appeared in *ND22*. OCTAVIO PAZ, who contributed the introductory essay on Tomlinson's work, holds the leading place in contemporary Mexican letters. Bilingual editions of his poetry, all available from New Directions, include *Configurations, Eagle or Sun?*, and *Early Poems 1935–1955*.

GANGA PRASAD VIMAL was born thirty-seven years ago at Utrakashi and has studied at Allahabad and Punjab universities. He has published eleven books in Hindi: novels, short stories, poetry and literary criticism, all of which have earned him a place among the leading writers of his generation in India. At present he teaches at Delhi University. K. P. SARADHI, recently deceased, was a noted critic and translator of Telgu and Hindi literature. His co-translator, MILLEN BRAND has completed two books of poetry and two novels, and his renderings from the Spanish have appeared in the anthology *For Neruda, For Chile*.

Work by various members of the VOU group has appeared in several New Directions anthologies, as far back as 1938. An association of poets and artists founded in the 1930s, it has been instrumental in bringing to Japan the methods and techniques of the European and American avant-garde.